Praise for *The Lean Turnaround Action Guide*

"In *The Lean Turnaround Action Guide,* Art Byrne offers a priceless gift to the reader: the exact process he has followed in turning around dozens of companies over 30 years. Some readers can simply paint by the numbers. Others may need to modify or even improve Art's process. But no organization's leaders reading this book can claim they have failed to act for lack of knowing what needs to be done and how to do it."

—Jim Womack, coauthor of *Lean Thinking* and *The Machine That Changed the World*

"Reading *The Lean Turnaround Action Guide* reminds me what a tremendous teacher, coach, and friend Art was for me at The Wiremold Company. Art is a superb leader with an unrivaled set of Lean turnaround success stories to his credit. I am awed by the way Art writes about the detailed tactical and cultural change elements of Lean transformation. While the Lean journey of UGH Corporation may be fictional, the lessons in this Lean treasure couldn't be more realistic."

—Marc Hafer, President, Simpler Consulting

"As a Wiremold alumni, reading Art Byrne's *Action Guide* was déjà vu. It is the mirror image of the beginning of our Lean journey, and the next best thing to having him at your side, guiding you through the steps of becoming Lean. Even if you are well down this path, you will find things that you probably overlooked. This is an opportunity for everyone to learn from one of today's best Lean leaders."

—Orest (Orry) Fiume, Vice President Finance (Retired), The Wiremold Company

"An absolute must-read for any executive interested in how Lean is a full business strategy, or any Lean officer tasked with supporting it. This no-nonsense account of how to turn around any company and shape a Lean strategy with the people themselves, straight from an author who has led more than 30 Lean turnarounds, will help you draw a clear and direct map to success."

—Michael Ballé, author of *Lead with Respect, The Gold Mine,* and other Lean books

5 6 7 8 9 LCR 23 22 21

ISBN: 978-0-07-184890-9
MHID: 0-07-184890-8

e-ISBN: 978-0-07-184891-6
e-MHID: 0-07-184891-6

Design by Lee Fukui and Mauna Eichner

Library of Congress Cataloging-in-Publication Data

Names: Byrne, Art, 1945- author.
Title: The lean turnaround action guide : how to implement lean throughout your company / Art Byrne.
Description: New York : McGraw-Hill, [2017]
Identifiers: LCCN 2016027125 (print) | LCCN 2016039669 (ebook) | ISBN 9780071848909 (alk. paper) | ISBN 0071848908 | ISBN 9780071848916
Subjects: LCSH: Corporate turnarounds--Management. | Value added. | Organizational change. | Organizational effectiveness.
Classification: LCC HD58.8 .B969 2017 (print) | LCC HD58.8 (ebook) | DDC 658.4/013--dc23
LC record available at https://lccn.loc.gov/2016027125

McGraw-Hill Education books are available at special quantity discounts to use as premiums and sales promotions, or for use in corporate training programs. To contact a representative, please visit the Contact Us page at www.mhprofessional.com.

I would like to dedicate this book to my wonderful wife, partner, and best friend Mariko Byrne. She is the one who encouraged me to write a book in the first place. She typed all of my handwritten manuscripts for *The Lean Turnaround* and kept pushing me forward when I got off track. Likewise, she has been my constant source of encouragement in getting this book to the finish line. Along the way she has nursed me through two cancer surgeries and had one of her own while still managing to have five holes-in-one on the golf course herself (I, by the way, have none). I hope that she has five more aces in the years to come.

Contents

Foreword

Over the years I have learned several things about Lean. One is that CEOs only listen to other CEOs, probably with good reason. The other is that Lean will only succeed when it is an integral part of the strategy of the organization, actively led and supported by the CEO. When this happens, the results are truly impressive and cause big headaches for the competition. Step by step, example by example, industry by industry, this very different approach to running a business is changing the world.

In this and his previous book *The Lean Turnaround*, Art Byrne convincingly demonstrates that Lean is a *strategy*—and not just the latest cost-cutting process improvement methodology. Indeed, he argues it is the most powerful strategy you could have to leave your competitors standing.

A Lean strategy is all about growth through continuing to deliver more value to customers, which can only be done by improving the processes that create this value, which comes in turn from teaching everyone a fundamentally different way of thinking about working together and continually improving their work. These cumulative capabilities then feed into the design of next generation products and services, and so it goes. Instead of relying solely on a select band of experts and tough management to ensure compliance with the answers they come up with, this strategy mobilizes everyone in a virtuous circle of steadily improving business results.

Note that this is not just a one-off success story told by consultants but a well-tested method Art has used in turning around many businesses. Art was previously an executive at GE, where he learned about traditional, or modern, management at the source. He became all too aware of the limitations of GE-style management, which until recently has been hailed as the most successful in the world.

It is significant that Art learned to see this better way of leading and managing directly from members of the team that developed the fabled Toyota Production System and taught it to their suppliers in Japan. He was one of a small group of U.S. managers who had the courage to try it for themselves, learning what it takes to make this work and deliver superior results.

At the same time he was learning this, Jim Womack and I were looking for examples beyond Toyota. In *The Machine That Changed the World,* we benchmarked Toyota's ability to design and make its cars with half the time and effort and a fraction of the defects of its Western competitors. This led to a stream of speaking requests and questions from managers about how they could follow Toyota's example. We also ended up learning from the same group at Toyota and very quickly found Art and his colleagues. We learned a lot from observing what Art was doing at Wiremold and ended up describing his story in *Lean Thinking.*

Jim and I discovered that writing a book is one thing, but if it resonates with readers this leads to more and more questions. Indeed, this stream of questions has guided our research into what makes Toyota's example so significant ever since.

This was the same with Art's own book, *The Lean Turnaround,* in which he described the Wiremold story and what he learned from it in more detail. This popular book only generated more and more questions—detailed and practical questions from other CEOs and venture capitalists. Art answers these questions one by one in this book, where they are woven together into a coherent whole business story.

I am sure you will recognize questions you might have asked Art as you read this book. However, reading is one thing; putting these ideas into practice is another. Art has demonstrated many times that Lean can be done outside Toyota, with similar results. There is therefore no excuse anymore for not following his example. Share and study this book with your management team, find someone with deep experience of doing this to challenge and mentor you, and get going. Once you have embarked on this path it will be awfully difficult for your competitors to catch up with you. This is the management system of the future. Good luck on your journey.

Daniel T. Jones
Coauthor of *The Machine That Changed the World, Lean Thinking,* and *Lean Solutions*

Acknowledgments

A business/strategy book like this doesn't just pop into existence on its own. First of all, you have to gain some knowledge about the subject matter, in this case using Lean principles to turn around any company, yourself before you can pass on what you have learned to others. In my case I was fortunate to be taught Lean by the founders of the Shingijutsu consulting company of Nagoya, Japan. Mr. Iwata, Mr. Nakao, Mr. Takenaka, and Mr. Niwa all had spent their careers at Toyota Motor Corporation with much of their time spent working directly for Taiichi Ohno, the father of the Toyota Production System. I was lucky to have learned from the best just how big a strategic impact Lean can have on any company.

But having the knowledge is only a starting point. Putting it into a book so that the readers can actually understand and take away something that will benefit their business is a whole different thing. It turns out that writing a book isn't that easy, and as a result an author needs help and advice along the way. I have been fortunate to have had a lot of help, but a few names stand out and need to be specifically acknowledged.

Tom Ehrenfeld, with some initial help from Emily Adams, was the principal editor of my first book, *The Lean Turnaround*. As far as I was concerned I was done writing books after that, but McGraw-Hill, my publisher, had other ideas. The first book turned out to be quite popular, so McGraw-Hill wanted a sequel with even more detail about how a company actually accomplishes a Lean turnaround. Tom, who has edited Lean thinkers such as Jim Womack, Dan Jones, John Shook, Michael Ballé, and many others, helped me with the notion of simply creating a company and a management team and bringing them through the process. Tom provided steady guidance all along the way. He asked great questions, made insightful edits, and did it all while allowing me to retain my "voice" as the author.

Knox Huston of McGraw-Hill has supported this book with great energy and passion from the very beginning, helping with careful edits and wise advice about creating a sequel that provides something new and valuable. I also want to thank his predecessor, Mary Glenn. Erin Mitchell has produced terrific visual elements that help tell the story. Additionally, I want to thank readers of earlier drafts of this manuscript: Michael Ballé, Ed Miller, and Jim Booth have shared insights on ways to make it better. Marc Hafer of Simpler Consulting has been a great source of support and encouragement.

Orry Fiume, who was part of our team at The Wiremold Company as chief financial officer, is one of the better Lean minds in the United States. He is the coauthor along with Jean Cunningham of the bestselling book *Real Numbers: Management Accounting in a Lean Organization* and a true authority on Lean accounting. Orry provided many valuable suggestions and comments to each succeeding draft of this book as we went along. I greatly value his thoughts and insight. When Orry says, "Art, you can't say it that way," or "this doesn't make any sense," I just say yes sir and follow his advice.

Dan Jones and Jim Womack are of course the bestselling authors of two of the most iconic Lean works ever done, *The Machine That Changed the World* and *Lean Thinking*. I first met them back in 1995 when they were working on writing *Lean Thinking*. They visited us and decided to include The Wiremold Company as a chapter in the book. We have been good friends ever since, and I consider myself to be very lucky and very honored to have had Jim write the foreword to *The Lean Turnaround* and for Dan to write the foreword to this book. I am very blessed as I can't think of anyone else who could say that. They both continue to make enormous contributions to the worldwide Lean movement, and I hope they never stop.

Introduction

The State of the Lean Movement

Most companies today have heard about Lean. Many have tried it in some form or other. Unfortunately, although the concepts are very simple, implementing Lean is not, and as a result few companies have benefited. Most that have put forth a serious effort have failed and gone back to their traditional batch ways. This does not have to be the case. I was fortunate in my career to have learned from four Lean sensei, all of whom spent their whole careers working under Taiichi Ohno, the father of the Toyota Production System. I always saw the Toyota Production System (TPS) as a tremendous strategic weapon—the basis of how you run your company. I have used this approach to turn around various companies for over 30 years; and it has always been successful. My purpose in writing this book is to share this with others so that they can be successful as well.

If we go back far enough, we can find elements of what we now call Lean scattered here and there for several centuries. I think most Lean thinkers would agree that the basis of today's approach started in 1913 at Highland Park, Michigan, when Henry Ford combined interchangeable parts, standard work, and a moving line into what he called flow production. This was an enormous advance and worked brilliantly as long as you only wanted a single model in only one color—black. It did not hold up well when customers demanded variety.

The real foundations were developed much later in Japan by Toyota Motor Corporation after WWII. In his book *Toyota Production System*,* Taiichi Ohno, a pioneer of the Toyota Production System in those years, gives full credit to Ford and his early work for inspiring Toyota's approach, noting that both systems are based on "the work flow system." Yet while Ford had huge warehouses, Toyota,

* Taiichi Ohno. *Toyota Production System* (English translation). New York: Productivity Press, 1988.

responding to current challenges, had none. Toyota started as a manufacturer of looms founded by Sakichi Toyoda. His invention of a new weft breakage automatic stopping device in 1896 was the basis for jidoka (autonomation with a human touch), which along with just-in-time are the pillars of the Toyota Production System. Sakichi also introduced the core philosophy of "the complete elimination of all waste," which remains the foundation of TPS (and Lean). His son, Kiichiro, the founder of Toyota Motor Corporation, inherited this philosophy. He understood that the best conditions exist for making things better when machines, facilities, and people work together to add value without creating any waste. The result of this thinking was the just-in-time production method. When Eiji Toyoda took over after Kiichiro, he along with his production manager Taiichi Ohno, outside help from Shigeo Shingo, and outside influence from Kaoru Ishikawa, W. Edwards Deming, and Joseph Juran ensured and perfected the just-in-time approach—which is the basis for what we know today as Lean. Most of this took place between 1949 and 1975.

By pursuing the practice of "daily improvements" and "good thinking, good products," Toyota not only has become the world's largest automotive manufacturer (as of this writing) but has given the rest of us a system and approach that can be used to improve any company. Many outsiders attribute Toyota's success to any number of factors. Sure, they pursue "conventional" strategies like becoming the world's largest automotive producer, expanding geographically, drastically reducing the time it takes to introduce new products, and being a leader in new technologies such as hybrid cars. But any way you look at it, TPS is the core underlying *strategy*.

The outside world knew little about what Toyota was doing until 1977, when an article by Fujio Cho and Y. Sugimori about the logic behind TPS was published in a U.K. engineering journal.* It was not until after the oil shock of 1979, however, that the world started to notice that Toyota was doing something very different. In their seminal book *The Machine That Changed the World*, Jim Womack, Dan Jones, and Dan Roos helped highlight the vast differences between the results achieved by Toyota and those achieved by all the other auto companies. Even so, we didn't really get it. What we heard was "just-in-time manufacturing"—a phrase that led people to see this as simply an inventory reduction program and not a strategy.

Womack and Jones clarified this for everyone in 1996 in *Lean Thinking*, in which the authors drew from extensive case studies of companies applying TPS

* Y. Sugimori, K. Kusunoki, F. Cho, and S. Uchikawa, Toyota Production System and Kanban system: Materialization of just-in-time and respect-for-human system, *International Journal of Production Research*, *15*(6) (1977): 553–564.

in various industries (including my experience with The Wiremold Company) to codify the key practices in ways that extended far beyond Toyota. The authors recommended that to practice Lean, people should specify the value desired by the customer, identify the value streams of each product providing that value, remove the waste from each step, and let the value flow continuously aided by pull signals between the steps and then manage to perfection so that the waste and the time needed to serve the customer continuously fall. This was clear and correct. Unfortunately, we didn't get this one, either, and as a result, I've seen that Lean thinking has become commonly known as Lean manufacturing.

The missed opportunities of this wrongheaded approach are huge. When you think of Lean as "some manufacturing thing" rather than an incredible strategic weapon, then mistakes get made and the whole approach gets underutilized. Even in manufacturing companies, calling something Lean manufacturing leads to misuse. The CEO then sees it as something to help him get more productive (i.e., reduce head count) and delegates it down to his VP of operations. Lean then becomes one of 10 different company initiatives and nothing else changes. The sales department continues to operate in basic ways that prevent Lean practice—offering discounts for large batch orders, for example, and doing stupid sales tricks at the end of the month to move next month's demand into this one. The purchasing department continues to buy 6 to 12 months of material at a time in order to get a few cents each off the cost. And naturally, if you have a nonmanufacturing company, you figure that something called Lean manufacturing couldn't apply to you, so you don't even try.

After nearly 30 years of the Lean movement outside of Toyota, this is a sad state of affairs. All is not lost, however. I believe that the number of companies that are aware of Lean, have tried or are about to try Lean, or are well down the path is growing all the time. There are no reliable statistics on the penetration of Lean in the overall economy. In manufacturing, based on my own observations and input I get from the leading Lean consulting companies in the United States, my best guess would be that perhaps 35 to 55 percent of all companies have some experience. This is a wide range. Just 10 years ago I would have put the estimate in the 20 to 30 percent area. This is encouraging. Even so, very few of these companies succeed. They may just be going slowly, or they could have tried and already failed. I hope I am wrong, but at this point, I think that only 4 to 7 percent of all companies have successfully implemented Lean. By successfully I mean that they have implemented this approach across all aspects of their business—not just in manufacturing or operations—and have become a Lean enterprise where Lean is the core culture of the entire organization.

Art's Lean Turnarounds by Industry

- Lightbulbs
- Lighting Fixtures
- Hand Tools
- Power Tools
- Heavy Truck Components
- Drill Chucks
- Encoders
- Temp./Flow Instruments
- Specialty Bolts
- Swiss Screw Machine Parts
- Tachographs
- Tank Level Sensors
- Counting Instruments
- Air Conditioning
- Aircraft Engine Parts
- Jewelry (Rings)
- Surge Protectors
- Wire Management Systems
- Hospitals
- Life Insurance
- Coolers and Freezers
- Hot Tubs
- Bathtubs and Showers
- Wet Shaving Razors
- Staplers and Punches
- Label Manufacturing
- Beverages
- Voting Machines
- Warehouses
- GFCI Fixtures

Figure I-1. Art's Lean turnarounds

In an effort to improve these ratios, several years ago I wrote *The Lean Turnaround.* This book was based on my own experiences in various companies over the past 30 years (see Figure I-1). It was aimed at CEOs and senior executives: if I could get them to understand the strategic nature of Lean, there might be more success stories.

Writing a book has been an interesting adventure, to say the least. I was simply trying to help other companies get on the Lean path. I fully expected to be a "one-and-done" author. After all, I am a businessman and not a writer. It was rewarding to receive many favorable comments on the book. Even so, people consistently asked, "But how do you really implement a Lean turnaround? What is the secret sauce?" They were surprised to hear me describe Lean as a powerful and comprehensive business strategy—their prior understanding was that it was more a "set of tools" to use as needed to cut costs or fix problems. I guess this should not have surprised me, as much of the Lean literature has focused on one specific tool or another. Even those who could grasp the concept of Lean as a strategy struggled with how they would actually implement it in their company. They could see all the obstacles and even hear the objections of their senior staff team who had been taught the traditional batch approach and didn't want to change. I guess you could say they wanted a silver bullet solution that they could just buy off the shelf, plug in, and, voila, they would be Lean. They could conceive of "doing Lean," but the idea that they had to "be Lean" was beyond them. They were looking for a step-by-step guide.

Why a New Book?

Having raised these questions as a result of writing *The Lean Turnaround,* I felt obligated to do my best to answer them—hence this more detailed version, *The Lean Turnaround Action Guide.* There is no secret recipe; Lean is just a few simple ideas and a lot of hard work. Yet teaching this can be a challenge since Lean is all about learning through doing. Then my editor, Tom Ehrenfeld, asked me a simple question:

"Why don't you just do one? Take the reader through a Lean turnaround the way you would do it." Brilliant! The more I thought about it, the more I liked the idea: this is the best way to answer both questions, help everyone learn along the way, and have a little fun as well.

So, we are going to buy a company and then lead the management team, step by step, through a Lean implementation that will vastly improve its results and increase its enterprise value. The company is a manufacturing company, as this allows for the most robust comparisons to what other companies have done. Even so, I will bring in nonmanufacturing examples as we go along. That's because Lean applies to all settings. And, in my experience, the gains from implementing Lean in nonmanufacturing companies are almost always larger than those for manufacturing companies. As a result, it is important to show you nonmanufacturing results.

Our company is The United Gear and Housing Corporation, or UGH. We are going to take it from being an UGH to a WOW. UGH's profit and loss history and forecast is shown in Figure I-2. It is what I would characterize as a midsize company. Its headquarters and main plant are in Cleveland, Ohio. UGH has a total of seven plants throughout the United States and ships to its national industrial distributor network from two distribution centers in Memphis, Tennessee, and Reno, Nevada. Approximately 75 percent of its sales are off-the-shelf products it has designed and sells through its distributors; 25 percent are custom products sold directly to end-user original equipment manufacturers (OEMs). Its products enjoy a good reputation in the marketplace. UGH is one of the top three competitors in its category and as a result is a well-known name in its industry.

Turning to the results and forecast in Figure I-2, you can see that the company is doing well. Sales have grown each year and are projected to grow at a compound rate of 3.6 percent over the next five years.

The gross profit margin has increased over the past three years and is projected to add another whole point at the end of five years. The EBIT (earnings before interest and taxes) margin will show similar gains over this same period. In addition, sales per employee, a measure of productivity, although flat recently, is projected to improve at a rate of 3.1 percent annually over the next five years. Inventory turns, although low, are expected to improve slightly but at least are going in the right direction.

At the same time, the company operates in a traditional way, which is to say that UGH is the epitome of a batch manufacturer. It has had long (two- to three-hour) changeover/setup times on most of its equipment for as long as anyone can remember. The equipment is arranged in functional departments by type of machine, which is typical of any batch manufacturer. The combination of these two

United Gear and Housing Corporation
Traditional Batch Version

$ millions

	A 2013	A 2014	A 2015	F 2016	F 2017	F 2018	F 2019	F 2020	2015–20 AAGR%
Sales	$512.0	$532.0	$550.0	$568.0	$588.0	$609.0	$632.0	$657.0	3.62%
Gross Profit	152.6	159.6	165.6	170.4	178.2	185.1	193.4	203.7	
Percentage	29.8%	30.0%	30.1%	30.0%	30.3%	30.4%	30.6%	31.0%	
SG&A	106.5	110.8	115.2	120.0	124.2	128.5	133.6	139.6	3.9%
	-	-	-	-	-	-	-	-	
EBIT	$46.1	$48.8	$50.4	$50.4	$54.0	$56.6	$59.8	$64.1	4.9%
%	9.0%	9.2%	9.2%	8.9%	9.2%	9.3%	9.5%	9.8%	
Inventory	$108.9	$116.4	$116.5	$116.9	$124.2	$124.7	$129.0	$129.5	
Inv Turns	3.3	3.2	3.3	3.4	3.3	3.4	3.4	3.5	
Headcount	5,689	5,911	6,111	6,242	6,323	6,344	6,449	6,257	3.1%
Sales/Employee	90k	90k	90k	91k	93k	96k	98k	105k	

Figure I-2. UGH history and forecast

things (long setups and functional physical layout) creates manufacturing lead times that average six weeks. As a result, the company manufactures everything to a forecast. With six-week lead times, the forecast is rarely accurate, and the company experiences many customer service problems as a result.

UGH has spent a great deal of time, energy, and money trying to improve its forecasting. In fact, during our due diligence we found that developing a new forecasting model is one of the top three strategic objectives. The problems caused by the current system cause internal finger-pointing and heated discussions within the company, especially between sales and marketing and operations. We got the sense that sales and marketing and operations have never really gotten along, although no one would actually admit it.

The pressure to meet customer needs when the forecast is wrong causes a great deal of expediting within the company. In fact, there is even an expediting department within operations. But this often results in quality problems that are an issue with the customers. The six-week lead times also give rise to quality problems and make it difficult to get at the root cause of the problems when they arise. To offset these issues, the company is forced to carry more inventory than it really needs, "just in case" something goes wrong.

UGH's CEO, Jerry York, has been with the company for 16 years, the past 9 in his current role. Prior to joining the company, he spent 12 years with two other industry competitors. His principal background is in marketing and sales. He is quite outgoing, and people generally seem to like him. The morale in the company has been good, although, as you might expect, everyone is a little apprehensive about us being the new buyer. We have a reputation for being fully committed to the Lean approach to running a business, and no one knows exactly what that means. As a result, we can expect people to default to the worst rumors and think that Lean is just a way to cut head count.

As part of buying UGH we made it clear to Jerry that implementing Lean completely would be part of the deal and fundamental to both the company's success and his (and of course ours as investors). Jerry agreed to commit to our approach. He was even smart enough to admit that he would need some help. We explained that I would become chairman and work closely with him and his team to implement Lean in an aggressive way.

This will be difficult for Jerry. He will have to learn many new things quickly. This in turn will change the way he sees things and the way he manages the business. Not every CEO can make the transition and change behavior so that he or she can go from manager to leader. It is a stark difference. Leading requires showing and teaching people new ways—not just telling or ordering them to do something. CEOs who are insecure or are wedded to the command and control model have an especially hard time making the change. In fact, most of them can't.

We have extensive experience in knowing how much improvement is just sitting there waiting to happen—meaning that we look at things with "Lean eyes." UGH's results and forecast look like every one I saw doing 21 acquisitions at Wiremold and at almost every private equity deal we examine at J. W. Childs Associates. While I was CEO of The Wiremold Company, we increased our gross margins by 13 full percentage points and took inventory turns from 3x to 18x. Several of my J. W. Childs portfolio companies saw similar gains in both gross margins and inventory turns. The trick will be to teach Jerry and his team how to see things differently, how to take the proper actions to change not only the way things are done but, more important, how everyone thinks so that UGH can have a strong and sustainable kaizen (continuous improvement) culture.

I'll work hard at this, and so will Jerry. You can come along for the ride. I hope you enjoy it.

1

Kickoff Meeting

OVERVIEW

Converting any company to Lean is almost impossible if the CEO and the senior management team don't lead the charge. As a result, prior to the introductory Lean meeting that will be held for more than 100 hourly and salaried UGH associates later in the day, the UGH turnaround starts with a senior management team meeting that provides an overview of what kinds of results the new owners expect. The expected financial improvements include increasing gross margins by 5 to 7 points, freeing up at least $70 million in cash from inventory, and growing the enterprise value 100 to 150 percent over the current plan. These are shocking goals—just as hard for people to grasp as the need to see Lean as the company's strategy, to lead it from the top, and to focus on transforming the people. In this chapter, UGH's management team is primed to run a successful Lean turnaround. They learn that Lean is all about removing waste from their value-adding activities in order to deliver more value to the customer. The future Lean leaders need to understand value from the customer's point of view. Most important, they need to understand that because Lean is a "learn by doing" activity, they are all expected to get their hands dirty and will be on many kaizen teams going forward. There should be no illusion that UGH's leadership team will just magically discard everything they have learned in the past and jump on the Lean train.

Meeting with the Senior Management Team

So, let's get UGH off on the Lean journey. This initial meeting is held in a small, dilapidated conference room in UGH's main plant in Cleveland, Ohio. In other words, the initial Lean meeting takes place right in the middle of UGH's value-adding activities just outside the door on the shop floor. In fact, the noise, vibrations, and unique odor of the plant permeate the room. Perfect.

Art Byrne: Good morning, everyone. My name is Art Byrne, and I'm an operating partner at J. W. Childs Associates, a Boston-based private equity firm—and your new owners. I am now also serving as the chairman of UGH. Prior to this I was the CEO of The Wiremold Company, a group executive at the Danaher Corporation, and before that, general manager of several businesses for The General Electric Company. I have been implementing Lean since the beginning of 1982. In that time, I have always followed the same approach, and it has always worked. As a result, we will be following the same approach here.

Before we get into that, let's go around the room and introduce ourselves. It's great to have you all here. I've met most of you during the acquisition process, but just to refresh my memory, tell me your name, your title, and your years of service with the company. (See box, "UGH Senior Management.") Do any of you have prior experience in Lean, just-in-time, or something similar?

UGH Senior Management

Jerry York, CEO, 16 years with the company

Dick Conway, CFO, 18 years

Scott Smith, VP of Sales, 25 years

Ellen Minor, VP of Marketing, 3 years

Judy Rankin, VP of Human Resources, 10 years

Steve Mallard, VP of Engineering, 14 years

Frank Gee, VP of Operations, 20 years

Gary Cook, President UGH Custom Housings, 12 years

Steve Jones, President UGH Automotive, 15 years

Sam Watson, President UGH Small Gears, 8 years

John Flynn, President UGH Specialty Gears, 17 years

Frank Gee: First of all, thank you, Art, for coming to help us. I'm vice president of operations and have been with the company for 20 years. Please try to understand the background. We tried to implement just-in-time about three years ago, and it nearly bankrupted us. As a result, I think you will find that Lean brings up bad memories here, and so you are probably going to face a great deal of resistance.

Art: I wasn't aware of that. How did you go about it, and what happened?

Frank: Well, we were told that if you lowered the water, so to speak, by lowering your inventory, then the "rocks" (i.e., problems) would be revealed. Once you can see them, then you can fix them and lower the water some more. The problem was that when we took inventory turns from 3.0x to 3.6x, so many rocks popped up that we couldn't respond fast enough, and our customer service went to hell. We had no choice but to go back to our old batch ways and build back the inventory. In fact, we even went to bigger batches than in the past.

Art: Sorry to hear that. Unfortunately, your story is pretty common. That is because you went about it the wrong way: you had no plan for how to fix the rocks once they were exposed. But don't worry—we will take it a step at a time and eliminate the rocks one by one as we go along.

Frank: I certainly hope so. I don't want to live through that nightmare again. So, how will we learn enough quickly enough to avoid the problems this time?

Art: Frank, the only way to really learn Lean is by doing it. That is certainly the way I learned, and so will all of you. You will all get a chance to be on many kaizen, or continuous improvement, activities. To get you going, however, here is a list of six books that I would like each of you to read (see box, "Lean Reading List").

Lean Reading List

1. *Toyota Production System: Beyond Large Scale Production* by Taiichi Ohno

2. *A Study of the Toyota Production System: From an Industrial Engineering Viewpoint* by Shigeo Shingo

3. *Lean Thinking* by Jim Womack and Dan Jones. This 1996 book helped launch the word *Lean* into our business vocabulary as a way to think about the Toyota Production System. The authors were part of the original team that coined the phrase at MIT, and this book takes you through the business rationale of starting with the customer and moving all the way through the

value stream. The authors were early in recognizing that Lean is above all strategic—so this book will help you understand it in a broad way.

4. *Learning to See* by Mike Rother and John Shook. This book will give you the tools and perspective to help you "see" and then eliminate the waste in your value streams. It takes you step by step through the process of mapping your work and understanding how to improve it.

5. *Better Thinking, Better Results* by Bob Emiliani. Professor Emiliani shares a great case study of a Lean conversion (the company in the book is in fact The Wiremold Company). Told largely by the managers from the company, this book pays attention to the details that others might miss. It gives you great insight into how the various management team members felt as they went along the Lean journey. More important, they tell you of the changes they had to make themselves in order to make Lean successful.

6. *The Lean Turnaround* by Art Byrne. This book is aimed at senior executives and emphasizes that Lean is the core strategy to turn around any business. It outlines the key management principles that must be present to have a successful Lean turnaround. It also walks you through how to implement a Lean turnaround and leverage your success in the marketplace.

It is important to start with the Ohno and Shingo books, as the Toyota Production System is the basis for what we more commonly refer to as Lean today. Ohno was the father of TPS; Shingo had a front-row seat as an outside consultant and collaborator. As TPS will be the basis of everything we do, it is important to get a foundation in what they created and why. Pay special attention to the philosophy that lay behind their thinking. Knowing why something was done, the business and human resources rationale, is more important than what was done.

Scott Smith: Is there a time frame in which you expect us to finish these books? Will there be a test at the end?

Art: [*laughing*] No, Scott, there is no time frame and there will be no test. The more you can understand about the "why" of Lean, the easier it will be for you to understand things as we go along.

How Should We Think About Lean?

Jerry York: I also want to welcome you to our company, Art. We know that this can be good for us, but we have concerns. Many of us have heard that Lean is basically a manufacturing thing—a bunch of tools to lower your costs and reduce your head count. Don't most people in fact refer to it as "Lean manufacturing" and say it works pretty well as a cost reduction approach?

Art: Jerry, thank you for putting this on the table. And I want to make it clear that this is not true. Unfortunately, what you described *is* the way most people perceive Lean. They see it as a cost-cutting approach focused primarily on operations. As a result, they delegate it down to the VP of operations and keep everything else in a traditional batch type of approach (I'll explain more about this later). They rarely succeed. They will get some gains here and there, but they will suboptimize their potential and never become a Lean enterprise with true leverage in the marketplace.

Jerry: Then how should we think about it?

Art: The proper way to understand Lean is as a strategy. In fact, Lean is the greatest strategic weapon in running a business—any business—that you will ever see. Relative to most companies, UGH is doing just fine. However, using Lean as a strategy can boost shareholder value dramatically higher than what would occur if you stayed on your present track.

Let me share the key things you must do as a management team to be successful in converting to Lean. Let's call them the management musts. I'll write them on the board here:

Management Musts

Lean is the strategy

Lead from the top

Transform the people

Financial Expectations

All of these need to be in place if we are to be successful. We will talk about each of them in more detail as we go along. But first let me outline what we expect from UGH as financial results over the next five years:

1. Improve both your gross margins and EBIT margins by 5 to 7 points

2. Reduce inventory by over $70 million

3. Increase enterprise value by 100 to 150 percent more than your current forecast

Dick Conway: Art, are you serious? I mean, how do you even come up with such huge numbers? Even if we make some gains, won't it be discouraging when we fail to meet these crazy goals?

Art: Dick, I know this may seem strange to you, but I have the benefit of decades of doing this work and seeing this type of result over and over. I came up with these targets based on (1) knowing what other companies have achieved with Lean and (2) my own observations walking around your plants. In fact, my experience tells me that with a team as good as this one is, I wouldn't be surprised if you didn't do even better.

For now, however, I want you all to understand that the only way any company creates value for all its stakeholders is by delivering more value to your customers than your competitors can over long periods of time. This value can come in many forms: the best products, the most reliable customer service, the fastest response/turnaround times, the best quality, the easiest company to deal with or partner with, and of course competitive (though not necessarily the lowest) prices. The key is to be able to understand how our customers view value and be able to respond to that.

Scott: I think we have a pretty good handle on what our customers see as value. The problem is how we deliver that value. We seem to get in our own way a lot of the time.

Art: Scott, that is not surprising. All of the inventory I see lying around is a symptom of other problems that cause stress for your customers. In order to solve this, you have to improve your own value-adding activities by removing all the waste that exists. As an example let's take lead time. You have a six-week lead time on average. You have all probably taken this for granted as something that is pretty much the standard in your industry and that can't be improved upon. In fact, I bet there is a long list of logical-sounding reasons why this is as good as it gets.

Frank: You're right about that. We've looked at this every which way over the years. In fact, we got our lead times down from eight weeks just a few years ago, but we haven't gotten past the six-week barrier. Our setup times are too long, our suppliers are unreliable, our customers always have big pop-up orders, our forecasting is no good, and it goes on and on. Like you said, it is a long list. Six weeks is probably the best we can do.

Art: But what if your lead-time was two to three days while the rest of your competitors were still at six weeks? Wouldn't that give you a strategic advantage?

Scott: You bet it would! My sales guys could gain serious market share with that type of turnaround time. They wouldn't have to spend so much time listening to our customers complain about our long lead times. In fact, I bet we could get a lot of new business at full book price instead of always having to offer a discount to offset our lead times.

Art: You're right, you could. People will always pay for speed. Think of the premiums UPS and FedEx get over the U.S. Postal Service. More important, however, you would be much more responsive to your customers instead of making them conform to your long lead times.

Reduce Setup Times to Cut Lead Times

Frank: Look, before you guys get carried away, I just told you that a six-week lead time is the best that we can do. How are we going to overcome that?

Art: Frank, I'm sure that you have been working hard to reduce lead times, and I commend you for that. The fact that you have gone from eight weeks down to six says a lot. We're getting ahead of ourselves here, but while we are on the subject, let's start by attacking the root cause of long lead times in most manufacturers: long setup times. Setup reduction is a foundational activity for Lean. If you don't attack it up front, you can't bring down your lead times, you can't switch from batch to flow, and you can't compete on speed. Fortunately, doing this is quite easy using the SMED (single minute exchange of dies) approach developed over many years by Shigeo Shingo. The principles apply in any industry even where there are no machines, just desks and paper or something like hospital beds. Here are a few examples of setup reductions that we did at Wiremold on various pieces of equipment over the course of a one-week kaizen event (see Figure 1-1).

Wiremold Setup Results

Equipment	Setup	Reduction
Rolling Mill	720m to 34m	-95%
150 Ton Press	90 to 5	-94%
PM Punch Press	52 to 5	-90%
Hole Cut Mill	64 to 5	-92%
2.5″ Extruder	180 to 19	-89%
Injection Molder	120 to 15	-88%

AVG. SETUP REDUCTION = 91%

Figure 1-1. Wiremold setup reductions

As you can see, the average setup reduction was cut 91 percent in just one week. You can't spend much money in that time frame. In addition, all of these times came down much further as a result of additional SMED activity. The injection molding machines, for example, got down to a range of one to two minutes.

Frank: Art, those are certainly impressive times, and you're right that you can't spend a lot of money in just one week. So I guess you are telling me that not only can setup times come way down but that setup reduction is not capital intensive? This blows a big hole in our historical assumptions that reducing setup times is capital intensive. And to be fair, we have different types of machinery than in your example. Do you think we can still reduce setup times?

Art: Yes, Frank, I'm sure you can. And once you've removed the first layer of waste, then you go back again and again to keep removing more. The idea of continuous improvement is not a dream. It is the reality of how a Lean company behaves every day. There is no such thing as "but when will we be done?" when talking about continuous improvement.

Lean Strategy

Jerry: Art, can you say more about how Lean is a business strategy? Does that mean Lean applies to any business?

Art: Excellent question. Yes, Lean applies to any type of company. In fact, in my experience nonmanufacturing companies usually get more gains from Lean than manufacturers do. Often they get dramatically more. At their core all businesses are the same. Let me write on the board a bit more:

What Is a Business?

A group of people

A collection of processes

Delivering value to a set of customers

Every business fits this definition. I think everyone would agree—until, that is, the moment you start discussing *their* business. Then, all of a sudden, although they agree in principle, they tell you all the reasons why their business is so much more complicated—which ends up as a long list of excuses why they can't get better.

Let's go a little further into this definition. Your current people are probably the ones that created the processes you use to deliver value to your customers. It only stands to reason that to change the processes you have to change the people. And by that I don't mean throw them all out and get new ones. Instead, to be successful with Lean you have to teach your people how to see things differently and solve problems so that you can get better and better. That's why I believe that Lean is "all about the people."

Jerry: But Art, focusing on the processes and the people seems inwardly focused. How can this be strategic?

Art: Simple: *the focus is always on delivering more value to the customer.* And this can only be done by improving your processes: this is the only thing that will improve your future results. Traditional companies don't seem to understand this. They tend to spend much of their time looking backward, at last month's results. They analyze them and have big monthly reviews. But why? Last month's results have already happened. There is nothing you can do about them now. What you can do, however, is focus on fixing your processes. Better processes lead to better results.

Jerry: All that makes a lot of sense, but I'm still having trouble understanding how focusing on fixing our processes is really focusing on the customer. For example, we were talking earlier about setup reduction. If I have a team spend a whole week reducing the setup on a particular machine, what has that got to do with the customer?

Art: It has everything to do with the customer. Let's say you and I are competitors and we each own the same machine that we bought from an outside equipment manufacturer. The only difference is that I can change my machine over in one minute and you take one hour. Who has the lowest cost and the best customer service?

Jerry: I suppose you do in that case. But what if it takes multiple machines to make the product?

Art: Most of the time it does take multiple machines. So, only when I get them all to very low setup times, say, under 10 minutes, will I be able to have an effect on my lead times and thus on the customer. I can only do one machine at a time. Even so I never lose sight of the objective. I want to go from six-week lead times to two to three days. This will have a big impact on the value I can deliver to my customer. So, even if it takes some time my focus is always on the end point—the customer.

Jerry: OK, thanks; now bear with me a bit more. I think that the next question that is on all of our minds is how are we going to go about this conversion from our current batch state to Lean, and what will our role be in this?

How Will We Change Everything We Do?

Art: Great question. We are going to use a simple approach that starts with a clear strategy, focuses on implementing the four Lean fundamentals, and uses a continuing series of kaizen events to both improve the processes and convert the people to Lean thinking and seeing. This will require a shift from your current functional organizational structure to a "value stream organization" with fewer layers and more direct connection to the customer. We will talk about this in greater detail later, and I will help you create a value stream structure.

To make this as simple as possible, all Lean conversions, manufacturing or nonmanufacturing, are about going from batch, your current state, to flow (see box). The batch company makes to a forecast. This usually results in a "sell one—make 10,000" approach. The Lean company, in contrast, tries to get as close as possible to the "sell one—make one" ideal, and always at the pull of the customer. Pretty much polar opposites.

Flow Production Exposes Waste

From	To
Batch production	Flow production
Push scheduling	Pull scheduling
The objective is one-piece flow.	

This is a huge shift. And you will need help. As I said before, Lean is a "learn by doing" activity, but in addition to starting the work, you will need some Lean expertise to guide you along the way. I'll help as much as I can, but I won't be with you for the number of weeks in the year to have a big enough impact. Instead I want to hook you up with a top-notch Lean consultant who can be with you at least one week per month to start with and probably more as we go along. In addition, I think we should hire an experienced individual to launch a Kaizen Promotion Office (KPO) whose full-time work will be organizing, running, and following up on kaizen activities as well as training all your associates in the Lean principles so they can begin to see the waste.

Frank Gee: Consultant? Really? We haven't had very good luck with consultants in the past.

Jerry: I second that for sure. Most of the consultants we have worked with charge an outrageous amount to come in, pore over our own data, do some fancy PowerPoint presentations, make some recommendations that we had already considered, and then leave.

Art: Don't get me wrong—I generally agree with your feelings on consultants. I have had the same experience, and I usually hate using them as well. But what I'm talking about here is quite different, even though I did use the term *consultant.* Back when I was a group executive at Danaher Corporation and we started using Shingijutsu as our Lean sensei, they referred to themselves as "Insultants." To be honest they function much more like trainers or coaches. They teach your people to see waste and develop approaches to eliminate it. We never got a PowerPoint presentation or, in fact, any type of presentation from Shingijutsu. They just spent their time out on the shop floor making things better. And it worked. As a result, you should plan on working with a good Lean consultant/trainer for many years. They contract on an annual basis. A company this size should probably start with at least 20 consulting weeks per year.

Frank: I'm not sure I fully understand this yet, but I'm open-minded, and we sure could use the help.

Jerry: OK, I think we get the general direction, but what is our role as managers going to be going forward? How do you expect us to act and why?

The Senior Management Team's Role

Art: Lean principles are in fact pretty simple—what Taiichi Ohno called common sense. But they are about 180 degrees different from the traditional management approach in almost every area. Look at the differences in Figure 1-2.

Judy Rankin: Art, I have to say that this is a pretty scary list. It basically tells us that *everything* we have been doing is the exact opposite of what you expect us to do going forward. Tell me, how do we get people to buy into that?

Traditional vs. Lean

Traditional	Lean
• Complex	• Simple/Visual
• Forecast/Budget Driven	• Demand Driven
• Excess Inventory	• Make One – Sell One
• Speed Up Value-Added Work	• Reduce Non-Value-Added Work
• Long Lead Times	• Minimal Lead Times
• Quality Inspected or Sorted In Functional Departments	• Quality Built and Designed In
	• Process/Value Stream Teams

Figure 1-2. Differences between traditional and Lean management

Art: Judy, your point is well taken. To make the switch, you have to change the thinking of everyone in the company. It is as if I walked in here today and said that everything here is no good and has to be changed. Now, I'm being a little overdramatic, but the changes are big enough that it will feel a little like that. This type of change can't be managed in the traditional sense. It has to be led, and it has to be led from the top. That means this entire management team has to come together and lead the charge.

Jerry, as CEO, is of course the key. He and I have already talked about that. If he is not willing to be the out-front, hands-on leader of this change, then it will never work. I tell anyone who asks, "If you can't get the CEO to lead, don't start down the Lean path." Of course as investors that is unacceptable to us, so I'm glad that Jerry is willing to make the change.

Dick: Well, I'm glad to hear that Jerry is committed [*laughing*]. I guess that means the rest of us can go back to business as usual.

Art: Dick, on the contrary: that doesn't let the rest of you off the hook. Certainly Gary, Steve, Sam, and John, as presidents of your subsidiary companies, have the same role as Jerry does for UGH in their own units. But even the staff-level functional leaders here in the main part of the business have to lead the charge and support the changes in their areas.

It is critical that you function as a single unified team. Teamwork, not only at your levels but throughout the whole company, is important if Lean is to be successful. I don't want to hear about squabbles between sales and operations, for example. The customer only sees you as a single entity, UGH, so internal fighting is counterproductive.

Judy: Art, I get the impression that when you talk about teamwork being critical you are putting a very different emphasis and meaning to it than what we think of as teamwork now. Can you elaborate a bit?

Art: Certainly, Judy, and you make a good point. Teamwork in Lean is a much bigger deal than the way you think of it now. All functions have to work together in a coordinated way. You can't have sales soliciting large batch orders while the plant is trying to level load production. You have to know what each other is doing and how it ties into the overall objectives of UGH. This will take a level of teamwork that you haven't experienced yet. And not just at your level. Teamwork has to be present all the way down to the value-adding employees.

Scott: OK, I get the teamwork part, but you aren't planning on doing kaizens in areas like mine? Dick and I have almost all office workers.

Art: Of course we will be doing kaizen in your areas. No area will be exempt, and some of the biggest gains will be in the office areas. In fact, one of our first kaizens should be in the customer service area, as errors here cause big trouble for us later on in the process due to the wrong information being given to operations, shipping, and billing.

Jerry: That makes sense. A lot of our customer complaints come from shipping the wrong amount or having the wrong pricing or even shipping it to the wrong address. Most of this can be traced back to order entry errors, some of them made by the customers, by the way. In any event, this would be a good place to start. What other things do you want to see from this team as we go along?

Art: One of the key things that all of you have to do is to show your commitment to the shift to Lean on an ongoing basis. The best way to do this is for each of you to be on five or six weeklong kaizen teams per year. And I don't mean just poking your head in to see how it is going. I mean being a full-time participant on the team for the whole week.

Dick: Art, with all due respect, are you kidding? All of us are going full speed day in and day out. How are we ever going to fit that in?

Art: This is a big commitment—but it is extremely important. First of all, it shows every employee that the senior leadership team is fully behind the shift to Lean. More important, it shows that you have your priorities straight and are investing your time where you will get the biggest return due to the increased value that you will be able to deliver to your customers.

But I think this is enough of an introduction for now. We have a meeting this afternoon with about 100 of your people to kick this off, and I will give you more insight into why we want to go in this direction, along with the key principles that are involved, at that session. I even plan to give you a much deeper understanding of kaizen and why it is such a good methodology to use in converting everyone to a Lean way of thinking while at the same time drastically improving our value-adding activities.

Hey, don't look so serious. This will be a lot of hard work, but you will be amazed by the results and should have a lot of fun along the way.

Summary Points

- Lean is not a manufacturing or operations "thing" but the greatest strategic weapon in running any business that you will ever see.
- The only way to learn Lean is by doing it.

- There are three fundamental "management musts":

  Lean is the strategy

  Lead from the top

  Transform the people

- Lean is all about removing waste from your value-adding activities to get to a state of continuous improvement, allowing you to deliver more value to your customers than your competitors can.

2

UGH's Lean Training

OVERVIEW

Now that Jerry York's management team has been given an overview of how Lean can turn their company around, it's time to join 100 UGH employees for a kickoff meeting about why the company wants to make the shift. What are the expected results, the fundamentals that will form the basis of the turnaround, the strategy that will be followed, and the kaizen approach that will be used? UGH's associates need to understand the rationale behind the changes that will need to be made. Removing the waste and competing on operational excellence will enable them to deliver more value to their customers, gain market share, grow the company, and secure their jobs. As most of this is almost the exact opposite of the approach they have been following, it's critical to spend time answering questions to help them understand. The more they accept that Lean is a better approach to running UGH, the easier it will be to implement.

Why Lean?

Jerry: OK, everyone, let's settle down and get started. First of all, it's great to see you all here. We don't get a collection of our best people together often enough. Having you all here today is important as we are about to kick off a whole new chapter in the history of UGH. This is our first training session, but it will be repeated later in the day for the second shift and a couple of times tomorrow so that everyone gets to hear from us firsthand. It will also be repeated in our four subsidiary companies using both a video of today's session and some hands-on training.

As you know, we were recently acquired by J.W. Childs Associates, a Boston-based private equity firm. JWC has a reputation for using Lean as a business strategy to get the most out of its investments, and we will be no exception.

Today we are kicking off UGH's Lean journey, and I can tell you that JWC's expectations of what we can achieve are very high. I'm excited, but I have to admit that I will be learning Lean right along with the rest of you. To get us going faster, I've asked Art Byrne, a JWC partner and our new chairman, to get us started with an overview of Lean, why we want to do this, and how we plan to go about it. Art has been doing this in various companies for over 30 years, so he has a lot to tell us. Art, it's all yours.

Art: Thanks Jerry! It is a pleasure to be with you all today. I can tell you that we are very excited about our investment in UGH. You are doing well, your products have a good reputation in your markets, and, above all, we believe you have a great group of talented people. At the same time, we think that you have a huge upside potential. We base that on what other companies have been able to do using a Lean strategy versus what you are doing now. The best way to help you understand this is to show you a few examples of what others have done and see what this type of results would mean for UGH. So let's start with the first example, my old company, The Wiremold Company.

As you can see in Figure 2-1, Wiremold has a long list of impressive results. Let's start with the fact that gross profit increased by 13 full points, from 38 percent to 51 percent, over about a nine-year period. Think of what that would mean for UGH. We would go from 30 percent gross margin to 43, which would result in *$71 million additional profit*. Most of that would fall directly to the EBIT line. UGH's EBIT last year was a little over $50 million, so this would have the impact of more than doubling our earnings—which in turn would double our enterprise value.

Wiremold Results

- Lead Times from 4–6 weeks to 1–2 Days
- Productivity Up 162%
- Gross Profit Up from 38% to 51%
  Machine Changeovers from 3 Per Week to 20–30 a Day
- Inventory Turns from 3X to 18X
- Customer Service from 50% to 98%
- Sales More Than Quadrupled
- EBITDA Grew from 6.2% to 20.8%
- Operating Income Up 13.4 X
- Enterprise Value Increased by 2,467%

Figure 2-1. Wiremold results

Next you will note that inventory turns increased from 3 turns, your current level, to 18 turns. If, based on last year's balance sheet, you were at 18 turns, you would only need $21 million of inventory versus the $117 million you have now. That frees up $96 million of cash—something that I call "sleeping money." This surplus cash is just lying around waiting for someone to pick it up. This amount also happens to represent almost two years of your current EBIT earnings ($50 million). I don't know if you'll reach Wiremold's levels, but there certainly is a lot of potential cash available here.

In addition, Wiremold's sales more than quadrupled over a nine-year period. Our operating income rose by 13.4 times. And best of all, the enterprise value increased by 2,467 percent. One of the keys to all of this was the progress that people made on changeovers of their equipment. You will note in Figure 2-1 that machines with a changeover rate of 3 per week were eventually being changed 20 to 30 times per day. Think of the impact that has on everything else. You need less space due to lower inventory, the workplace (you may hear me refer to it as the gemba, which is a Japanese word referring to the actual work site) can be more compact and much safer, your quality is better, your costs go down, your lead times drop dramatically, and your customer service goes way up.

Frank: Art, those are certainly impressive numbers. Being the manufacturing guy here, I'm particularly impressed with what you just mentioned about setup reduction. If we could get our equipment to change over 20 to 30 times per day, we would have a whole new ball game here at UGH. Can you give us a more detailed example of what is possible?

Art: Sure, Frank, I'd be happy to. When I first got to Wiremold, I was out on the shop floor one day looking at one of our bigger rolling mills. I asked, "How long does it take to change this over?" I was told 14 hours, although sometimes it takes a little longer. "No, no," I said, "We can't have that. We need to be able to change it over in less than 10 minutes." I'm sure you can imagine the reaction—"Who is this nutcase, and why did we get him as our new CEO? He has to be out of his mind." But we started to do kaizens on the changeover time. In this case it required four or five kaizens because we had to alter the machine in simple ways. As a result, it took something like nine months to one year. The end result, however, was a six-minute changeover time. More important, we picked up a few new Lean converts as well. They went from "Who is this nut?" to "Gee, what is his next crazy idea?"

Jerry: Art, the setup results on this rolling mill are certainly impressive. In fact, we are all a little shocked by the big Wiremold gains you are sharing with us. At the same time, I have great confidence in all our associates and am sure that given a little help we can get similar results. [*Looking around the room*] Don't you all agree? So I assume that you would say that the people conversion is more important than the actual setup results, right?

Art: By far the people conversion is more important. After all, the setup reduction didn't happen by itself. The people made that happen, just as I'm sure that the people at UGH will make it happen here as well. It is, however, a great example of how you and all your people will convert to Lean. It will be on a project-by-project basis, a few associates at a time. Participating in something that you are sure is impossible and then helping to make it a reality makes you feel really good. It also makes it hard to deny that Lean can provide great value.

Dick Conway: Art, maybe we can accomplish great things, but starting with the Wiremold results is a little intimidating. Do you have any easier examples?

Art: I can share some additional examples, but I don't think you should expect them to get easier. Our next example (Figure 2-2) is American Safety Razor, one of our former portfolio companies. ASR at the time (2002–2006) was the leading producer of private label wet shaving products for the U.S. and European markets. As you can see in Figure 2-2, it almost tripled inventory turns, brought its customer service results from 85 to 98 percent on time, while at the same time increasing EBITDA margin by six full points. To put that in perspective for UGH, a six-point gain in your EBITDA margin last year would translate into earnings of $83.6 million versus the $50.4 million you actually did. By the way, it also freed up $65 million in cash, which helped realize a 3.5 times return on our investment when we sold it, but more important it was a great result for the people of ASR both financially and from the pride they took in achieving the gains and creating a better work environment.

American Safety Razor Results		
Item	**Result**	**Change**
Inventory Turns	2.5 times to 6.2 times	+148%
Working Capital as a % of Sales	34% to 15%	-50%
Customer Service	85% to 98%	+15%
EBITDA Margin	17% to 23%	+35%
Cash Freed Up from Working Capital	$65 million	n.a.

Figure 2-2. American Safety Razor results

Barbara Mooney: [*Barbara, wearing a bright red hat with a jaunty white feather, stands up, and the room goes quiet. Art looks over at Jerry York, who catches Art's eye and shares an expression that is half grin and half grimace.*] Art, my name is Barbara Mooney. I work out in the shop, and I have been working here for over 30 years. This is a good company with a lot of good people. I don't know how you can compare us to these other companies. Our products are different. More important, my guess is that these companies got their results by using Lean to cut head count. Isn't that what this is all about?

Art: Nice to meet you. Thirty years is a long time. I bet you know more about this company than almost anyone. Barbara, let me reassure you that Lean is not about cutting heads. None of these companies got their results that way. In fact, the opposite was true. The focus was on removing the waste and growing the business. This is the way we want to get productivity gains as it is the best way to protect our workforce. This is the approach we will use at UGH as well. So please, relax, we plan to work smarter, not harder. We will only be successful if we grow our people, not if we get rid of them.

Dick Conway: Art, every example seems to show we could double our earnings and free up a ton of cash from inventory. Let's assume we can do that—which, frankly would be shocking all by itself. But to Barbara's point, what about growth? More specifically, what about new product development? Do you have any examples of what can happen here?

Art: It just so happens that my next example has thrived on new product development—Sturm, Ruger & Company (Figure 2-3), which is listed on the NYSE. Around 2005 John Cosentino, who was the other group executive with me at Danaher Corporation and served on my board at Wiremold, got on Ruger's board. He initiated the move to Lean, replaced much of management with proven Lean talent, and brought in Shingijutsu. And boom, look what happened. Sales quadrupled, and it gained 21 points of gross margin over just seven years. Don't worry, I won't embarrass you by even trying to calculate what this would have translated into for UGH. Let's just say . . . a lot.

Sturm, Ruger & Co., Inc.

Results 2006-2013

	2006	2013	Increase
Revenues	$168M	$688M	4.1x
GM%	17%	38%	2.2x
EBITDA ($/%)	$6M/3%	$196M/28%	33x
Inventory T/O	1.6x	6.7x	5.1 Turns
RONOA	1%	108%	WOW!
Units Sold	478,000	2.2M	4.7x
Market Size (Index)	100	186	1.9x
# Engineers	<10	>80	90%
% of Revenue (New Products)	<5%	65%	
Sales/Employee	$150,000	$289,000	1.9x
Profit Sharing	5%	>30%	6x
Share Price	$5.86	• Hit $85	14x
Enterprise Value	<$200M	>$1.4B	7X

Figure 2-3. Sturm, Ruger results

I want you to pay the most attention to the percentage of revenue accounted for by new products (those introduced in the last five years). This number went from under 5 percent (which is practically none) to 65 percent today. You won't see this very often. This dramatic change was driven by a switch to quality function deployment (QFD) as the new product development process. This is a Lean approach to new product development that we will discuss in more detail a little later. It is a simple visual approach that will really help our growth and give us market-leading products. As a rule of thumb it will cut product development time by 50 to 75 percent.

Just in case I haven't gotten you to understand "why Lean" yet, the next example (Figure 2-4) shows the types of increases in equity value that have been achieved by six different companies over various time frames. We have already talked about Wiremold and Ruger. John Cosentino and I were, as co-group executives, responsible for getting Lean started at Danaher along with one of my presidents, George Koenigsaecker. We were also somewhat responsible for getting it started at United Technologies—John as head of Otis Elevator–North America and me by introducing Shingijutsu to Pratt & Whitney and leading the first kaizen events at Carrier Corporation. PCI Group/Rau Fastener was owned by John Cosentino during the period shown. Whitcraft Group is a Hartford, Connecticut, area manufacturer of aircraft engine parts that John and I invested in and served on its advisory board.

Tale of the Tape				
Increases in Equity Value				
	Start	End/Now	# Years	Gain
Danaher	$0.40/sh	$75/sh	26	>188x
United Technologies	$6.00/sh	$120/sh	23	>20x
The Wiremold Company	$30M	$770M	9	>26x
PCI/Rau Fastener	$0.4M	$11.5M	2	28x
Whitcraft Group	~$4.0M	~$80M	12	>20x
Ruger	$5.86/sh	$64/sh	7	12x
OVER $170B OF SHAREHOLDER VALUE CREATED				

Figure 2-4. Increases in equity value

As you can see, all but one company increased equity value by over 20 times. But more important, in my opinion, were the people results that each of these companies achieved. Their growth created significant growth opportunities for all the people who worked there. They had a cleaner and much safer work environment. They created a learning environment in which everyone could learn and grow. And certainly the wealth that was created was shared with all the employees. I don't have specific examples for each company, but at Wiremold, the employees, through their participation in the 401(k) plan and the fact that we matched their contributions with company stock, were the biggest single shareholder when we sold the company. They got the biggest share of the wealth that they collectively created.

Jerry: Art, those results are certainly impressive. Now, the one question that was in the back of my mind as you were going through this is, will this work for nonmanufacturers? My next-door neighbor, for example, runs a hospital. Would it work for him?

Art: Of course it will work for him. In fact, he will probably get better results on a relative basis. I just happen to have a hospital example. This (Figure 2-5) is Virginia Mason Medical Center in Seattle, Washington. When it started its Lean journey, CEO Gary Kaplan flew 30 of his most senior doctors and administrators from Seattle to Hartford, Connecticut, to visit Wiremold. We explained that what we do and what they do is the same. "We take a piece of raw material, in our case steel or plastic, we run it through a series of processes where we punch holes in it and attach stuff to it, then we put it in a box and sell it. You also start with a piece of raw material, in your case a human body, and you put it through a series of processes where you punch holes in it, attach stuff to it, then put it in a car and send it home (no bodies in boxes, please)." They laughed at this, but they got the point, and so we spent the next couple of days explaining how we pulled raw material through our processes. Shortly after they got back to Seattle, Gary flew them to Japan to visit Toyota and some of Shingijutsu's more advanced clients.

Virginia Mason Results
2000-2010

- Nurses Spend 90% with Patients vs. 35%
- Time to Report Lab Results Down 85%
- Cost of Supplies Down $1 Million a Year
- Hospital Liability Costs Down 49%
- A/R Days >90 Days Down 74%
- Surgery Center: Cases per Day Up 60%
- Pharmacy: Order to Available Time Down 93%
- Margin $s: $0.7M in 2000 to $41M in 2010

Figure 2-5. Virginia Mason results

Look at their results. Their nurses now spend 90 percent of their time with patients, versus 35 percent on average for most hospitals. Time to report lab tests to patients has dropped 85 percent. In the surgery center, the number of cases per day per operating room increased by 60 percent. Best of all, they went from earning just $700,000 when they started their Lean journey in 2000 to earning $40.9 million in 2010.

Dick Conway: Art, I'm still having a hard time believing that we can really double our earnings and free up an odd $100 million in cash from inventory. How exactly did these companies get these great results?

Art: All of these companies focused their energy and efforts on finding and removing waste from all of their processes, be they office, factory, supply chain, or whatever, in order to be able to deliver more value to their customers. Removing the waste became the daily work and driving force behind each of these companies. They didn't do it as a cost reduction program. Yes, they got major cost improvements as you can see in their results, but simply reducing costs wasn't the driver. They all understood that removing the waste was strategic. The focus was on increasing their ability to deliver more value to their customers and thus gain market share and grow.

This is the same approach we want to follow here at UGH. For us to become a Lean enterprise with a Lean culture, everything must change. Let's start by talking about our understanding of waste.

Waste

Toyota tried to help us all here by defining the different types of waste so that people could more readily identify waste and thus be able to work on removing it. All of these are still relevant today.

The Seven Wastes

1. **Overproduction.** Making more products than can be sold.
2. **Waiting.** Operators or machines waiting.
3. **Transportation.** Transporting parts.
4. **Processing.** Processing itself.
5. **Inventories.** Raw material, work in process, and finished goods.
6. **Moving.** Operator and machine movement.
7. **Defects.** Making defective products.

As Taiichi Ohno explains, "If we regard only work that is needed as real work and define the rest as waste, the following equation holds true whether considering individual workers or the entire line:

$$\text{Present Capacity} = \text{Work} + \text{Waste}$$

"It is our job to find and remove the waste, thus increasing capacity, which in turn allows us to shorten our lead times and be much more responsive to our customers' needs."

Jerry York: I like Mr. Ohno's simple equation. It suggests to me that doubling your capacity doesn't have to be capital intensive; you can just eliminate waste and get the same result. This helps to explain why Lean is strategic and not just some cost reduction program. Can you break this down further for us so we can start to understand how to get at the waste?

Art: Sure, Jerry, great question. We can divide everything we do, in any type of company, into three broad buckets:

1. Work that adds value
2. Non-value-added but necessary work (like closing the books at the end of the month or complying with government regulations)
3. Work that adds no value and is just pure waste

In any traditionally managed company, the portion that is waste is normally well over 60 percent of what is going on. First you want to attack the pure waste. But as you go along you can eventually improve the value-adding and non-value-adding but necessary areas as well.

Dick Conway: Art, as the CFO here, I have to take exception with your statement that closing the books each month is non-value-added. I have a lot of people in my department, and we think that what we do adds a lot of value to this company.

Art: Dick, thank you for bringing this up. I'm not trying to insult your whole department. I said closing the books is non-value-added *but necessary*. Our banks, our shareholders, and your management team all need this information. But from the customer's point of view this work adds no direct value. Just ask yourself if you could go ask for a price increase because some request from your bank or from the financial accounting standards board will take you three more days each month to close the books. Of course not. She would laugh at you.

Batch to Flow

Art: Another way to look at how to get at this waste is to understand that going from a traditional functional organizational structure to Lean is always in effect going from batch to flow. We will be approaching it this way, so it is helpful to understand the differences.

Barbara: Art, it's me again. Do you see us as a batch company? If so, should we feel insulted?

Art: Yes, Barbara, I do see you as a batch company. But I don't mean that in any negative way, so please don't feel insulted. In my experience, just about every company batches in one form or other. It is this approach that gives rise to most of the waste and inefficiencies that exist in today's businesses.

For industry, I think batching has just naturally evolved. Manufacturing was a craft activity with several very specific crafts or skills needed to make a product. As we moved to more of a machine-based approach, people were trained to run one specific type of machine. The idea of "one man, one machine" was quite common. Then for productivity's sake we started to group similar machines together so that one man could operate two similar machines. As this equipment got more sophisticated it took longer to change over. This problem was solved by the finance department's "invention" of economic order quantities (EOQs) that told us the ideal lot size that needed to be run based on the time it took to change over the equipment. Lot sizes got bigger. Waste grew. Lead times expanded.

Frank: Art, we are certainly organized by type of machine, so I guess we fit your batch definition. But how are we being affected? Can you be more specific about what type of problems, or I guess I should now say waste, it causes?

Art: Sure Frank, Figure 2-6 shows a typical layout for a batch manufacturer. Equipment is arranged in functional departments by type of machine. In order for a product to get made, it has to travel to and from a number of these departments.

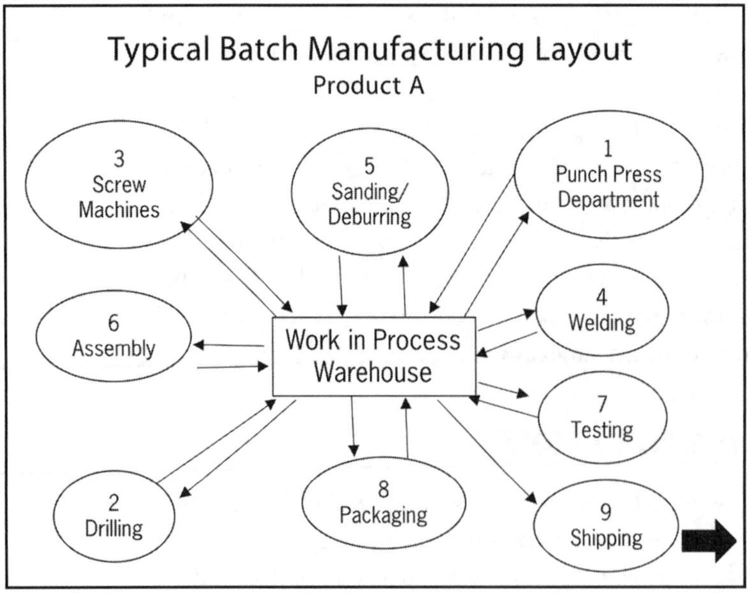

Typical Batch Manufacturing Layout
Product A

Figure 2-6. Typical batch manufacturing layout

The machines all run at different rates, so the time it takes in any one department is different from all the other departments. Once the work in one department is finished we need a place to put the product until we are ready to send it to the next department. We created a large work-in-progress (WIP) inventory storage area in this layout to deal with this. We also have large warehouses for raw material, packaging supplies, and finished goods (which I didn't show in this example). In effect we have created a maze: getting product through it requires lots of sophisticated planning (MRP systems) and long lead times. It was all put together logically, but the waste that exists here is phenomenal. And, to be more specific, this looks a lot like what you have here at UGH and explains in a simple way why you have six-week lead times and low inventory turns.

Jerry: We can't be the only guilty ones. What about my neighbor in the hospital? Am I the only batch guy in my neighborhood?

Art: Jerry, batching is everywhere. Think of the distributor whose philosophy is "you can't sell from an empty wagon." He batches in the way he orders (three to four months' worth at a time). This in turn causes extra movement of products, extra storage space, costly excess inventory, and of course the risk of obsolescence. A hospital batches in the way patients move through the various departments, technicians do lab tests or read MRIs or x-rays, and even in the way patients are discharged. A bank will batch loan applications through several departments of "specialists" and take three weeks to make a decision when the actual touch time labor might only be 10 minutes.

Hand from the audience: Hi, I'm Carol Pope from sales. I want Jerry York to be a hero in his neighborhood. What is the solution to our batching?

Art: Thanks for the question, Carol. The solution to this is to move to "flow" in production or processing. Take the bank loan application. You want to create a system where once I pick up a loan application, I don't put it down until it is done. I may have to physically pass it from one expert to the next for this to happen, and that means they have to sit right next to each other, but it will be "flowing" through the process until it is done. The same is true in manufacturing. You want to arrange the machines such that once you pick up a piece of raw material you keep it moving (i.e., don't put it down) until it is a finished product. The graphic in Figure 2-7 shows what a one-piece flow cell of this type should look like.

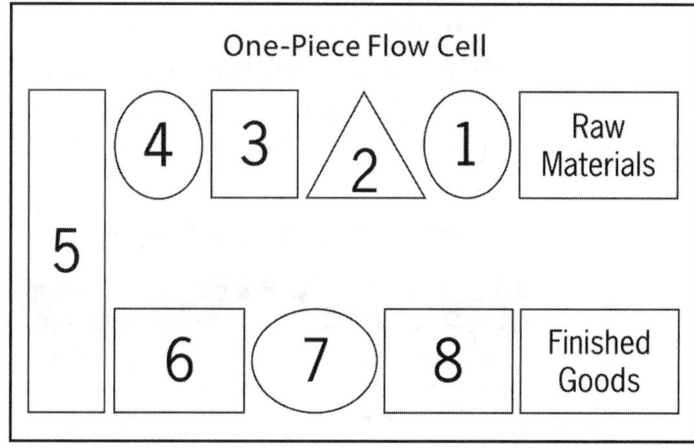

Figure 2-7. One-piece flow layout

Taking this one step further, the following example shows

how a traditional batch company might schedule its production versus a Lean company. For simplicity, this company makes only four products: A, B, C, and D.

Batch Company Schedule

Week 1	Week 2	Week 3	Week 4
Product A	Product A	Product B	C 3 Days, D 2 Days

Lean Company Schedule

Every Day
A B A B A C A D A B A C A B A B A D A C

This is quite a contrast. Think of what happens in the batch example when someone wants to order product C or D in week one. There is no plan to make this product for three weeks in the case of C and over three and a half weeks in the case of D. That means that the only way to deal with this is to carry a lot of inventory or to force the customer to wait. The Lean company, in contrast, can respond to the customer's demand almost instantaneously and with very little inventory. This is the kind of capability you are trying to build in the transition from batch to flow.

Dick: Right now we are the first example above. And it feels like a pretty big leap from where we are to the Lean company schedule. How should we think about this? What is the strategy?

Art: To help you better understand the difference between batch and flow, the table titled "Contrast Between Batch and Flow" assumes that we have two companies in the exact same business. Each does $100 million in sales. The only difference is that one uses batch and the other uses flow.

Contrast Between Batch and Flow

	Batch	Flow
Sq. feet of space	300,000	150,000
Inventory turns	4x	16x

	Batch	Flow
Inventory dollars	$17.5 mil	$3.8 mil
Gross margin	30%	40%
Lead time	6 weeks	2 days
Defect percent	1.7%	.6%
Customer service	93.4%	98.7%
Productivity	3.0%	9.0%

As you can see, the Lean or flow company has significant advantages. Similar gains are available for service companies. I once did some kaizen work for an insurance company. The focus was on underwriting. When the company started, it took 48 days on average to respond to an application for insurance; the typical underwriter could underwrite 15 lives per week. We got to the point where over half of the applications were being responded to in less than 20 days and the underwriter was doing 88 lives per week. There was still a lot of upside, by the way. For a $500 million per year revenue hospital, a kaizen proved that increasing bed turnover by 25 percent (which seemed to be quite doable without capital spending) was worth approximately $60 million per year in gross margin. The main thrust here, of course, was moving from batch to flow.

Strategy

Art: I mentioned earlier that Lean is a strategy, a way to run your business. But what would this strategy look like if you had to write it down? Well, here, in Figure 2-8, is the strategy we developed at Wiremold. I believe any manufacturing company can just copy this strategy and use Lean as the way to achieve these goals. I want you to use this approach here at UGH.

The overall objectives—being number one in your markets and competing on time—are admittedly straightforward and a bit generic. The time-based competitor part may seem a little odd to you, but it's essential to Lean. Removing the waste always lowers the time it takes to do anything. More important, companies that compete on time can charge more for their rapid response and are very hard to catch.

Wiremold Strategy

Be the Leading Supplier in the Industries We Serve and One of the Top 10 Time-Based Companies Globally

1. Constantly Strengthen Our Base Operations
   100% On-Time Customer Service
   50% Reduction in Defects—Each Year
   20% Productivity Gain—Each Year
   20x Inventory Turns
   Visual Control and the 5S's
2. Double In Size Every 3 To 5 Years
   Pursue Selective Acquisitions
   Use QFD to Speed New Product Introductions

Figure 2.8. Wiremold strategy

Hospital Strategy

Become the Quality Leader In Healthcare In the USA, And a Global Leader In Time-based Competition

1. Constantly Strengthen Our Base Operations
   10% Gain in Patient Satisfaction Each Year
   50% Reduction in Defects Each Year
   20% Productivity Gain Each Year
   20X Inventory Turns
   Visual Control and the 5s's
2. Deliver Value To Patients In Order To:
   Grow and Gain Share
   Be the Employer of Choice in Our Markets

Figure 2-9. Hospital strategy

As you can see, all of the goals in the Wiremold strategy are stretch goals. To go from 3 turns, where we were at the time, to 20 turns, for example, requires a whole new way of thinking. You can't get there by just doing what you currently do, only slightly better. You also can't get there overnight because in order for this to happen almost everything else has to change. Instead you should think about it as a 5- to 10-year journey where you add a turn or two of improvement every year. One of my portfolio companies that also started with inventory turns of about 3x now has 8 of its 11 plants at over 20x turns, and yet it is still budgeting for a 1.5x improvement in turns each year and is getting it.

I think you will start to understand the opportunity better as we go along. For now, our approach is to constantly remove the waste so that we can compete on our operational excellence. To do that you first have to define what operational excellence means. The five items under section 1, in Figure 2-8, "Constantly Strengthen Our Base Operations," provide a road map for this. Focusing all your energies on achieving these targets forces you to look forward at where UGH is going, and not backward at where it has been as the "make-the-month" boys do. It also is the approach that will drive you to a continuous improvement culture.

The same approach can work for nonmanufacturers as well. The list of things that define operational excellence will vary, but the concept remains the same. As an example, Figure 2-9 is what the same strategic approach for a hospital might look like.

How Will We Implement Lean?

Judy Rankin: Art, this is a great overview of waste, batch to flow, strategy, and all. Unfortunately, all of it is almost the exact opposite of what we have been doing. How are we going to make the change? Is there a particular method we will use?

Art: Well, yes, Judy, I want UGH to use the kaizen method to implement Lean. A typical kaizen event will last for one week (although there is nothing sacred about this—two-week, three-day, or even one-day kaizen events will also take place) and be conducted by a team of 8 to 10 of our associates. It will be a full-time activity for the whole week, and the targets the teams will be given will all be stretch goals.

But I want you to understand kaizen in a broader sense, not just as a series of improvement activities. The box shows what can be accomplished through kaizen events.

Kaizen Events Will Drive the Following

1. Core activity to remove waste and/or solve problems
2. Key training vehicle to teach all associates a new way to think and act
3. Get everyone on board to support change
4. Become the way we will create a learning environment
5. Critical path to UGH's Lean/kaizen culture

Steve Jones, president of UGH Automotive Division: Art, because my division sells into the automotive industry, I have heard the word *kaizen* before. I always thought it was just another way of saying continuous improvement. Our customers talk about running "kaizen events," but I never heard anyone say that kaizen could have such a broad impact as you just outlined.

Art: Yes, Steve, it will impact all those areas. As I said before, Lean is a "learn by doing" approach to running your business. Most of your learning will therefore come during the kaizen events, which will be our principal approach in the early going where the most dramatic change has to take place. These will be well-organized events with specific goals and some formal training up front to help you understand the methodology.

The Traditional Approach

Art: To get an appreciation for the power of the kaizen approach, it is best to contrast it to the more traditional approach to problem solving. Most companies approach problem solving or improvement activities by forming a team. While cross-functional, the team will probably consist primarily of salaried employees. These important people are all very busy with their day jobs. As a result, the team will start out with a plan to meet once per week to address the situation they have been assigned. Sound familiar?

Judy: In fact, that is our normal approach—and works for us. Is there something wrong with that?

Art: Well, as the team moves along, people start to discuss various approaches or fixes to problems and goals. These proposals often create additional requests for more data. After perhaps several months and lots of analysis, the team will agree on a plan of action. Please take note that at this point, the entire output from the team is just a "plan." Any actual change activities will take place sometime in the future. But first, the "plan" will have to be reviewed and approved by senior management. And nothing will have been actually done.

This is a pretty common approach for most companies. There is an aversion to risk built into this. Management wants to make sure that any proposed changes have a high degree of certainty and perhaps just as important fit into the current way of doing things. Many times this means that you have to respect the current functional departments or other management silos and not step on anyone's toes.

Judy: But again, so what? The team was asked to come up with a solution to a problem—and it did. Maybe it took some time. But I think it is prudent not to rush into things and make mistakes.

Art: Yes Judy, but let me reemphasize the Lean notion of "learn by doing" when it comes to this. Sticking with the old, slow, cautious approach won't get you much change. It certainly won't let you improve quickly. I think that the comfort most companies have with this traditional approach goes a long way toward explaining why companies make the choices they do when they decide to go down the Lean path.

Kaizen Is for Doing

Jerry York: Art, as Judy mentioned, our general methodology is just as you describe. I guess what we are all wondering is, how does the kaizen approach differ from this?

Art: The kaizen approach we will use is a "doing" activity as opposed to the "planning" activity we have described. Equipment that you may not have moved since it was first installed in the plant 10 to 15 years ago will be moving by the afternoon of the first day. You will get big results by the end of the week, as shown on the chart in Figure 2-10. These are actual, and typical, results from a one-week kaizen event. I have seen this happen over and over again. The main reason is that during a kaizen the team members are assigned full-time for the week (or whatever the kaizen duration). This short, intense effort focuses on obtaining some stretch goals in a set period of time—an approach that really distinguishes kaizen from any other problem-solving mindset. It is what makes it so powerful.

Before the traditional team holds its second planning meeting, the kaizen team has already achieved some very significant improvements in your business. (Again refer to Figure 2-10.) You get fixes, not "plans." But there is a lot more going on here than just that. To begin with, a kaizen team has a mixture of salaried and hourly employees (versus the mostly salaried composition of the traditional team). You need to include people who actually do the work you are focusing on as well as the leader of their area. You also need a couple of people who can implement things on the spot like someone from the tool room or from maintenance (perhaps from IT and building services if you are not a manufacturing company). The rest of the team can be managers, engineers, sales force members, union heads, or whatever mix you think would be best. The best ideas for improvement will normally come from the people who do the work. Having them participate in the improvements will also help ensure that the changes stick. It also gives everyone a sense of empowerment and an excitement that positive changes can finally start to happen.

Typical Results of a One-Week Kaizen

- Cut Lead Times 90%
- Reduce Staffing from 10 to 5
- Reduce Inventory by 70%
- Reduce Floor Space by 50%
- Reduce Defects by 60%
- Reduce Travel Distance by 90%
- Cut Setup Time by 90%
- Connect the Customer to the Shop Floor

Figure 2-10. Typical kaizen results

Barbara: Art, do you mind if I speak my mind about this?

Art: Barbara, I am getting the idea that you will whether I mind or not. And in fact, I'd love to hear what you have to say.

Barbara: This sounds like a great approach. But I don't know how it can work in an environment like ours. No one here ever listens to improvement ideas that come from the people on the floor doing the work. At least they never have in the past. So how will this kaizen thing change that?

Art: Well, Barbara, I'm disappointed to hear this but not surprised. And I want to thank you for asking this question. The fact is that most traditional companies are so focused on "making the daily numbers/making the month" that they don't listen to their people. UGH is certainly not unique in this regard. On a kaizen team, however, everyone is considered equal. If you and Jerry York were on the same team, we would expect you both to contribute to solving the problem assigned to the team. In fact, if you were the one doing the job on a daily basis, we would expect you to have much better ideas than Jerry on how to improve the work.

Barbara: Art, I love the idea of mixed teams of hourly and salaried employees, but I still don't understand how you think this will change our culture.

Art: Another good question. The culture change comes from a number of things. First of all, getting great results through this work starts to create a sense of teamwork. Lean is a "learn by doing" approach, and kaizen events are where the learning is actually happening. Teaching everyone on the team how to see waste is eye opening for everyone and helps create the learning environment that Lean thrives on. It starts to build a sense of "well, gee, if we could solve that problem we can solve anything" within the entire organization. Stretch goals are no longer an issue once you have been on a couple of kaizen teams and experienced just how much can be done in a week. Your kaizen culture will build event by event over time. The more kaizens you do, the faster it will happen.

Barbara: Nice words, but I still think you are a little too optimistic here.

Judy: When you say that the more kaizens you do the faster you build your Lean culture, what sorts of targets should we be shooting for?

Art: You should set a goal to get everyone on a kaizen team at least once within the first year. Another good target is to run two kaizen events per week in each facility. If you can do more than that, it would be even better. Of course many of your key people will be on multiple kaizen events in the first year. This is especially important for the CEO and senior staff. They should each be on four to six weeklong kaizens every year.

Training

Judy: If we commit fully to this approach, it will have huge implications on how we conduct training, Art. From what I can see, Lean is a radical departure from what we have been doing. So do we need to create a large training program in order to make this shift?

Art: Judy, thanks, and please don't! Just share the advantages of Lean companies with people the way I'm doing now, sharing results like I showed you earlier, to teach the reason UGH is going down the Lean path. Help people understand the Lean fundamentals and some of the Lean tools that will help everyone see waste. Your introduction should emphasize that to be successful every employee will be expected to help find and remove the waste. This might be a three- to four-hour session like the one we are having now. It should be mandatory for all employees and, as you go along, for new hires or the employees of new acquisitions.

The main training tool, however, will be participating on kaizen teams. Kaizen teams will help you actualize the learning as people implement Lean in a real time, on the shop floor environment or wherever they do their work. Kaizen is the "doing" part in "learn by doing." To help make each kaizen as effective as possible I recommend that everyone on a kaizen team get a two- to three-hour refresher course on the Friday afternoon before the kaizen is to begin. This should cover the basic Lean fundamentals, how to do time observations, how to use the standard work and standard work combination sheets and similar tools that they will be using during the kaizen starting on Monday morning. Putting the training to use right away is the best way for people to remember it.

Barbara: Art, now I really think you are crazy. How can a couple of hours of training before the start of a kaizen have any effect at all? That almost sounds too simple. How do we leverage this minimal training?

Art: The real leverage from kaizen as an approach is the fact that your entire workforce is getting trained as you go along. As I mentioned before, the kaizen teams will be split fairly evenly between salaried and hourly people. They will be trained in how to identify waste and what can be done in a simple, inexpensive way to eliminate it. The target is to get everyone on a kaizen team as soon as possible and then to get them on multiple kaizen teams after that. Your outside consultants can handle four teams of about 10 people every time they come. If you start out with 20 weeks of consulting time per year, then 800 people can be on a consultant-led kaizen team each year. Adding in the internal kaizens run by your KPO (Kaizen Promotion Office), we could easily double or triple this number. Obviously if you are a bigger company you can just scale the whole thing up.

Frank: I see how this could work. At the same time, won't we have to be developing our own internal Lean expertise at a much higher, more detailed level? I mean we can't have outside consultants here all the time; I hate consultants. Who will be our Lean trainers when they are not here?

Art: You will need to train your own internal Lean experts. All of the senior management team, for example, will have to commit to becoming Lean experts over time. Their path to this is to be on many kaizen teams. At the same time, you can use your Kaizen Promotion Office (KPO) as the main vehicle to train your internal experts. For people in the KPO, kaizen is their full-time job. You should select people for the KPO who you think can advance two or three more levels within the company. Don't just think of salaried people either—your hourly workforce will surprise you if you let them. The KPO staff can learn initially from your outside consultants by having them follow them around whenever they are here. They also will learn by running internal kaizens when the consultants are not here. Rotating people into the KPO for, say, two years to really learn Lean and then promoting them out to run various operations is a great way to build and spread the knowledge.

Jerry: Did you certify them as Lean experts in some way?

Art: No, we never tried to certify them or call them "green belts" or "black belts." I always figured I was running a business and not a karate class. I was looking for results, not how many people I could certify. Moving them out of the KPO and into broader operating jobs was a big reward and was giving great results.

Judy: Any other Lean training tips?

Art: Yes, another excellent training tool is to take groups of 20 to 25 people to visit more advanced Lean companies. At Danaher, Wiremold, and now with my private equity portfolio companies, I have always used this approach. It helps people see how high is up, so to speak. I send or take people to Japan every year. We can see maybe eight different companies over five days. It is a real eye-opener. At the same time every participant has to commit to implementing something they saw during the trip when they get back home that will more than cover the costs of their visit.

Kaizen Culture

Barbara: Art, you've talked about taking your top guys to go learn Lean while drinking beer in Japan, but us folks grinding it out on the shop floor don't have the time for this type of trip. How do you propose that all of us can get on board?

Art: Barbara, I've got a feeling that I'm going to really enjoy working with you! Don't expect to be going to Japan next week, but don't think it couldn't happen at some point. And when it comes to getting everyone on board, my answer is the same: kaizen. In fact, the shift is particularly noticeable in the hourly workforce. For the setup operator who used to struggle for three hours to change over a machine, doing it now in five minutes saves a lot of hard work. People get that immediately. Early on at Jake Brake, I remember moving a bunch of machines into a cellular configuration and getting pushback from several of the operators that the machines were too close together. "It isn't safe," they said. Two weeks later when I visited this cell, I saw that they had moved the machines even closer and cut the size of the cell in half. They understood that this made their work even easier and much safer. The fact that the hourly workforce is a major component of every kaizen team makes this shift in attitude occur even faster.

The same is true for middle management, but here the shift is often slower. Your better managers and engineers will get it right away and help lead the charge. Even so, you are likely to have individuals in this group who are wedded to their traditional approach. As you discover who they are, you need to give them more attention. Putting them on more kaizen teams will help, but a good old-fashioned "career discussion" is sometimes needed. Often those who are initially the most reluctant eventually become the biggest advocates for the shift to Lean.

Barbara: Well, here is something we can agree on, that management is the problem and will be the most difficult to change.

Art: They are always the hardest to change, Barbara.

Continuous Improvement

Jerry: Art, are there other things than just kaizen that we should be doing?

Art: Yes. As your Lean turnaround moves along, a state of continuous improvement is what you are aiming for. This goes beyond just kaizen events and gets to the stage where every person in the company is eliminating waste and making improvements every day. You want to leverage the collective knowledge of all your people. Kaizen events as mentioned are great for making the very difficult transition from batch to flow. But kaizen events need to be built upon. Employee suggestion programs are a great example: they build on the progress made by the initial kaizen events with many small, easy-to-implement ideas for improvement. Each of these improvements can be considered a kaizen. The key with this type of approach is to make sure it is managed at the local level with the immediate supervisors approving and implementing the ideas.

The countermeasures that should flow out of your daily management meetings at the point of value adding are another form of simple, easy kaizen. They are corrective actions to a problem that may have popped up today that you don't want to see reoccur. They could also be in response to longer-term problems that you want to put an end to. In addition, the traditional quality circle approach to problem solving at the local level is a good ongoing way to remove waste once some initial kaizen events have established a new cell, for example. At Wiremold's China plant we had many assembly cells with from 10 to 13 operators. Each one had its own supervisor. We required each of these supervisors to come up with one improvement idea each week that could be implemented. They used their teams to help generate the ideas. We made sure that ideas implemented in one cell that applied to other cells were implemented everywhere. The ongoing kaizen leverage off of this simple program was tremendous.

Jerry York: We've covered a lot of ground. Let's take a short break and come back and learn about the Lean fundamentals that we will be implementing.

Summary Points

- Converting to Lean happens on a project-by-project basis, a few associates at a time.
- Lean is not about removing waste as a cost-cutting approach: it is a strategic method to boost value for the customer. It applies just as powerfully in healthcare, financial services, and any other business.
- The essence of Lean is moving from batch to flow. "Batching" exists in virtually every traditional business and leads directly to waste, partly by creating large inventories that are costly and also by hiding and preventing immediate responses to errors.
- Actually participating on kaizens and hitting stretch goals together creates a powerful sense of teamwork and a learning environment that continues to build and build. Kaizen is the "doing" part of "learn by doing."
- Lean enables you to compete on time by accelerating your ability to deliver to customers with ever-decreasing lead times.
- You can't become Lean by doing what you are doing now, only slightly better: it requires a completely new way of thinking.

3

UGH Learns the Lean Fundamentals

OVERVIEW

In order to make the switch from traditional management (batch) to Lean (flow) you have to introduce and establish the four "Lean fundamentals":

Work to takt time

One-piece flow

Standard work

Pull system

These four fundamentals allow you to see the waste that is covered up in the traditional batch approach. Takt time, for example, brings the customer directly to the gemba and makes clear what the rate of production needs to be based on customer demand. Understanding this lets you see the waste in the current processes: lead times of six weeks when the actual touch time labor is only three minutes or staffing of eight when only three are needed.

One-piece flow allows you to realize the gains that are evident from the takt time analysis. It is also the key to productivity and quality gains as it allows you to see the whole process at a glance and solve problems in real time and in a permanent way. Standard work, or standardized work if you prefer that term (they have the same meaning), provides a baseline for improvement. Without such a standard there cannot be consistent quality and productivity. And lastly, pull is what connects the whole value stream and makes the Lean ideal of "sell one—make one" possible.

It is critical that the UGH team understand these fundamentals.

The Lean Fundamentals

Art: All right, let's get started. In order to make it easier for us to see and remove the waste, we will use four simple guidelines. I call these the Lean fundamentals, as they are the foundation on which our new Lean enterprise will be built. We will apply these fundamentals to every problem. They are:

Work to takt time

One-piece flow

Standard work

Pull system

We will cover each of these in detail. Collectively they will change the way you think about everything that happens at UGH. Above all, I want everyone to know that *these Lean fundamentals apply to any business.* They are just as important in the office, or processing claims at an insurance company, or in a hospital.

For example, I was once asked to lead a kaizen in the emergency room of a hospital. The specific request was to solve the problem of mental patients in the emergency room. These patients were disruptive and took up an excessive amount of staff time and resources. My first response was "You want to do what?" as I had no experience with anything like this.

To solve the problem, I just applied the Lean fundamentals. My first question was, "What is the takt time?" In other words, what is the rate at which mental patients enter the emergency room? Then I asked, What is the flow? What do we do with them when they get here? Can we create a separate flow for these patients? Next: What is the standard work? We need a unified, repeatable method to deal with these patients that everyone can follow. And lastly, can we pull them through the emergency room, get them treated and on their way, and track this visually so that everyone can see the current state? Using this approach made the solutions self-evident. The hospital created a special "flow" for these patients that took them out of the mainstream right away, got them the care they needed, and freed up resources to deal with everything else that was going on in the emergency room.

Takt Time

Barbara Mooney: Art, first you throw Japanese words like *kaizen* at us, and now you are switching to German with *takt time*. Are you saying that after all this time beating us up for how we do things, you've decided it's time to show some tact? [*The whole room laughs at this one, including Art.*]

Art: Barbara, as usual you are right. *Takt* is a German word used to indicate the beat of music. For Lean we are using it to represent the beat of the customer. It is the rate of incoming demand that your organization has to satisfy. For example, let's say there are 450 working minutes in a day on one shift and that the incoming demand each day is for 450 units. Or, if you are a service company, 450 requests for service. That means that the takt time is 60 seconds per unit or per customer. The formula is:

Time Available / Daily Customer Demand = Takt Time

If demand doubles to 900 per day but there are still only 450 minutes available in your one-shift operation, then takt time will drop to 30 seconds and so on. This concept applies anywhere. "What's the takt time?" should be the first question you ask in any company when you start a kaizen. It is like asking, "What are we trying to do here?" You are trying to satisfy the customer and deliver more value to him or her over time than anyone else can. As a result, knowing the rate of customer demand or takt time is critical to figuring out how to respond.

Scott Smith: But Art, we are already spending a lot of time and effort trying to respond to customer demand. What will takt time do that we aren't already doing?

Art: Scott, right now you are trying to respond to the customer by using a forecast of demand that typically is three to four months long. You separate the customer from the shop floor, and as a result, instead of having the shop floor respond directly to customer demand as we do in Lean, you are telling the shop floor to produce according to what the forecast tells you. With a six-week lead time and a forecast of three to four months out, your chances of correctly guessing what the customer will want are almost zero. Most companies go a step further and hardwire the whole thing using MRP and other systems to make sure that the shop floor only sees the forecast and never sees the customer. This is not only illogical but drives most of the waste that we see in traditional companies. Using takt time will connect the customer directly to the shop floor team making the product he wants to buy.

Scott: I still don't get it. Can you give us an example?

Art: Sure. Let's look back on the chart I showed you earlier (Figure 2-6) that shows the layout for a typical batch manufacturing plant. You will note that all of the machines are organized into functional departments. For example, department 1 might contain all of the punch presses. Department 2 might be all of the drilling machines, department 3 the screw machines, and department 4 all of the welding.

For this example, it takes eight different operations or steps to complete Product A. These departments are spread all over the factory, and in fact there are many more of them, but we are just showing the steps that are relevant for Product A.

Because the departments are a long way from each other, we need a system to move Product A through the maze that having functional departments has created. This will require routings, move tickets, and labor tickets to keep track of everything. These are wasteful and of course just add to the complexity and the cost. The parts will be "pushed" from one department to the next using the routings and a sophisticated MRP system. This will require a central work-in-process (WIP) inventory warehouse to store the parts when they return from one department before they are ready to go to the next department. This is depicted in the middle of Figure 2-6 along with the directional arrows that show the movement to each department and back to the WIP warehouse.

Now, let's say I push a pallet of parts out to department 2 for processing, but the operators are not quite ready for them. The material handler doesn't know this, so he just dumps the pallet off in department 2. Unfortunately, it is now in the way of the other work going on in department 2, so the operators move the pallet again. After several days they go retrieve it and start working on the parts for Product A. Just after they start, an emergency expedited order hits the department, and they have to stop making Product A and switch to another product that has suddenly gotten priority. This could happen or they could have a setup problem getting Product A to run or they could have a series of machine breakdowns that would delay Product A. To allow for all of these and other reasons, the lead time for Product A to make it through this maze and become a completed product is about six weeks. In the meantime, the work in process moves multiple times and travels long distances. Of course it gets tired, so it has to rest. In fact, it spends most of its time waiting (resting) in the WIP warehouse, and the WIP inventory keeps building. Does this sound familiar?

Frank: It certainly does. You have just described the way we have always operated. How would it change if we applied this concept of takt time?

Art: Well, we do this by creating a percent loading chart (as shown in Figure 3-1). In this case we know that the takt time is 60 seconds. Then we go observe the manual time for each operation on Product A in each department and plot the results on the chart. The results are quite uneven, as shown. In fact, the chart shows that we cannot keep up with customer demand because the operator in department 4 is over takt time. Once we have this information, we want to reconfigure the work such that each operator is fully loaded to takt time. To do this we take the total time in seconds, 165, and divide by the takt time of 60 seconds, (165/60 =

2.75) to determine how many total operators we need to do this operation. In this case we can go from eight operators to three for a productivity gain of 62 percent.

So, without spending any money and by just employing the concept of takt time and doing some simple time observations, we have discovered a major opportunity to eliminate waste and get a 62 percent productivity gain. But this isn't really the strategic part of this. The strategic gain is that we now understand that the actual touch time labor to make the product is only about three minutes (3 operators × 60 seconds each)—yet we have *a six-week lead time* for the same product due to the way we are currently configured. This means that you can offer a two- to three-day lead time when your competition is still at six weeks or greater.

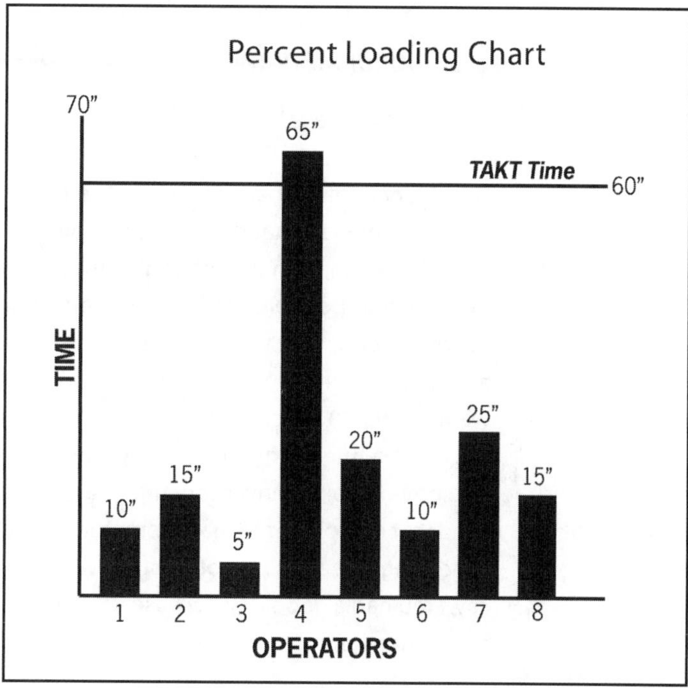

Figure 3-1. Percent loading chart

This is how the Lean fundamentals can help you see opportunities that you couldn't see before. The hard part comes when you try to implement your observations. To do this you need to move to one-piece flow. This will create a lot of resistance.

One-Piece Flow

Dick Conway: Art, I have a hard time with this. It seems completely illogical. How can one-piece flow be better than high-speed automated production? Aren't there economies of scale involved here? One-piece flow sounds like it will be much slower.

Art: Dick, I'm not surprised you are having a hard time with this conceptually. Most companies do, as it is the exact opposite of their traditional approach. But remember, we don't have to go any faster than the takt time as this represents the rate of customer demand.

Traditional Manufacturing Example

Let's say that it takes 10 machines to make Product B. But when you come in today, one of them is broken and can't make any parts. The machines are in their traditional functional departments, and there is pressure from finance to make the absorption hours so that the results for the month will look good. So the decision is to go ahead and run the other nine machines at full blast to get as many absorption hours as possible. Now because one machine is broken we can't make a single thing today that we can sell to a customer. In addition, because the machines all run at different speeds we will be piling up parts in uneven amounts. Maybe we make 2,000 covers but only 300 bases, for example. The inventory buildup is of course a huge form of waste by itself. Even worse is the fact that I tied up my equipment making inventory that I can only sell at a later date when I could have used that equipment to make something that I can sell today. The whole approach is nothing but a big pile of waste, but at the end of the day the finance guy will say, "You had a good day because you were still able to produce 95 percent of the absorption hours."

Art: What you want to do is go get one of each of the machines that it takes to make Product A and lay them out right next to each other in a cellular layout as shown in Figure 2-7. Get the machines as close to each other as possible and leave no room for inventory other than the standard amount of work in process that is required (normally one piece per machine). We normally think of a cell as U-shaped as shown in Figure 2-7, but a couple of parallel lines work just as well as long as they are near each other (close enough to stand in the middle and reach either side). Once you have a flow cell, if one of the machines is broken (per the preceding example), you no longer can run the other nine. The whole cell shuts down and you put an intense focus on fixing the one machine that is broken. This is the exact opposite of the traditional approach shown in the example.

John Flynn, president of UGH Specialty Gears Division: But Art, shutting down the whole line is pretty severe. I would expect that this is not the only problem that putting things into a one-piece-flow will uncover.

Art: You are correct about that, John. One thing becomes clear right away: the fact that you have excess machine capacity. This has always existed but was hidden by your batch state and six-week lead times. Now, when you run the line at takt time to meet customer demand, this will jump out at you. The finance guy may have an especially hard time with this. Don't let it bother you. Having excess capacity is in fact normal and actually a good thing.

The second thing that will become very clear right away is that, in their batch state with long lead times, these machines were not well maintained. They break down all the time and stop the entire line. You have to fix the problem immediately. One-piece flow intentionally forces this immediate response. You also have to develop a total productive maintenance (TPM) approach to prevent any breakdowns from occurring in the future. You have to commit to the mentality that unplanned downtime is simply no longer acceptable. This won't happen overnight, of course, but you need to take the steps to put in a daily/monthly/yearly maintenance program that will eliminate future downtime.

One-piece flow will also quickly highlight any problems you have with your vendors. These issues could concern delivery or quality; they will also shut down the line until you fix them. On the plus side, one-piece flow allows you to easily observe what is going on—bottlenecks, for example—and put fixes in place that lead to future gains.

Gary Cook, president of UGH Custom Housings Division: Art, what does one-piece flow do for product quality? We follow the traditional approach of having a strong quality department that can "inspect in" the quality. This costs us some money, but it gives our customers peace of mind.

Art: One-piece flow is the key to quality improvements. In my experience it is pretty common to get a 10 times or better gain in quality once you are in a one-piece flow. This will occur naturally and is something that you get for free. Let me explain. In a batch configuration with a six-week lead time, when something goes wrong it may be six weeks before you discover this when you go to assemble the final product. At this point it is very hard to determine what went wrong. You might get lucky and narrow down the problem to something that happened in department number 5. So now you go to department 5 and you find that the part could have been made on any of 10 different machines. It could have been made on one of two different shifts by a total of 20 different operators. In addition, we could have been using raw material that came from one of three different vendors, but by the time we discover the problem we can no longer determine whose material we were using. Pretty tough problem to solve immediately—let alone get a permanent solution. Oh, and of course you have six weeks of bad inventory that you have to deal with in some fashion.

Once you have the product in a one-piece flow, everything changes. Now when you discover the problem you know whose raw material you are using. You know which machine caused the problem and who the operator is. You only have eight pieces of work in process to deal with. So not only do you have all the information you need to solve the problem, you can get a permanent solution.

One of the key ideas in Lean in any setting, and that one-piece flow supports, is that you build quality into the product at every station in the line as opposed to trying to "inspect in" quality at the end. It's a simple and powerful shift in how people think about their work.

Barbara: Look, you guys, we are all for better quality. But what about the people? I mean you start out timing what they are doing with stopwatches to compare it to this takt time thing, and then you want to totally rearrange the way the work is done and create cells. Cells exist in jails, not on our shop floor. You realize that if you were the operator it would make you nervous to have someone out there timing what you do? Then if you put everything together into these cell things, you're asking the operators to do maybe eight different jobs when today they only do one. I don't think our associates will be very happy with that. Why will this be good for them?

Art: Barbara, once again you are asking the right questions. Moving to Lean requires us to focus on both the customer and our people. Delivering more value to the customer is what will protect the jobs of all our people. At the same time, focusing on the people will result in making their work easier and safer in a better, cleaner, more visual workplace. We are using stopwatches to time and then improve the work—not the worker. This is key: we are not timing the people; we are timing the work, and we will make sure that they understand that so they won't be nervous or worried. When we move things into a cellular flow, the most important consideration is how to make things easier and safer for the operator. We want to make the operator's motions as natural as possible and eliminate bending, lifting, climbing, searching for tools, sorting out parts, and any other wasted or unsafe motions. You are correct that our associates will have to become multiskilled. But you should look at that in a positive way! They will be learning new skills that in turn will make them more valuable and make their jobs more interesting.

So when you say, "but what about the people," my response is that switching to Lean is all about people, who have the most to gain as we make the change. It has been the case in every other Lean conversion, and it will be true here at UGH as well.

Standard Work Sheet

Jerry: Art, I can see the benefits of one-piece flow. But what do we do to make this happen? How do we go about establishing these cells?

Art: Good question, Jerry. There are some rules to follow in creating a cell. The standard work sheet is a good guideline to use. You should have a standard work sheet posted at every cell. As you will see on the illustrations in Figures 3-2 and 3-3, this is simple yet provides all of the necessary information. The form shows:

1. The machine layout in a simple but effective way (forget the blueprints and fancy drawings—you don't need them)
2. The sequence of operations
3. The amount of allowed work in process (i.e., standard work in process)
4. The location where quality inspections take place
5. Where safety precautions are needed
6. The takt time for the operation
7. The cycle time of the operation
8. The number of operators
9. The scope of the operation
10. The process name, part number, model name, and name of the department head and local supervisor

This chart tells everyone what is supposed to be happening in a simple format that can be easily understood by everybody. With this resource, by just going out and observing the cell you can tell if quality work is happening or not. More important, you can see right away, in most cases, where the problems are and as a result can take immediate countermeasures. This is completely different from a batch operation where the product has to pass through multiple functional departments over weeks of time. Seeing what is going on in this environment is virtually impossible.

The local supervisor is responsible for creating the standard work sheet and making certain that it is updated as waste is eliminated and the standard work improves. Getting the operators to follow and maintain this on a daily basis, however, is critical for getting everyone on board. Filling out the forms is not difficult, but getting everyone to follow the standard work is. People will naturally revert to their prior batch behavior and do the job their own way if you are not diligent.

Standard Work Sheet
Process Name
Sleeve Cylinder Machining
Model Number
23456-78901
Model Name
Sleeve Cylinder
Scope of Operations
From
Pick up raw material
To
Put down finished product
Date prepared:
Department Head
Supervisor
SF 210
NB 201
NS 103
NS 102
AL 101
Raw Material
Finished Product
SD 205
SD 206
SF 320
FN 410
HS510
HS320
SJ 600
Quality Inspections
Safety Precaution
Standard Work in Process
# of Pieces of Standard Work-in-Process
14
TAKT Time
95
Cycle Time
81
Operator Number
1/1

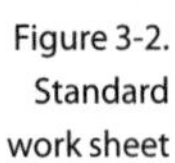

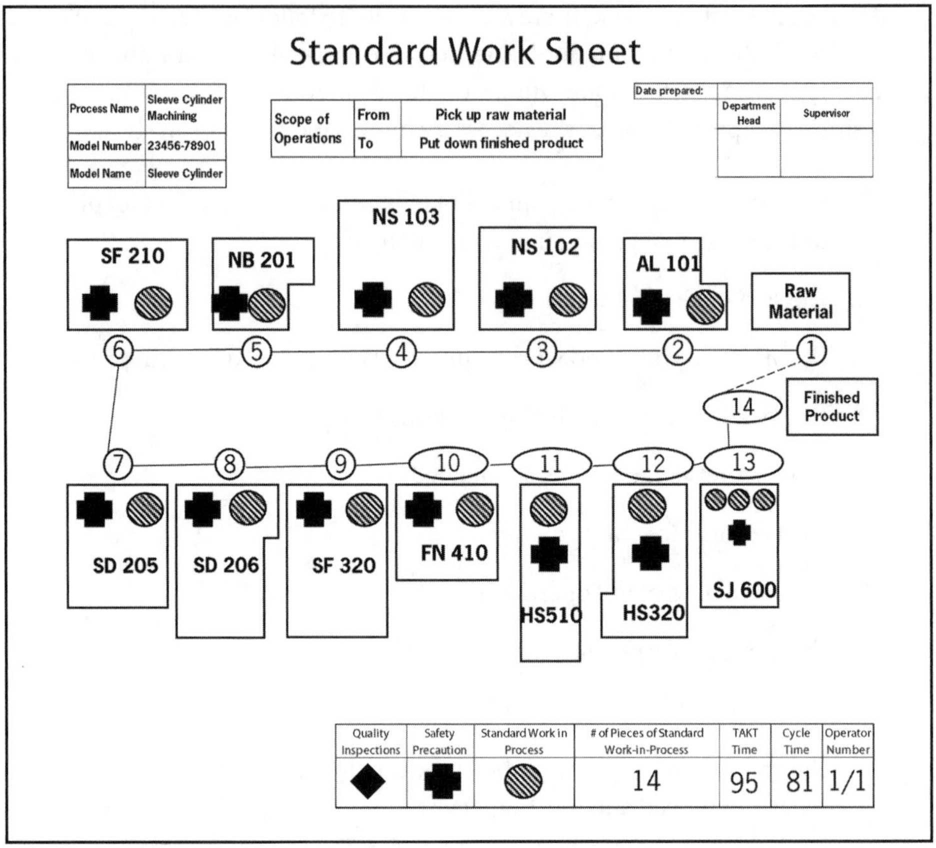

Figure 3-2. Standard work sheet

Standard Work Sheet Examples

The standard work sheet in Figure 3-2 shows an operation with 12 pieces of equipment and one operator. The standard work in process is 14 units, as there are three pieces at the last station. This might be a test station with a run-in time that is more than double the takt time. More important, we can see that there is one operator with a takt time of 95 seconds and a cycle time of 81 seconds, so this cell should be easily able to keep up with takt time. Even so, demand can change throughout the year even as the time available does not.

To deal with this we have a second standard work sheet in Figure 3-3. In this case demand has doubled and takt time has dropped to only 47.5 seconds. To adjust to this, we add a second operator. Now we have one operator with a 44-second cycle time and another with a 37-second time. Nothing else has really changed. All it took was some staffing flexibility to solve the problem. Perhaps another product line is soft at this time of year and we can pull the other operator from there. Maybe we need to add a temporary worker for a couple of months. There are many options. One of the things that this highlights is the absolute need for a very flexible workforce in a Lean environment. You have to cross-train people and remove any pay or work rule barriers that prevent you from having this kind of flexibility. That is always more difficult than creating a cell and will take more time.

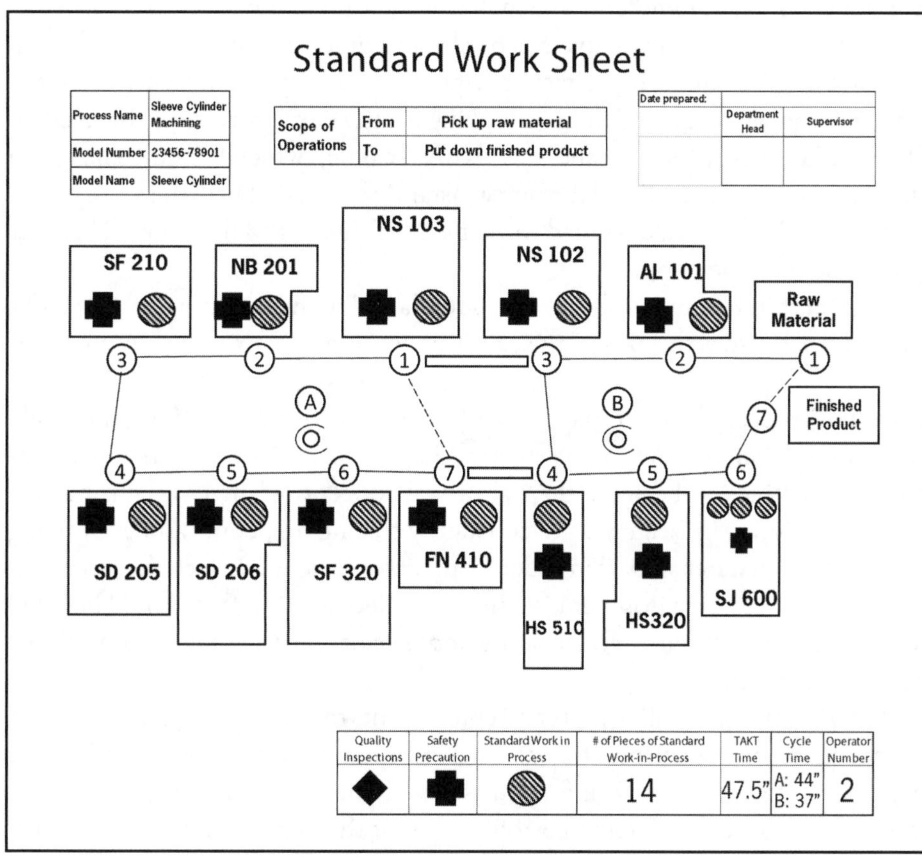

Figure 3-3. Standard work sheet for increased demand

Chaku Chaku Lines

Jerry York: The standard work sheets seem to focus on the layout of the cell. Is this what is most important, or is it something else? I'm thinking about the people here and how they should work.

Art: Good question, Jerry. You raise an important point: the layout of the cell is important, but the real focus in creating a cell should be on the operator. You want to minimize operators' movements and reduce if not completely eliminate their walking time. Any parts or components they need should be presented to them at the point of use in as close to one piece at a time as possible, and in the right orientation so they can move it into position without having to turn it around to reorient it. In other words, the operator should not be opening any boxes or trying to grab a part out of a big tangled pile. This can be accomplished by using a water spider (i.e., material handler) to deliver just the right number of parts to the operator at the right place, at the right time, and in the proper orientation.

It might be easier for you to envision this in a different setting. Take a surgeon and nurse as an example. If you were having brain surgery, you wouldn't want the surgeon to open you up and then go looking for the next instrument she needed. You want her totally focused and just saying "scalpel," which the nurse hands to her. Then she says "scope," and the nurse instantly hands it to her. The same is true in a factory where the value-added worker is the surgeon and the material handler (water spider) is the nurse.

The chart in Figure 3-4 shows a layout of a cell with an external water spider delivering parts from the back of the cell. This combination dramatically increases the productivity of the operator (your value-added worker) with little additional cost as the water spider can typically handle a number of cells at a time. This really emphasizes the importance of the value-adding work. It is also why we don't want to make a distinction between the traditional concepts of direct versus indirect hourly workforce. In Lean, we are constantly freeing up people and converting some of them to water spiders in order to increase efficiency. In fact, the job of water spider in a Lean environment is a highly skilled position that should be filled by some of your better people—just the opposite of how we think of a traditional material handler role.

In addition to presenting parts and components to the operator, it is important to place all the necessary tools that might be needed at the point of use and within easy reach of the operator. Your first thrust should be to get rid of as many tools as possible, but those which remain should all be at the point of use. There is nothing worse than watching an operator waste time looking for tools or going back and forth to get tools.

What you are ultimately aiming for wherever possible is chaku chaku, or in English, load-load lines, where the operator's main role is to load and move the parts. This will require you to automatically unload the parts as the machine cycle

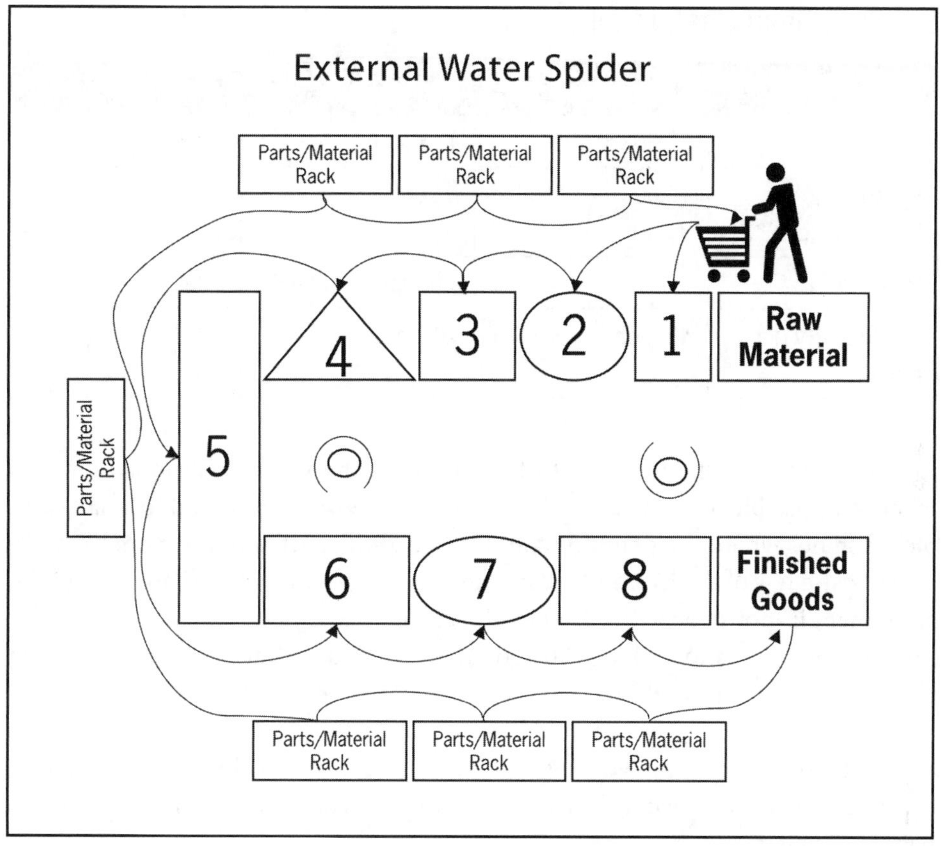

Figure 3-4. External water spider

ends. This is the only way you can get to the load-load state, which is the most efficient way.

Gary Cook, president of UGH's Custom Housings Division: Art, can you give us some examples of the types of gains you can get from these one-piece flow chaku chaku lines?

Art: Yes, but keep in mind that you can only really learn this by doing it. I can show you a load-load line, but until you have had to build one yourself you won't fully appreciate how efficient it is or understand all the problems that had to be solved to create it.

Let me share an example of the gains from a chaku chaku cell. The following table shows the results from one of my portfolio companies, a plant in Spain where we are making staplers:

Stapler Chaku Chaku Cell

	Before Kaizen	After Kaizen	% Change
Space	1,350 sq. ft.	150 sq. ft.	–89%
Finished goods inventory (pcs)	10,600	5,000	–53%
Head count	9	1 + water spider	–83%
Productivity per person	42/pph	200/pph	+376%

This small cell involves a lot of assembly at the various stations. Even so, wherever possible we distributed as much of the work as we could to small, simple machines where the operator could just load the part and move on. We were able to use a few of the machines from the old line, but mostly we had to build the equipment in-house or with the help of local outside tool shops. You will have to do the same as you move along. All good Lean companies have their own in-house ability to design and build or buy and alter simple devices to facilitate flow and help reduce setup time. You should be aware of this requirement before you start and be prepared to create your own skunk works or moonshine shop in-house. The need for this will become evident quickly, and you will easily free up enough people to staff it.

Standard Work

Gary: Thanks, these are good examples. I would guess that to make a chaku chaku line work you would need to have anyone who worked in the cell follow a strict work pattern. In fact, it sounds like part of laying out the cell itself creates the work pattern.

Art: Exactly. This won't work without standard work, which is another of the Lean fundamentals. Simple in concept but very hard to do in practice—especially if you are converting from a traditional batch approach. What standard work does is to create a work sequence and time standard for every step in a process. Say, for example, you have seven steps in the process. The sequence is 1 through 7, and the standard time for each step is determined by observation. You might have: Step 1 = 5", Step 2 = 12", Step 3 = 18", Step 4 = 9", Step 5 = 15", Step 6 = 22", and Step 7 = 7". The total time for this sequence is thus 88 seconds. At each step you would post the standard work required for that station, using pictures if possible, and step-by-step instructions.

Once the standard work has been established, this is the way anyone who does this job needs to do it. If you don't establish this consistency, how can you have reliable quality or consistent output (productivity)? I mean, if six people all do the same job and they all do it differently, your quality and productivity will also have six different outcomes. If you're a service provider and all of your employees don't provide that service the same exact way, however, you will probably have a lot of unhappy customers. Think about a restaurant: you probably won't go back if the same meal tastes different every time.

More important, if you don't have this baseline, what is the basis going to be for improvement? The goal of the local manager and cell team members and of the entire organization is to constantly upgrade and improve the standard work. This is done through a combination of formal kaizen activity and suggestions and improvements coming from the cell team itself and its leader. Toyota is the master at this.

Barbara: Art, we are not robots and we don't make cars. Everyone is different with different capabilities. How can you expect people to do the job the same way? Isn't this a veiled attempt to get everyone to work faster? What if someone can't keep up? Will they be fired?

Art: Barbara, I want to be emphatically clear about this: no one is going to get fired. Period. This is a huge misconception about Lean (done right). The best asset any company has is its people. We want to grow our people and improve their skills. Moving to a Lean approach will allow us to do that. Designing the standard work in such a way that the waste is removed and everyone doing the job can easily meet the standard work times is what this is all about. We don't want people to work faster; we want them to work smarter and safer. Establishing standard work and then improving on it is also a major part of creating a learning environment where every employee is contributing his or her ideas and learning new ways every day.

Frank: We have targets for how many pieces need to be produced in a day. Does that count as standard work?

Art: Actually, it doesn't. The typical batch company has standards for the product but rarely for the work that goes into making it. The thrust is much more, as you just described, on "making the forecast" than on how you do it. In fact, if you had five people doing an assembly job on the same product, chances are that none of them is doing it the same way. If you observed closely, you would probably see several of them doing the work differently themselves from time to time. Because the traditional focus is on the number of pieces you produce and not on *how* you make them, the move to standard work is quite a change and difficult to hold on to. People want to go back to doing it the way they used to. And any time you relax the pressure to enforce the standard work they will.

Standard Work at Veeder-Root

Back when I was a group executive for the Danaher Corporation, we had a great example of the benefits of standard work. This was at one of my Group companies called Veeder-Root in a plant in North Carolina on a line where we were making the mechanical reset trip odometers that went into all of Ford's Taurus and Sable cars. Final assembly consisted of a big table with about 12 operators sitting around it, each with a big pile of parts that she would assemble into the final product. The takt time was 82 seconds, but the actual cycle times were all over the place. They each had a different assembly method, but on average the times were in the 100- to 115-second range.

We thought about breaking the assembly up into smaller pieces and creating a couple of flow lines along with several other approaches. But as we continued to observe and time the operations, it became clear that one woman, the one who seemed the least rushed and most relaxed, had an assembly method that allowed her to assemble the part reliably in 75 to 77 seconds. We converted her approach into the standard work and taught everyone else to follow it. The results were dramatic. No one got down to her times by the end of the week, of course, but everyone got down into the 85- to 89-second range, and of course got better over time as we cleaned up how the parts were fed to them and created better assembly fixtures.

Frank: Well, how would we go about creating the standard work? Do you have forms and an approach for this as well?

Art: [*laughing*] Yes, we do. Start with a time observation form like the one shown in Figure 3-5. Go and observe and write down what is happening. You can use this same form to do your observations to create the initial percent loading chart we described earlier. Your main focus is on the manual time, both walking and the time to perform the work itself. If you observe 10 cycles for each process step, that should give you a good sample.

UGH Corporation

Process for Observation		TIME OBSERVATION FORM	Date:	Operator:
			Time:	Observer:

No.	Component Task	1	2	3	4	5	6	7	8	9	10	Component Task Time	Points Observed
TIME FOR 1 CYCLE													

Figure 3-5. Time observation form

As shown in Figure 3-6, you want to select the lowest average repeatable time as the standard time for that step. For example, if you have an operation that takes between 9 and 15 seconds, where 9 seconds occurs 2 out of 10, 10 seconds occurs 4 out of 10, and the rest are higher, then you want to start with the 10-second time.

Once you have the manual times, you need to get the machine times to make sure that you don't have some bottleneck operation that will cause the cell to fail. It is rare that the machine times will create a problem. Once you have both pieces you can then fill out the Standard Work Combination sheet (Figure 3-7). This brings

UGH Corporation

	Process for Observation	Final assembly and packaging			TIME OBSERVATION FORM							Date: 5/26/15 Time:	Operator: J. Smith Observer: B. Jones
No.	Component Task	1	2	3	4	5	6	7	8	9	10	Component Task Time	Points Observed
1	Screw base to cover	14	11	12	9	12	18	12	14	12	17	12	Base/cover fit Difficult to handle screws
2	Wrap plug & cord	5	6	6	7	10	6	3	14	6	15	6	Bad tape
3	Put in plastic bag	5	4	4	4	3	7	4	14	3	4	4	
4	Insert manual	3	3	4	3	5	2	3	14	2	3	3	
5	Make box	8	7	5	3	5	5	6	14	3	5	5	No fixture
6	Pack in box	3	3	4	3	3	5	3	14	2	3	3	
7	Label box	5	7	4	3	4	4	5	14	4	5	4	All manual
	TIME FOR 1 CYCLE	43	41	39	32	42	47	36	45	32	52	37	

Figure 3-6. Time observation form filled in

the whole picture together: the manual time, the machine time, and the walking time; plots it all in the proper sequence; and compares it to takt time. It is a very important analytical tool. It will tell you if the proposed cell will be able to meet takt time or not. More important, it will highlight the problems and allow you to focus on the fixes that are needed to stay within takt time. This sheet should be posted at the cell along with the standard work sheet itself.

Frank: [*laughing*] Somehow I just knew you were going to have another form that we could use to do this. I have to admit that the Standard Work Combination sheet looks a little intimidating at first. Even so, it gives us an approach that we

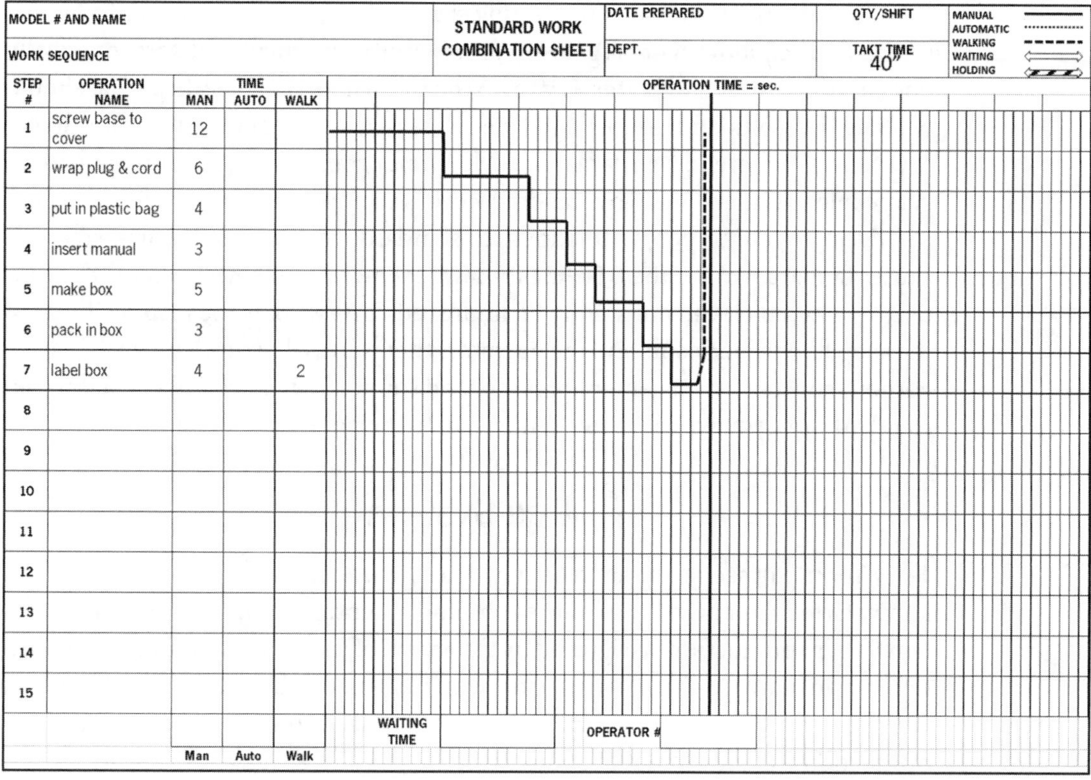

MODEL # AND NAME	STANDARD WORK COMBINATION SHEET	DATE PREPARED	QTY/SHIFT	MANUAL / AUTOMATIC / WALKING / WAITING / HOLDING
WORK SEQUENCE		DEPT.	TAKT TIME 40"	

STEP #	OPERATION NAME	TIME: MAN	TIME: AUTO	TIME: WALK	OPERATION TIME = sec.
1	screw base to cover	12			
2	wrap plug & cord	6			
3	put in plastic bag	4			
4	insert manual	3			
5	make box	5			
6	pack in box	3			
7	label box	4		2	
8					
9					
10					
11					
12					
13					
14					
15					
		Man	Auto	Walk	WAITING TIME / OPERATOR #

Figure 3-7. Standard Work Combination sheet

never had before that should allow us to start to see the waste more clearly. Should we establish standard work for everything up front or just do it cell by cell as we go along?

Art: Well, there isn't really a form for every occasion. Even so, the few I have showed you will be very helpful in allowing you to see the waste that you can't see now in your current batch state. You should establish standard work on a step-by-step basis each time you create a new cell or work area. This applies to service companies as well as manufacturers. Think about the back office billing operation of a large regional medical practice or processing loan applications for a bank or even for the accounting functions in any company. They are all processes that can be put into a flow and where standard work needs to be put in place. Establishing standard work and monitoring to make sure the standard work is being adhered to are two different things. The follow-up is much more difficult, and you will have to put forth special efforts to make sure it sticks.

Just remember that you are creating standard work as the best way for everyone to do the job with great gains in productivity and quality. If someone really does have an easier and better way to do the job, listen to her. Perhaps that should become the new standard work. Just be aware that it will take a lot of effort to get everyone to adhere to standard work. More important, it is even more difficult to get people to understand why standard work is so important.

Even so, getting people to adhere to standard work is only the first step. Because standard work is the baseline for improvement, you have to create the conditions whereby it can constantly be improved. This work is the responsibility of the shop floor supervisors and the operators themselves. It won't happen, however, without constant management pressure and support. Once you have established standard work you will be ready to move on to the final Lean fundamental, pull.

Pull System

Jerry York: Pull seems to me to be the easiest to understand. A few other CEOs I know started their own Lean journeys by implementing some form of kanban system [where production is triggered by the arrival of a kanban card] to create pull in their businesses. Couldn't we just start with pull and kanban cards first? [Kanban, which means "signboard" in Japanese, are physical cards or signs that control the production and movement of goods.]

Art: No, Jerry, sorry, but you don't want to start with pull. In fact, until you have drastically reduced your setup times, have everything running at takt time, and have everything in a one-piece flow and everyone working to standard work, pull won't do you much good. There would be nothing to pull against. I'm sure the other CEOs you talked to found this out. All they would have done is added kanban cards to their big batches of inventory.

Jerry: So . . . establishing pull isn't all that easy? Why?

Art: Like everything else in Lean, pull is the exact opposite of what you do now. Your current system "pushes" batches of things forward to the next operation. We want to reverse that and go to the preceding process to "pull" the parts we need. More important, we want to pull only what is needed, in the amount needed, and at the time it is needed. Everything is done at the pull of the customer whether it is an external customer or an internal customer. Your goal is to get your whole value stream on pull.

Sam Watson, president of UGH Small Gears: If our focus is on delivering more value to our customers, then I guess we should start by getting all our customers on a pull system.

Art: Good question, Sam, but as a matter of fact your customers are the last ones you want to get on pull. Your current batch state could not respond to the pull of the customer without massive inventory, and even then you would have problems. Instead you want to focus your initial efforts on establishing pull within UGH and simultaneously with your vendors. Internal pull can be established step by step every time you set up a new cell. You can establish simple kanban systems to make sure all the parts needed in the cell that are made internally get there on time and in the right quantities. Until your setups come way down, you will probably have to establish small "supermarkets" of parts to make this work. Eventually you should be able to eliminate the supermarkets or at least reduce them to minimum quantities.

How Kanban Reduces Batching

The internal kanban (depicted in Figure 3-8) travels between a production process and a small supermarket of parts that are stored nearby. When the parts are made, they are put in, say, a box (this container could be a wide range of configurations depending on the size and shape of the part) in a set amount (let's say 12 for this example). The production kanban card is then attached to the box and travels with it to the supermarket.

Part #	Description	Part Address	Qty	Cell 5212 Build Qty.
30-028	BRACKET W SCREWS 3007C		1.000	50
41402	INS G/V3000 SERIES		0.200	10
40372	LABEL P/S 5.00X3.875 65		0.020	1
28680	POLY BAG .002X5.0X8.0		1.000	50
40499	LABEL P/S 2.30X3.00 650		0.200	10
35006	BOX 6.625X3.000X6.625 A		0.200	10
26384	CTN RSC 200C 18.000X13.		0.020	1

Back of Kanban card shows all component parts needed

SHANKLIN CELL Label bar code	Part # **G3007C** QTY **50** 18 min.	FG ADDRESS **526/3/4** KANBAN # **10 / 20**

Front of Kanban card shows amount of time to produce one Kanban worth as well as the number of Kanban this card represents—could be #10 of 20 cards

Figure 3-8. Internal kanban card

When the person in the succeeding operation comes to pick the parts, he replaces the production kanban with its conveyance kanban, and the production kanban returns to the cell. The arrival of the kanban then tells the cell to make 12 more and put them in the supermarket. If the cell makes multiple parts, as many of ours did, then the kanban will be put in a simple heijunka box (load leveling) until enough kanban have been collected to tell the cell it needs to make more of this part.

Sam: How will we determine how many supermarkets to have and how big they should be?

Art: The size of the supermarket you will need and the number of kanban in the system, along with the size of the trigger point at which you have to start making a particular part, will be determined by your current state. The drivers will be your setup times and the volatility of your incoming orders. As both of these come down over time, you can shrink or often eliminate the supermarkets and everything that goes along with them. After all, your objective is not to build supermarkets, although you may need them temporarily until your processes get better. You want to build this out cell by cell, value stream by value stream as you go along. At first you will still be building to a forecast but using the kanban internally to help get things to the right place at the right time and in the right quantity. Eventually you will get to the state where nothing can get built without a kanban card. This should be one of your key objectives, by the way. You can still use an MRP system for all of the other informational things it can do for you, but you want to disconnect it from being able to run the shop floor.

Frank: Art, you are going to give me a heart attack. We run all of our production with our MRP system. Without that I don't know how we will keep track of anything. I certainly can't envision how we will, as you say, "connect the customer to the shop floor" using these kanban cards.

Art: Frank, you are too valuable to UGH, so you are not allowed to have a heart attack. But I do understand your concerns. Certainly we can't just get rid of using MRP to schedule production until we have put the alternative kanban system in place. We only can do this step by step and cell by cell as we go along. In the meantime, you will be caught between two different systems. This should put some positive pressure on you to get everything into a flow as soon as possible.

Once everything is in flow cells and setups have been drastically reduced, you can then connect the customer directly to the shop floor by way of kanban. First you have to establish the size of the various kanban cards. For example, a high-running product might be produced in pallet quantities, while a medium-size product might be in a large tote box quantity of, say, 72 products and a lower volume product only produced in quantities of 24 or even 12. Once the kanban sizes are determined, you can hook them to the incoming order entry system. As orders come in during the day, once you have enough orders for a product to equal its kanban quantity, then the kanban card should print out on the shop floor right next to the cell that makes the product. This will give you an almost instant connection to your customer and an ability to respond quickly.

Frank: Maybe I won't have a heart attack, but you are still hurting my head trying to envision all of this. It is so different from what we do now. For example, what are we going to do with all these kanban cards? Where do we put them, how do we handle them? What if we lose them?

Art: Well, you may in fact lose some kanban cards at first. And when you do, things won't get produced and customers will get upset. It's painful, but it forces you to deal with the problem. You have to train all your associates that kanban cards are like money. You have to make sure they don't get lost. There are simple methods to help with this. Once everything is made by kanban card, then it is easy to construct a simple mail slot system to load in the kanban cards and array them in a way that will show you at a glance what the current and future demand is for each product. Figure 3-9 shows an example from one of my portfolio company's plants in Belgium. This shows the heijunka (load leveling) box for one product code, with the days in the week going from left to right and each slot representing an hour of production. The colored zones tell when a product needs to be made. If the cards are only in the green and yellow, things are OK, but if a surge of orders throws things into the red zone, this is made visible immediately and action can be taken. The direct delivery area helps sort out those orders that can be directly shipped and do not

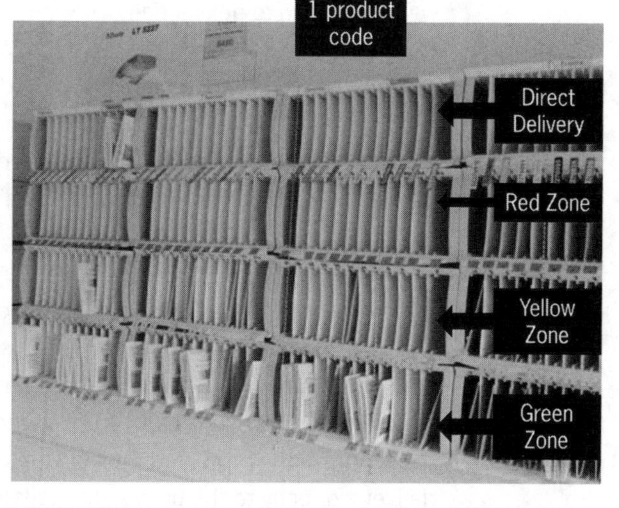

Figure 3-9. Load leveling system

need any internal storage. Often these are large orders with future dates that can be slotted into the schedule to help level out production.

Frank: But what about our suppliers? We can't run an efficient pull system unless they are part of it. I mean, we wouldn't try to produce everything internally by kanban at the pull of the customer and still buy in big batches from our own vendors, would we?

Art: Excellent point, Frank. You need to have your suppliers tied in to what you are doing. So, while building your internal pull system you should simultaneously be working on establishing a pull system with your vendors. In Lean you want to be in a position where you can make every product every day. This will give you the maximum ability to respond to your customers in the shortest amount of time. You want to be able to do this without carrying too much inventory. The only way to achieve this is by having all of your vendors deliver every day, or as close to that as you can get economically. Saying this and getting it done are two different things. First of all, most of your vendors are batch guys too. When you first ask for daily deliveries, they will say no. You have to keep pushing them. In addition, your purchasing people have been trained to buy in big quantities to get volume discounts, so this will make no sense to them. You will hear a lot of ridiculous excuses.

Wiremold Purchasing

At Wiremold, we started with our three local cardboard box suppliers. We had a separate warehouse just for cardboard boxes, and it took up a lot of space. When we asked them to deliver daily, they all said no. We kept pushing till we got one to try. We created kanban cards to attach to each bundle of about 25 boxes, and instead of the old box warehouse we stored them right next to where they would be used. Every time a new bundle was opened, we removed the kanban and put it in a box. At the end of the day we collected all the cards, and the next morning we handed them to the vendor during his daily delivery and said, "Here is the order for tomorrow."

At first we were attaching the kanban to the bundles when they arrived. This was extra work for us. At the same time our vendor had such long setups that he was struggling to keep up. We solved this by sending some of our KPO team to his plant and running several kaizens for him. We drastically reduced his setup times, which cut his costs and reduced his inventory. Next we taught him how to attach the kanban as he produced the boxes and how to group the product together and deliver it directly to the production cells for us. We also had to work out the billing issues so we got one bill per month instead of having to deal with individual invoices on every shipment, which was swamping our finance department.

This enabled us to consolidate all our business with this one vendor in return for lower prices. When the other two vendors came back saying, "Hey, where are our orders?" we said, "Well, you wouldn't do daily deliveries." "Oh," they said, "we didn't know you were serious; we can do daily deliveries now." The problem was they were too late. We created the same type of system with all of our vendors. Our biggest supplier was our steel vendor. He was over 300 miles away, yet we got six to eight truckloads of steel every day. We used to carry three to four months' worth of steel, and this went down to a day and a half to two and a half days' worth. When he decided that now that he was our single source he had some leverage on us and tried to raise our price, we were able to show him how much volume he had picked up as we eliminated a few of his competitors and that we were perfectly willing to reverse the process. A price increase would cost him at least half his volume. We never heard any more noise about a price increase.

Art: Pull systems done correctly will link your supply chain together and dramatically improve your results, especially in the areas of lead time reduction, reliability as a supplier, and, of course, costs. This all sounds very simple and easy to do. I caution you it is not. It gets quite complicated and needs to be constantly managed. If you have 10,000 SKUs, then some multiple of that number of kanban cards will need to be created and managed. Your demand patterns will change, and so you will have to constantly update the number of kanban you have in the system. You may have a seasonal sales pattern, so kanban will have to be added to the system in advance of this and taken away afterward. There are many variations. The gains are well worth the effort.

Jerry: What about the customers? When and how do we get them on a pull system?

Art: Yes, thanks for reminding me. As I mentioned before, you have to get your internal pull system in shape first. Once you do, you will probably find that getting your customers on pull will not be that easy. They work off of their own MRP systems and tend to order everything in batches. You taught them to do this by offering volume discounts and having a six-week lead time. Now you have to teach them to order in a different way and be able to explain to them why this will be good for them. Your objective is simply to get them to tell you what they sold every day. You can then treat this as an order and make sure it is on the next truck to them.

For example, let's say you deliver to them every Monday. Every day they tell you what was sold in the prior week and you put it on next Monday's truck. This should allow a typical distributor to go from holding four months of your inventory and instead hold only two to three weeks' worth. This is giving your distributor a lot of cash. You are delivering value to your customer in a big way. But don't be surprised if they don't recognize it right away. They have been trained to drive down the cents each cost and not to worry about inventory. If you offer a 4 percent price reduction worth $50,000 or a three-month reduction in inventory as shown above worth $500,000, don't be surprised if they go for the price reduction. You will have to work with them and educate them. Stay with it. Once you convert them, you will lock them in as a customer as the switching costs to go back to a batch vendor (your competitor) are high. They would have to add back the $500,000 in inventory that you had helped them eliminate.

Scott Smith: I'll tell you right now that if our switch to a Lean strategy enables my sales team to give this kind of cash back to our distributors, we will be the most loved company in our industry. There is no question in my mind that we could gain a lot of market share. I'm still a skeptic that we can achieve all the goals you have laid out for us, but I'm all in for the change if we can do this for our customers.

Jerry: Scott is certainly right about the leverage this would give us with our customers. To do it, though, we need to have everyone all in, as Scott calls it. But it has been a long day, and I want to thank everyone for participating and asking great questions. What do you see as our next steps, Art?

Art: Thanks, everyone, for your participation today. I especially want to thank Barbara for asking a lot of good questions. Some of you may have felt a little embarrassed by her questions, but don't be. We need every one of you to challenge us with these types of questions if we are to be successful at removing the waste. As for next steps, I want you to pick a Lean consultant (trainer) and establish a Kaizen Promotion Office (KPO). Next, in about three weeks I'll be back with your management team to help establish a value stream organizational structure. Once these things are in place we should be able to start our kaizen activity. Then the real fun will begin.

Summary Points

- The four Lean fundamentals of takt time, one-piece flow, standard work, and pull apply to any business. They reveal opportunities that you would not be able to see otherwise.

- Takt time is the rate of customer demand that you are trying to respond to in order to deliver the most value.
- Flow reveals problems as they happen and forces you to fix problems as they occur—in any process. It is the key to quality improvements.
- Build quality into the product at every station in the line as opposed to trying to "inspect in" quality at the end. It's a simple and powerful shift in how people think about their work.
- Switching to Lean is about the people: making their jobs safer, easier to perform, and ultimately more secure.
- A standard work sheet tells everyone what is supposed to be happening in a simple format that can be easily understood by everybody. It helps you see whether quality work is happening or not when you observe the cell.
- Standard work establishes a baseline for improvement.
- Pull is the last of the four Lean fundamentals to implement: having products "pulled" by customers when they need them (not produced in batches and "pushed" onto them).

4

Organize for Lean

OVERVIEW

The next steps for UGH after the initial training sessions are to pick an external Lean consultant to work with and to begin the search for external candidates to head up the Kaizen Promotion Offices (KPOs), and then to create a value stream organization with strong team leaders. At this meeting, the functional department heads come with a list of three or four people from their organizations that they think could be good value stream leaders.

Most companies start down the Lean path while maintaining their traditional functional organizational structure—a huge mistake. As behavior follows structure, this approach makes the already difficult job of converting to Lean almost impossible. The switch from batching things through a series of functional departments to flowing product quickly from raw material to in-the-box requires a corresponding shift in the organizational structure.

The right structure is a value stream organization with team leaders responsible for entire value streams. These might be product families if you are a manufacturer, health specialties such as heart or bones if you are a hospital, or sales channels if you are in the business of selling life insurance. The value stream leader should have all the equipment needed to make the product family complete. The company's operational excellence targets can then be deployed down to and owned by the value stream leaders. This not only flattens the organizational structure but also ensures that everyone in the company is working on the same set of stretch goals. These operational excellence targets will drive the company's future results. Getting this alignment in place before starting serious kaizen activity will really help change behaviors and increase your chance at a successful Lean turnaround.

This meeting will be an important step on UGH's Lean journey. Picking the value stream leaders will probably break a lot of old taboos, so it ought to be fun to listen in on the conversation.

Value Stream Structure

Jerry York: OK, let's get started. At our last session Art gave us some clear homework: select a Lean consultant we can work with, pick a leader for the Kaizen Promotion Office (KPO) here in Cleveland and in each of our four subsidiary companies, and create a value stream structure to facilitate our move to Lean. Each of you participated in the selection of our Lean consultant, and as you know we have an advanced search under way, both internally and externally, for our KPO leaders that should be finished in the next couple of weeks. Our goal today is to pick the first value stream team leaders for our main Cleveland headquarters, and later we can do the same for our four subsidiary companies. Based on the information Art has provided us, I have put together this rough outline of what we are trying to do.

Value Stream Structure Rationale

1. Behavior follows structure
2. Functional = Batch; Value Stream = Flow
3. Value stream leader owns UGH's operational excellence goals
4. Value stream leader responsible from raw material to the customer
5. Value stream leader owns kaizen results
6. Value stream/KPO leaders responsible to make kaizen results stick
7. Organizational shift to value streams sends strong message to all of UGH

Art, do these make sense to you? When you say value stream structure, what do you mean? Can you give us a couple of examples?

Art: Sure, Jerry. For UGH, I think that the right value stream structure will be by product family. I'll explain that in more detail in a moment. First let me give you a couple of examples from other industries that might be easy to understand. I'm sure that you are all familiar with hospitals. Almost every hospital is organized in a silo type of structure, which is similar to your functional departments but even more fractured: silos within silos. To get treated as a patient you have to go across many silos, which causes not only delays (waiting), but errors in the cross-silo communication that can be hazardous to your health.

The crazy thing is that hospitals have natural value streams. They just don't manage that way. For example, a medium-size urban hospital might have $500 million in annual revenue. Inside it is a natural value stream for the heart and everything related to that. There is another natural value stream for bones and maybe one for babies. The heart value stream might be $150 million of total revenue, but there is no one in charge of it. Instead there are cardiologists, heart surgeons, heart surgery physician's assistants (PAs), and cardiac nurses. This group relies on centralized services such as admissions, the blood lab, radiology, transportation, pharmacy, the laundry, food services, sterilization, and the like, all of which operate their own silos their own way. Pulling this all together, giving it a leader, and operating it as the Heart Value Stream would allow for much more efficiency, better patient outcomes, and fewer errors and quality problems.

Or let's take a life insurance company that currently operates in silos but could benefit from a value stream structure. In this case the work wouldn't be organized along product lines but by distribution channel, because that's where the real differentiation occurs.

For UGH, a product family structure would work best. You already have seven distinct product families that you report on financially, but no one is in charge of them. There is no owner. Instead you rely on functional departments coordinated by an MRP system to get the products made.

This makes you just like the hospital, where functional silos do things their own way for their own benefit. The value-added workers are completely removed from the customer, and in most cases they only see components of the final product and not the actual product itself. Management focuses on making the numbers for its own functional department and is expert in blaming other departments when things go wrong and they can't make their numbers. No one is focused on UGH's operational excellence goals. They are just trying to "make the month" by hitting the monthly targets. Making the number takes precedence over the customer, inventory turns, productivity, quality, lead times, and a number of other things that determine your ability to provide value to your customers and grow. In effect, no one is in charge. There is no owner and little responsibility.

Instead of this, I want you to assign a team leader (in other words, a value stream leader) for each product family. The leader should be given all the equipment necessary to make that product family complete from raw material to the finished product. This not only brings everyone on the team closer to the customer but also removes the excuses and finger-pointing that go on in a typical batch company when something goes wrong. The team leader has to own the results all the way from your vendors to the customer. His or her focus will always be on the customer and achieving UGH's operational excellence targets.

Frank: But Art, I'm not sure we have enough equipment to do that. We have a number of machines where we only have one of them but they make parts for several of the different product families.

Art: Frank, it will always feel like that initially. Don't worry. First of all, you will be surprised at how much of your current equipment can be moved and dedicated to a particular product family. Because you never tried to look at it this way, it is easy to assume the worst. For those few machines that you only have one of—and there will be a few but less than you think—ownership should be given to the team that gets the most parts off that machine, and they should then be required to supply the other teams with parts through a simple supermarket system. You can't move all the machines at once, but over a period of time, kaizen by kaizen, they should be brought together in a particular product team area.

The team leader not only should be given all the equipment needed to make his product family complete but also needs to own the company's operational excellence goals that I showed you as part of the strategy statement (Figure 2-8). This provides a clear focus on what to work on and a means for comparing the progress each of the teams is making.

Jerry: Art, what would this look like structurally?

Art: The structure of the product family, or value stream, team is shown in Figure 4-1. First of all, in a manufacturing company like UGH, the team leader reports to the head of operations. In our major division, which is located here, that is you, Frank. The team leader also has a dotted line reporting relation to Jerry and this management team, as we will discuss a little later. You don't have to change your basic structure: you can still have a CFO, a VP of sales, a VP of marketing and HR and engineering and so on. Even so, you will have to assign someone to represent your department to each team leader of a product family team. They won't be full-time on the product team but will attend their weekly meetings and give input from your function.

Frank: Your chart shows someone called a buyer-planner. What is that? We have a purchasing department and a production planning department.

Art: Under the team leader the most important position is the buyer-planner. I'm sure you never heard of this as most companies don't operate this way. Creating

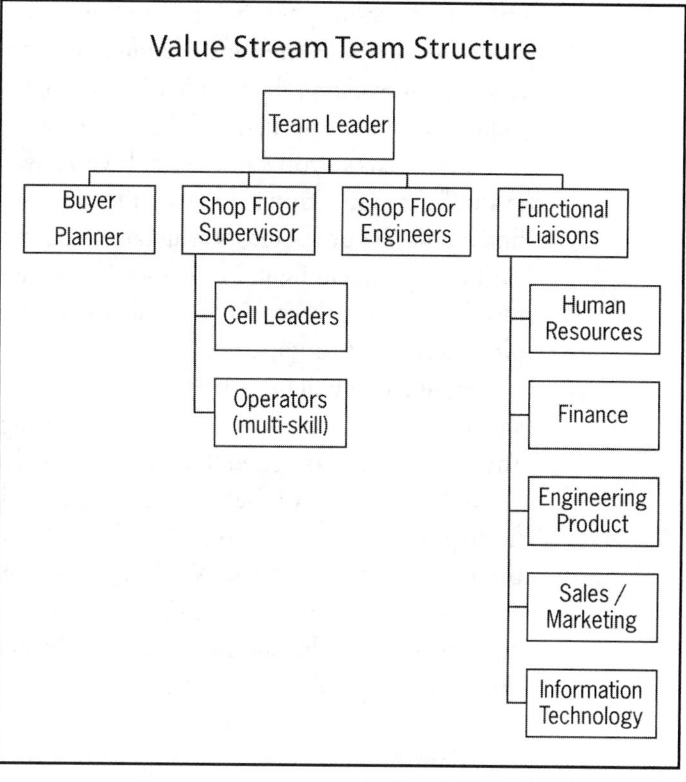

Figure 4-1. Value stream team structure

this position basically eliminates your centralized purchasing and planning departments and instead incorporates these functions in one person per team at the value stream team level. The theory here is that if one person does both functions, they can't fake themselves out (where purchasing is buying something that planning is not planning to make or vice versa) like the centralized functions can.

Frank: What about the shop floor structure under the team leader?

Art: Under the team leader there should be a shop floor manager for each shift, overseeing what happens on the shop floor. Under that position are various cell leaders. These are all hourly employees that you select based on capability (not on the more traditional seniority approach favored by a union). They can be paid an extra dollar an hour or so for this and are responsible for two to four cells depending on size and complexity. Their job is to keep the cells moving, use the kanban system to determine what to make next, and shift resources around as needed to meet demand. They can also step in and do the work if need be as well. They are a critical part of keeping everything running smoothly. If you pick the right ones, you will be surprised at how much ownership they will take for their cells and how much respect they will get from their team members.

Frank Gee: It would seem that the flow cells you talked about earlier would only work if you had operators who could run multiple machines. Our current approach is much more "one man, one machine" in nature. Will this be a big problem for us?

Art: Well, your operators will have to be multiskilled, just like those at any Lean company. I think Wiremold had something like 65 separate job classifications when we started, and we eventually got it down to 5. As you move from batch and "one operator per machine," to flow, where an operator might run six to eight machines and be trained and qualified on a similar number of other machines, you have to remove the job classification barrier. Responding to the customers' needs requires a lot of flexibility, and this has to be reflected in the skills of your operators.

This will take you some time. If you have a union, as we did at Wiremold, for example, the reduction in job classifications will have to be agreed to. Then you will find many of your operators reluctant to learn new skills. It scares them. They think, "What if I fail, will I get fired?" Getting our assembly operators who were used to just doing assembly type work to also learn to do simple machine setups, for example, took a lot of convincing.

Frank: That will be a challenge for sure. I hope you can give us guidance along the way. I also need some help understanding what you did with your engineers. You seem to have assigned them to the team leaders. Is that correct?

Art: Yes, as part of the value stream teams we also split up our centralized shop floor (mechanical, industrial, and electrical, for example) engineers and assigned them to the team leaders. We thought of them just as shop floor engineers. We wanted them to get their hands dirty at least five times per day. We saw them as problem solvers who should be constantly making things better for whatever team they were assigned to. If we had a big project in one team, we could always borrow a few engineers from the other teams to put more resources on it.

Many of these shop floor engineers were individuals we hired into Wiremold after we started down the Lean path. We needed them to design new products using the QFD approach in order to give us the growth we targeted. We made a decision early on that we didn't want to hire any engineers who had previously worked for batch companies. We felt that they would bring their batch thinking with them and we would have to spend a lot of time "unlearning" them.

As a result, we hired most of our engineers directly out of school. We made it a rule that they had to spend the first two years on the shop floor before they could design new products. We didn't want them designing things we couldn't build, and we also needed to immerse them in our Lean way of thinking. What was interesting was that when their two years were up, about half of them wanted to stay on the shop floor and delay their move to design. They said they were learning so much and having too much fun to go into design just yet.

Steve Jones, CEO of UGH Automotive: Art, that is a nice story, but this idea of breaking up the engineering departments and assigning the engineers to value stream teams makes no sense to me. My engineers take great pride in being part of a team of similar engineers—industrial engineers, for example. They have a centralized office where they work together and share ideas. It gives them a career path within their specialty. They respond to written requests and can cover anything in the plant. Can't we keep them in their departments and just do the other value stream things you are suggesting? I'm worried that some of them might quit if we assign them to the value stream leaders.

Art: Steve, all of those are valid concerns. Especially if you want to stay at your current state and not improve. Keeping your existing silos will do little to remove the waste and make the type of progress that I know is possible here at UGH. You will have to handle this one with some care. Be honest with your people but explain why we want to make the change. The idea of them getting their hands dirty at least five times a day will come as a shock to them. At the same time, I know that the change will energize them. They will be a key part of a hands-on team trying to deliver more value to the customer. And don't worry; as I mentioned earlier, if you need to pull a couple of engineers off their product family teams to focus short term on an urgent problem in another team, you still can. As for worrying about promotional opportunities, this approach will broaden their skills and give them even more chances to advance.

Jerry: Art, help me understand how the support functions work with the team leaders.

Art: Sure. There needs to be a representative from each of the functional staffs, such as engineering, marketing, finance, HR, and so on, that attend team meetings and have a dotted line reporting relationship to the team leader. They make sure that the team gets the proper support from each function and that the communication lines work well. These individuals don't sit with the team leader but attend weekly or even daily meetings.

Oh, and speaking of sitting, we had the team leader, the buyer-planner, and the shop floor manager all sit on the shop floor as close as possible to where their equipment was located. It was noisy (which meant they complained about it at first), but it gave the team members instant access to the leader and facilitated better decision making. I recommend you follow the same approach here at UGH. It is not traditional for sure, but that is part of the point. The changes you will be making are huge. You need to show people that you will be going about it in a totally different way. Little things like where the team leader sits really matter.

Jerry: I think we have a good idea of the structure and why we want to do it from a business perspective. So I guess we should switch gears now and start picking the team leaders? Before we do that, I have a question. As all of these team leaders will report to Frank and be responsible for making product on the shop floor—shouldn't they have a manufacturing background? For example, are our current foremen of the functional departments good candidates, or should we be looking elsewhere?

Art: The value stream team leaders do not need to have a manufacturing background. That is traditional thinking but not Lean. A couple of your current foremen might make the transition, but I hate to say that it's unlikely. People with lots of manufacturing background tend to be experts in certain types of equipment and have been trained in a "make the forecast, just do what I say" mentality. What you want in the value stream team leader is a self-starting problem solver capable of running a small to midsize business because that is what you are giving them. They will be responsible not only for making the product but for all your key measurements: customer service, inventory turns, productivity, quality, and 5S, as well as the visual workplace. In addition, they have to be team players capable of leading and being able to deal with people both above and below them. You can't have them out there yelling at people and ignoring the inputs of all their associates. Most important, they have to be capable of training their team members in problem solving to eliminate the waste. They have to carry the Lean message all the way down through the organization. They have to support and encourage their people. In addition, they have to be able to interface with the customers, your sales force, and inside sales.

Jerry: Wow, that's a lot of stuff. Do you think we can find the right people internally?

Art: Absolutely you can. I'm sure all of these skills are present in a number of your people. You just have to shake off your old way of thinking and stop trying to restrict people to traditional functional silos.

Judy Rankin: Art, Jerry asked me to lead the actual selection process for the first team leaders, and I'd like to ask for some help from you. You asked each of us to bring three or four candidates from our own organizations to discuss. How do you want to do this? Should we just start by putting all the names up on the board? Then what? Who will pick, or do you somehow expect us to do this jointly?

Art: Yes, exactly, let's start by putting all the names you brought up on the board. I assume that most of you know all of them, so you should be able to have a good discussion and come to a joint team decision on who the team leaders should be. Teamwork is extremely important in a successful Lean turnaround, and this should help you to build teamwork among your senior team.

Judy: OK, here goes. [*She proceeds to write down the names.*]

Art: Are there any others that should be there?

Scott Smith: I can think of several really good people who are not up there. Our corporate auditor, Dan Grace, for example, is one of the brighter people we have and seems to get along with everyone.

Dick Conway: Well, I didn't put him on the list because he's one of my best resources. And we may be able to get him a promotion in the finance department.

Judy: I can think of a couple of other names that people have not put on the list for similar reasons. But if these team leaders are going to be a key part of our Lean turnaround and becoming team leaders puts them on a great career path, then I don't think we should be holding back any names.

Jerry: That makes sense, Judy. Let's make sure we get the best names on the list. Who else did you have in mind?

Judy: Well, Scott didn't put the head of inside sales, Betty Wagner, on the list—she is terrific. Frank didn't list Tom Fairbank, who is one of our better engineers. And Ellen didn't offer up Suzy Whaley, who is probably our best product manager. I think all of them have the skills and personalities that Art outlined as important for a team leader.

Jerry: I agree with you. Let's put those names up on the board.

Jerry: OK, what about Suzy Whaley and Tom Fairbank? Frank and Ellen, do you want to argue about putting them on the list?

Frank and Ellen: [*in unison*] No, boss, they should be up there.

Judy: Let's go through each of the names and see if we can get some consensus candidates. Who wants to start?

Steve: Judy, several of the names up there have a bad reputation in my engineering department. I don't mean they are not smart, but they are a pain in the ass to deal with. They are late with everything, they withhold information, and they often yell at people in meetings.

Judy: Anyone else want to comment on the names on the list?

Dick: Yes. I also see a couple of names on the list that people in my department have complained about in the past. One is the same as Steve mentioned, and another is a different name.

Jerry: I see that Frank has put a couple of current functional foremen on the list. I think they are both good guys, but Art mentioned that traditionally trained functional leaders have a hard time making the switch to value stream leaders. Should we keep them on the list? Art, any thoughts here?

Art: I don't know either of these two candidates, but like I said, it is unlikely to see traditional foremen make the switch, though not impossible. In fact, both at Jake Brake back in my Danaher days and at Wiremold, we had a couple of former foremen who were very successful at becoming value stream leaders. Frank, what is your take on these two?

Frank: My feeling is that these two could make the switch. They are both bright and quick learners. They are self-starting problem solvers who don't need a lot of daily supervision. And when faced with problems they tend to make the right decisions on their own. They are also the only two of my foremen who are actually enthusiastic about Lean. And I'd say that the most important qualification for both of them is that they are very good with people both up and down the organization. They will be able to teach and encourage people to become problem solvers.

Judy: Well, that seems to touch all the bases that Art mentioned earlier. Anyone have any objections to keeping them on the list? I don't see any objections, so let's move on.

This discussion continued for a while as everyone gave his or her opinion on the list of names. The team eventually settled on 10 names from which to select 7 value stream leaders. In the process, although they didn't realize it at the time, they were building a new spirit of teamwork in the leadership team. They started to feel more comfortable being able to openly express their opinions even when they involved employees in someone else's organization. At the same time, they were better able to accept the criticism of their peers. So, not only were they creating the new value stream structure, but in addition, a lot of learning and team building was occurring.

In the end they kept Frank's two foremen and added the corporate auditor, the young shop floor engineer Tom Fairbank, the woman from marketing, another woman from the IT organization, and one of the new product development managers from Steve Mallard's engineering department. They all felt pretty good about the choices and, more important, about the team process through which they were picked.

Judy: Now that we have the team leaders selected, I assume we should notify them and get their acceptance. Then what? Should we go ahead and announce this before the first kaizens even while everything is still physically organized in a batch state?

Art: Before you make the announcement you should divide up the people and the equipment and other resources that will report to each team leader. Don't worry that the equipment is still spread all over the place. That can only be corrected over time. It is important, however, for the team leaders to know what people and equipment they are responsible for on day one.

Jerry: What about their responsibility for our new operational excellence goals? We have targeted 100 percent on-time customer service, 50 percent reduction in defects each year, 20x inventory turns, 20 percent annual productivity gains, not to mention having visual controls and 5S in place everywhere. They get to own those right away for their teams even in our current batch state, right?

Art: Yes, Jerry, that is right, so once all this is in place go ahead and announce the new organization. It will send a strong signal to all your people that things are going to be different going forward. So how does that sound? How do you all feel about it?

Scott: I enjoyed the process of picking the team leaders, but I'm still a little nervous about having so many nonmanufacturing people being responsible for producing big chunks of our product lines all of a sudden. I guess that's just the traditional manager in me.

Jerry: Scott, I think we all share a bit of that feeling. Even so, the opportunity Art has outlined for UGH is so big that we have to get over our fears and move ahead. We all feel good about the leaders we picked, and it will be our job as a management team to make sure they are successful. I'd like to announce the new organization as soon as possible. Art, what are the next steps after this?

Art: After you announce the new organization, then we will be ready to begin the first kaizens. Let's plan on doing that in about three weeks. We already have a good idea what the first four teams will be. I'll be back for the kaizen week. Normally we would kick this off early on Monday morning, but Jerry has asked if I could spend some time with your management team, including the four division presidents who will all be here for the kaizen, talking about leadership in a Lean turnaround before we actually start the kaizen. So I suggest we start the kaizen kickoff meeting at 9 a.m. and we all get together at 7:30 a.m. to talk about leadership and anything else that is on your minds. Before we finish this session, however, do you have anything else you would like to discuss?

Frank Gee: Yes, I do. This is a little off the subject, but as we go about setting up our KPOs, how big should they be? Do we just hire in an experienced Lean guy or pick an internal person and that's it? Or are there some guidelines for KPO size? If so, where do we get the people?

Art: As a rule of thumb, I think you should think in terms of 2 percent of your workforce as a good size for the KPO. These will be people working full-time on kaizen activities and helping train your workforce in Lean and problem solving. You should be able to populate this primarily using existing people freed up from other activities balanced with a few good experienced external hires that can hit the ground running. Think of the KPO as a great training ground for future leaders.

Pick people, both hourly and salaried, that you think can go higher by at least a couple of levels in the company. Put them in the KPO for a couple of years to really learn Lean and then promote them to other functions like value stream leader, plant manager, and so on.

The KPO leader should be at least equal to the product team leaders in terms of title, pay, and so forth. He or she can report to you, Frank (that would be my preference), or, if you decide as a team, to Jerry. Either way will work. They should be setting up and running kaizen teams when the outside consultant is not present. They should also be teaching and training your people in how to see the waste and then how to remove it. The KPO will be a key driver of your Lean turnaround. Is there anything else you would like to cover?

Sam Watson, president of UGH Small Gears: Art, when you were explaining the Lean fundamentals to us, you mentioned that there were three foundational elements that would help us but said you would cover these at a later time. Is this a good time?

Art: Well, I was going to cover these at our first kaizen kickoff meeting, but I suppose now is as good a time as any. By foundational items I mean things that need to be in place for you to successfully implement the Lean fundamentals. There are three of them, as follows:

Foundational Items for Lean

Setup reduction

5S discipline everywhere

Visual control

Setup reduction is the most important of the three, especially for a machine-based company like UGH. It is important for nonmanufacturing companies as well, as almost every company has some form of setup, even if they don't recognize it as such. A hospital, for example, has to change over the beds between patients. This can take 45 minutes, but on a kaizen I ran once we were able to get it down to 10 minutes. The same would be true for high-fixed-cost operating rooms in a hospital that have to be changed after each procedure. If you don't drastically reduce setup times, you can't really have flow and pull. Your lead times will continue to be very long.

Unfortunately, most companies that start down the Lean path don't focus on setup reduction at all. If all their experience says that it takes two hours to change over a certain type of machine, and it always has, they just accept that as gospel and move on to something else. But if you asked how often they spent the time to watch a two-hour setup from beginning to end, the answer would be, "Well, never."

Judy: What do you mean by 5S, and why is it so important to a Lean turnaround?

Art: Judy, 5S refers to five Japanese words that translate to words that start with the letter *s*. Approximate English equivalents are shown in Figure 4-2. In effect they stand for cleanliness, organization, and discipline, which are all foundational building blocks for Lean. In effect, if a company doesn't have the basic ability to keep things clean and orderly, its chances of being successful with a Lean turnaround are low. Several of our acquisitions at Wiremold fell into this category. We always started right away with a couple of kaizens to show them what to expect (our standard work for acquisitions), but if their 5S was bad, we would have them spend the next six months doing nothing but 5S before we were willing to run another kaizen.

UGH CORPORATION

Visual Workplace—5Ss

1. SORT	Sort out necessary and unnecessary items and throw out the unnecessary items
2. SET	Everything should be placed in order, easy to use, and it should take very little time to find what you need.
3. SHINE	Make aisles, machines, tools, instruments, desks, etc. clean and keep the factory and office areas dirt free.
4. STANDARDIZE	Maintain cleanliness, arrangement, and disposal in all areas.
5. SUSTAIN	Demonstrate the discipline to maintain and improve your workplace always.

Figure 4-2. 5S

Steve Mallard: And the visual controls? This makes me think of kindergarten and all the artwork that was hung around the room. Just kidding. But what do you mean here?

Art: Well, Steve, you are actually not that far off. Figure 4-3 is a short list of some of the various types of visual controls.

UGH Corporation

Visual Controls

- Signals
- Floor Markings
- Bar Codes
- Supply Replenishment Cards (Kanban)
- Supermarkets
- Measurements
- Production Boards
- Color Coding
- Labels / Signs

Figure 4-3. Visual controls

Figure 4-4. Production control chart

Production Control Chart

CELL 304

TAKT Time = 60"

			CUMULATIVE		
TIME	PLAN	ACTUAL	P	A	COMMENTS
7-8	60	45	60	45	Slow start-machine warm up
8-9	60	50	120	95	Station #3 jam ups
9-10	60	61	180	156	n.a.
10:15-11	45	40	225	196	Ran out of boxes
11-12	60	55	285	251	Station #3 jam up
12:30-1:30	60	40	345	291	Station #3 jam up-no boxes
1:30-2:30	60	62	405	353	No problems
2:45-3:30	45	50	450	403	No problems
3:30-4:30	-	45		448	Worked one hour overtime

The main purpose is to make sure everyone involved in any process can see at a glance what the targets are and where they stand on an hour-by-hour basis in achieving them. It is valuable for management to get this input as they walk around so that they can take immediate corrective action. A great example is the simple production control chart shown in Figure 4-4.

This doesn't need to be sophisticated to be effective. We just used an off-the-shelf flipchart on a stand. Most traditional factories have no visual control. You don't know where you stand at any given moment. This is partly because things are made in batches in functional departments and partly because of the long lead times. In a six-week lead time situation, hour-by-hour status reports are meaningless. When you put things in a flow, however, and drive everything to takt time at the beat of the customer, knowing where you are hour by hour is critical.

Jerry: Thanks, Art. OK, everyone, this has certainly been an interesting exercise. I feel really good about the team leaders we picked but even better about the teamwork we showed in selecting them. We still have some follow-up work to do, but in just a few weeks we can start our serious kaizen efforts. I'm looking forward to that. I hope you are too.

Summary Points

- Organizing by value stream rather than department or function aligns the work around the customer and not around internal demands; it places responsibility on customer value, not "make the month" goals.
- What you want in the value stream team leader is a self-starting problem solver capable of running a small to midsize business because that is what you are giving them.
- Think of your KPO as a great training ground for future Lean leaders.
- Visual controls show targets and where everyone stands in achieving them; they help management to take immediate corrective action at the gemba.

5

Preparing for Kaizen and Lean Leadership

OVERVIEW

You can't simply manage a Lean turnaround; you have to lead it. Getting everyone focused on the company's operational excellence targets, for example, requires teamwork at every level of the organization. Leadership needs to understand this and constantly encourage everyone to work together. That's why the next step is to gather the leadership team and set direction and expectations for the kaizen kickoff.

Focus the kaizen efforts by starting with the most important value stream. Selecting the individual kaizen activities will depend on your type of company. For a machine-based manufacturer, for example, two setup reduction kaizens plus one flow kaizen and one office kaizen each time is a good starting point. For hospitals, improving bed turnover and getting discharges to occur earlier in the day, before noon, for example, might drive the economics. Other types of businesses might want to attack the biggest problem areas in their major value stream first. Remember that reducing setup times drives everything else in almost any kind of business.

Leadership must recognize that leading a Lean turnaround will require a completely different approach. They will need to manage forward instead of constantly looking backward in the traditional "make the month" approach. They will need to focus on the weekly progress on the operational excellence goals—thereby concentrating on improving the processes that will deliver more value to your customers. Along with this switch the leader will have to change his or her personal approach and become much more hands-on and out in front than the traditional manager. The Lean leader needs to be committed, consistent, accessible, and supportive of her people. The Lean leader also needs to go see, be willing to take the necessary leaps of faith, and above all, constantly drive the Lean fundamentals.

Preparing to Kick off the Kaizens

Jerry York: OK, everyone, I want to thank every member of our executive team (including our four division presidents) for joining me and Art in this meeting. Thanks also for getting started at 7:30. As you know, our reason to be together today is to kick off our first week of kaizen activity at UGH. The kickoff meeting will be at 9 a.m., and each of you will be on one of the four teams. You won't be a team leader or coleader, just a member of the team. As Art has explained to us, that means you need to be a full-time team participant for the week. Your title or position in the company means nothing on a kaizen team. Everyone is equal and should contribute equally. Get your hands dirty, become involved, and do what the leader or coleader asks you to do.

The reason we are starting a little earlier is that I want to take advantage of Art's insights into the management and leadership approach that we will have to take. Earlier Art explained that three "management musts" have to be in place: Lean is the strategy, lead from the top, and transform the people. I think we understand the strategy and people parts. We could use some help with the leadership part. Art, what do you recommend?

Art: Thanks, Jerry, and good morning, everyone. For starters, I want to explain that you really can't "manage" a Lean turnaround. You have to lead it. So this morning I want to focus on two main topics: your operational excellence targets and the leadership traits of a Lean leader. But first I'd like to briefly touch on two other things: the need for teamwork and the way you use hoshin planning to help you allocate your resources.

Let's start with teamwork. The way you think about teamwork is probably quite different from the teamwork required for a Lean turnaround to succeed. For example, if I asked if you functioned as a team, you would probably tell me yes, we do. But if I dug in a little deeper, you would probably say things like "we all get along with each other" or "we have common objectives."

Judy Rankin: Art, that's true. What's wrong with that?

Art: Nothing is wrong with it—for a traditional batch company. For Lean, however, you have to think and act as one. You need to support each other and be willing to give and accept criticism. You can't have any infighting, and it has to be very clear to the rest of UGH's associates that you are all on the same page. They should expect to get the same answer to any question from any one of you.

But that only scratches the surface. Becoming a Lean enterprise requires you to create successful, motivated teams throughout the entire company. Many people feel that the real key to Toyota's long-term success is its ability to form productive teams. Your new value stream teams need to come together to remove the waste and deliver value to your customers. As you move from batch to flow, you will be transitioning from a traditional "one man, one machine" approach to small teams of people trying to respond directly to the demands of the customer. They have to function as teams to be successful. Your current functional organization is the exact opposite of this. It creates internal squabbling and finger-pointing when things go wrong.

True teams work for each other and the customer and take responsibility when things go wrong. They don't look for someone else to blame. Your customer just sees you as a single entity, UGH. They don't care about your internal squabbles—all of which are just waste, anyway. Yet your current organizational structure will always create such problems. For example, you can't have operations trying to level load the factory while sales and marketing are out trying to generate large batch orders. You will be working against each other. To become Lean, everything has to change, and you all have to be on the same page to make this happen. You all need to be trying to level load the factory. Great teams need to be encouraged to try new things and not have to worry about failure. In fact, unlike your current rigid measurements, you should be encouraging a certain level of failure.

Dick Conway: Art, you can't be serious. You want us to encourage people to fail? People here believe failure is unacceptable because we have spent years punishing people for it.

Art: Yes, Dick, most traditional companies behave this way. It is part and parcel of the "make the month" mentality. When something goes wrong, look for someone to blame. But from the Lean point of view, we learn from our mistakes, from our failures if you will. You can't "learn by doing" without actively encouraging people to "do." In fact, my sensei, Chihiro Nakao, used to always tell me, "Byrne-san, if you don't try something, no knowledge will visit you." I love that saying.

Jerry: I think that we all understand the need for teamwork. And that my whole leadership team must all get along with each other as individuals. We do have some work to do, however, to function like a real team, especially in the way you are describing it. Will hoshin planning help us do that?

Art: Yes. Hoshin planning can help get you all on the same page as a team. Hoshin planning (another way of saying policy deployment) is the approach you

2015 UGH Corp. – Policy Deployment Matrix – Top Level (PD1)

Date: 1/15/16

Defect reduction: 50% per year Productivity: + 20% per year	Double in Size every 3-5 years	Inventory Turns = 20x +	100% Customer Service	Key Strategies (breakthrough) / Key Metrics Goals (3 years & current year) / Hoshins (key initiatives) / Team Support	Install Real-time Pull System from customer order thru operations	Develop new rigid packaging platform	Develop South American Beachhead	Add Plastic Processing capabilities and build market position
	○			**STRATEGIC ACQUISITIONS**				○
	○			**NEW MARKET POSITIONS**		●	○	○
○	○	○	○	**COMPETE ON SPEED TO MARKET**	○	○		
○	○			**DEVELOP STREAM OF NEW PRODUCT PLATFORMS AND DERIVITIVES**		○		
○	○	○	○	**ESTABLISH LEAN BUSINESS SYSTEMS**	○	●		
				Executive Team	○		☒	☒
				Admin (Finance, IT, HR)		○	○	○
				Rigid Packaging VST	○	☒	○	
				Plastic Assemblies VST	○		○	
				Artermarket VST	○	●	○	
				Global R&D / Engineering Team		○		
				Supply Chain Management Team			○	
				Marketing Team		○	●	
				Sales Team		○	○	
				Operations support team	☒	○	○	

Legend

☒	Leader
○	High Impact / Strong Support
●	Some Impact / Moderate Support
	Weak or No Impact

Figure 5-1. Policy deployment matrix

should use for your strategic planning. This is a whole subject all by itself, so I'm not going to spend a lot of time on it right now. You can learn the details of this approach and put it in place during your regular planning cycle after we get the kaizen efforts under way. But for now, and especially since we are talking about this regarding how you lead your teams, hoshin as I've always used it is basically a visual planning tool that will help you get all of your resources aligned behind your key strategic objectives. Figure 5-1 shows a high-level hoshin matrix as an example. You start with the operational excellence targets that are part of the strategy we talked about earlier. These are shown on the left side of the grid. These then drive this year's hoshins, or plans, at the top of the grid, which in turn are expanded into the responsibilities and resources needed to accomplish them over on the right side of the grid.

The intersection points on the matrix show how each hoshin supports one or more of the strategic operational excellence goals. As this gets deployed down in the organization, the chart highlights the person responsible for each hoshin and the resources you have assigned to it. This forces you to understand how many projects you can actually handle at any given time. The ones you can't allocate resources to right now will be put in the parking lot to be done at a future date. This will leave you with a limited number of "must do–can't fail" projects that you all agree will receive the proper priorities and above all resources. Getting everyone on the same page is key. Most traditional companies don't have this clarity and as a result attempt 10 top-priority projects when they can only resource 4. The end result is that almost nothing gets done.

You will learn more about hoshin planning as the main approach for this year's strategic planning cycle once we kick this off. First, however, I want you to start removing waste and learning from kaizen.

Manage to Your Operational Excellence Targets

Art: So, as we prepare for the kickoff of our hands-on work, I'd like to talk about how you run the company on a day-to-day basis. What are some of the key leadership traits that you will need to adapt to keep your Lean transformation progressing?

Jerry: Art, to be fair to our current leadership, I want to point out that our historical results have been pretty good. And we believe a lot of the credit goes to the way we have been managing the business. We have tight financial controls and do a thorough management review every month. Do you really think we need to change that?

Art: Thanks for raising this point, Jerry. I want to be clear that I'm not saying you are not doing a good job. What you have been doing is OK—if, that is, you want to stay on the same path you have been on and get the same kinds of results. But that is not what we want to do. We know that results like the ones I showed you earlier are possible here at UGH. To achieve them, however, you and everyone here will have to change your approach to how you run the business. To be more specific, we want you to manage looking forward, not looking backward at last month's results like most traditional companies do.

Jerry: What do you mean by that?

Art: I'm suggesting that you focus on where you want to be and not where you have already been. Think of it this way. What do you think UGH will look like five or so years out if you hit all of the operational excellence targets I gave you as part of the strategy? Better, or worse?

Scott Smith: Well I'm not sure we can hit those targets—they look pretty stretched from where we are. At the same time, if we did achieve them, boy oh boy we would be so much better as a company that there would be no comparison. Our customers would just love us.

Dick Conway: Yes, and our investors might love us even more as our enterprise value would go way up just like all of those companies you showed us earlier.

Art: And that is exactly my point. To get there, though, I need you change the way you run the company. You still have to close the books every month and review the results. But don't spend a lot of time with big end-of-month reviews. Instead I want you to manage to your operational excellence targets. Just as a reminder, these are:

- 100% on-time customer service
- 20% productivity gain each year
- 50% reduction in defects each year
- 20x inventory turns
- Establishing visual controls and 5S everywhere

This is what I mean by "managing looking forward." Focus on improving your processes: that is what will change your future results.

Jerry: I think my team understands what you are asking us to do and why. So how should we deploy this down in the organization? If our focus is going to be on removing the waste so we can hit our operational excellence goals, we'll need everyone in the company to be focused on doing this approach. But I guess that if the value stream leaders were all focused on these targets it would certainly help our teamwork.

Art: Correct. Every product family team leader (or value stream leader) has to own these goals for his or her value stream. Once per week all the team leaders should present their progress on these five goals to you and your staff. Give them each 10 minutes to present. Find out where they are having problems and ask what you as a staff can do to help them. Have your KPO pay extra attention to helping the teams that are lagging. Part of their presentation should outline what their plans are for next week. Make sure that you are all comfortable with these plans and that you feel they are being aggressive enough.

Don't expect miracles at first. Many of the teams will struggle. Your job as a management team is to help them, not criticize them. Keep the entire organization constantly focused on your vision of where you are trying to take UGH by achieving your operational excellence goals. Bit by bit you will get better. Driving for a set of stretched future goals will become the norm. Celebrate your wins. Publicize the gains. Create a monthly kaizen newsletter. Your people will be learning so much so quickly that even the constant pressure on these operational excellence goals will begin to feel like a fun challenge rather than a burden. The important thing is that you will always be "managing forward" by focusing on your processes, not your results.

Jerry: Well, this will certainly be different from what we have been doing. Do you really think it will give us a lot of leverage in making our turnaround?

Art: Are you kidding? Just think of how big these "small" changes can be. First of all, creating a value stream organization sends a strong message to everyone in the company that things will be different. Then you couple this message with new behavior: managing the company by having these value streams focus on your operational excellence targets. Then everyone can understand and align with your core strategy. Next you make it clear through these weekly review meetings that you are not only serious about hitting these targets but you understand that the CEO and senior management team's role is to do everything you can to support the value stream teams. After that you start an aggressive kaizen program with strong KPO support that teaches your people how remove the waste and make significant progress toward the goals in a rapid-fire way. Wow, you will have a completely different company.

Leadership Traits

Judy Rankin: Art, what you're proposing is a completely different way of working here, and I am sure that for most folks it will not come easily. How do we deal with this new culture?

Art: Judy, great question. Although these simple realignments will make a big difference, the real key to success in a Lean turnaround is leadership. The most important leader here will be Jerry as the CEO. I always advise companies that if you can't get the CEO to lead the shift to Lean, then you are better off not starting down this path. Just be the best batch company that you can be and hope that none of your competitors make the Lean turnaround. For UGH to be successful, however, it will take leadership from this entire executive team. Certainly the four division presidents are the CEOs of their businesses, but those of you with functional titles have to show leadership as well.

Jerry: Art, you keep describing our current state. How do we break out of this? Let's set aside the topic of resistance for now; won't our people be confused?

Art: Initially they might be, yes. The transition to Lean not only challenges the current state but proves, kaizen by kaizen, that there is a much better way. This new way of working will basically say to them what Iwata said to us years ago during our first kaizen at Danaher: "Look, everything here is no good, what do you want to do about it?" How do you think they will react? They created the current processes, and you patted them on the back for doing a good job along the way.

Judy: Well that is because we think that when people do a good job they deserve to be congratulated. Is that so wrong? Are you suggesting that we stop praising them when they do a good job and just tell them, "Everything here is no good, go fix it"?

Art: No, of course not. You always want to praise and reward your people for doing a good job. I'm just trying to point out why we say that Lean is all about people. What you are trying to transform is your people. You have to show them a different way to look at the work. You need them to buy in and contribute their ideas to removing the waste. This will take time, but more than anything it will take leadership. You have to make the case for Lean and keep making it. Forever.

I've put together a short list of traits that I think are important for the Lean leader:

Lean Leadership Traits

- Vision
- Commitment
- Drive the lean fundamentals
- Go see
- The soft stuff is the hard stuff
- Consistency
- Accessibility
- Take the leaps of faith
- Respect your people
- Set stretch goals

Vision

Art: Let's start with vision. People follow a leader because they believe that the leader has a clear sense of where he—OK, let's mix this up and say she—is going and that she is taking them to a better place. This means that the leader (think of it as your management team) needs a clear and unwavering vision of where she is trying to take the company. The vision of the Lean leader starts with a clear understanding of value from the point of view of the customer. She never starts down the Lean path for internal reasons like cutting costs. She understands that the only way to deliver more value to her customers is to improve her own value-adding activities to remove the waste first. This will allow the company to service all customers in a faster, higher-quality, and lower-cost way. Her vision is one of seeking internal perfection on behalf of her customers.

The Lean leader also has to have a vision for growth. Growth comes from a combination of providing the customer with higher quality, shorter lead times, and better customer service. It also comes from rapid new product development as a result of removing the waste from this process and linking all parts of the organization to the product development process, including "the voice of the customer."

Commitment

Jerry: I think that is a pretty clear outline of the vision that is needed, but what about the next leadership trait, commitment? I can come up with a lot of different ways to look at this one.

Art: Making the switch to Lean is so big that the organization needs daily proof that the leader (in your case the leadership team) is fully committed to the change. You have to be out front and visibly involved. One of the best ways to do this is to be on five or six full-week kaizen teams per year. This will send a clear message, and more important you will learn how to see things with a set of "Lean eyes"—which will reveal how much opportunity there is in your current operations.

The leader needs to talk about the Lean initiative and her vision for the company all the time. Anytime someone is around or in a meeting with the leader her commitment to Lean should be very clear. This will help spread the word. When you cannot be on a kaizen team, Jerry and his whole staff should attend the kick-off meeting, the daily leader's meetings, and the wrap-up meeting for any kaizens that are going on. This won't take much time but is a loud statement of your interest and commitment.

Another clear way to show commitment is to spend time every day on the shop floor. Check the visual control boards, talk to the operators, ask what problems they are having and what you can do to help. When everyone gets used to your constant presence they will feel reassured by your commitment and support.

Drive the Lean Fundamentals

Art: The Lean fundamentals that we discussed earlier are your path to removing the waste, switching from batch to flow, and delivering more value to the customer. You don't have to start off as a Lean expert, but you need to commit to becoming one. The more you understand about what is possible using the Lean approach, such as reducing a setup from three hours to one minute for example, the better you will be able to lead. In the meantime, you will speed your Lean turnaround by constantly asking about the Lean fundamentals everywhere in the business. Is everything running to takt time? Is everything in a one-piece flow? Is standard work in place and being followed everywhere? Do we have pull signals in place all the way from our suppliers to our customers?

Go See—Leave Homework

Jerry: Art, I think I understand these first parts, but what do you mean by "Go see"? Do you really mean it like it sounds?

Art: Yes, Jerry, that's it. It is easier said, however, than done. Remember that the traditional manager lives in his office or conference room where things are discussed and decided without anyone ever going to see the actual problem. The Lean leader is different—she will always "go see" the problem firsthand. Have it explained and demonstrated. Ask why, why, why, why, why to see if you can get to the root cause. Talk to the operators and get their input. The more points of view, the better the decision. Don't worry about who came up with the best solution. It won't matter. People need to feel good about the process.

Part of "go see" in my opinion is what you do when you visit one of your facilities. Never start a visit in the conference room. Always start on the shop floor. You should always be able to see physical changes since your last visit. Take a walk around. Have your team show you what they have accomplished since your last visit. Look for waste and opportunities to improve. Point them out as you go along. Make sure your people know that you expect them to take actions to correct the problems you are pointing out.

Taiichi Ohno's Approach

Nakao-san, Iwata-san, and the other Shingijutsu consultants who trained me all worked directly for Taiichi Ohno for many years. This is one of the Ohno stories they loved to tell. Ohno came to one of their factories, and while on a gemba walk, he asked about the setup time of a particularly complicated machine. When told it was about four hours, he said, "That is ridiculous; fix that before my next visit." They worked hard for the next several months, and when Ohno came back the time was down to one and a half hours. They were so proud and had the plant photographer ready to take pictures of Ohno watching the setup. Instead he said, "Look, I'm a busy man, get the time down a lot by next visit and then I'll watch it." By the next visit they were down to 50 minutes, and all excited with the plant photographer standing by. Again Ohno said, "Look, I'm a busy man, you can't expect me to watch something that takes 50 minutes." This kept repeating until they had finally gotten this setup to under 10 minutes, when he finally agreed to watch it and have the plant photographer earn his keep.

They all had a love-hate relationship with Ohno. He was tough and uncompromising. He never gave them the solution, just the objective. More important, he always followed up and gave them the next target. This was the "hate" part of the love-hate relationship. When they finally achieved a level that he thought worthy of praise, he gave them the "love" they craved. On balance, however, the best description is that they all revered him. He got them to do things they thought were impossible. They did it as a team and felt great about their accomplishments. At the same time, they understood that without Ohno pushing them they would have never gotten there. He went to see and followed up, something that needs to be adopted by all Lean leaders.

Art: Follow Ohno's lead when you visit one of your facilities. Leave homework before you depart. Clarify the physical things you want to see accomplished before your next visit. This might be two new cells, some freed-up floor space, reduced setup time on a couple of machines; it might be 5S and visual controls in a couple of areas. If you're a bank it might be a more efficient office layout to achieve flow. If you're a distributor it might be switching to picking by size and time instead of picking by order. I've attached one of my lists, Figure 5-2, from visits to the Barcelona, Spain, factory of one of my portfolio companies. Xavier, the plant manager, kept all of these homework lists and had almost always accomplished them all by the time I got back for my next visit. By the way, look at his results in the following table.

Spain Kaizen Results

	Before	After	Change
Customer service	91%	98%	+8%
Inventory turns	8x	20x	+150%
Space freed up	201k sq. ft.	100k sq. ft.	–52%

Figure 5-2. Barcelona homework

Barcelona, Spain Homework

Year-End Targets
- Free up 25–30% of floor space
- Inventory turns of 13X–14X by year-end
- 15% productivity gain
- 30–40% reduction in scrap

Press Area
- Focus on reducing all set-ups
    - Convert all dies and presses
    - Train operators
- Once part starts on primary press it needs to be completed in 2 days
- Clean up press area; paint, brighter lights

Widmans (plastic pocket machine)
- Sell automatic pallet mover—use money for something you need
- Move Widmans closer—man with 2 vs. 3

Lever Arch Line
- Get set up down to 10 minutes
- Redo layout to man with 2 vs. 3 people

Stapler Assembly
- Build feeding devices to go to a chaku-chaku
- Manning from 5 → 2

Kanban—from warehouse to assembly
- Finished goods targets; Widmans—8 days, LAF—10 days, Staplers—5 days, Staples—5 days

The Soft Stuff Is the Hard Stuff

Judy: Art, HR folks like me have heard this type of message quite a bit, and it can feel a bit abstract. What exactly do you mean by this?

Art: Your ability to lead people will dictate how successful you are at implementing Lean personally. Establishing trust has everything to do with how people see you behave. If the workforce sees the leader as arrogant or standoffish, you will stumble.

It's important to create a healthy work culture: a situation where everyone understands that it is hard to get hired and even harder to get fired. You can't have people running around afraid they are going to get fired for the slightest mistake. Never ask "who" when something goes wrong. At the same time your job is to make sure that the one asset that you have that can appreciate, your people, is in fact appreciating. One point of leverage is to do what you can to hire the right people first. We used a personality test at Wiremold to screen people before they were hired. This was a simple test with only about 30 questions, but it was very accurate. It separated people into seven personality types. One of those was the type of individual who would break through every barrier to get things done but was very hard for others to deal with and therefore not a team player at all. We needed people who could work in a team environment, so spotting this early helped us avoid disruptive individuals. It also helped us recognize the creative people and the self-starters and analytical minds that we needed to foster growth.

Be Consistent

Judy: That makes sense. In fact, I'm getting the impression that this Lean stuff is all just common sense. I assume that will be the same for the leadership trait of consistency.

Art: Exactly. A key role for the Lean leader is consistency. You can't bounce around with a new "program of the month" every month. You want to stay focused on implementing the Lean fundamentals—forever. To compete on your operational excellence, improving the work is the daily work. The leader has to consistently reinforce this message.

Another key part of being consistent is being predictable. Say, "Show me the data." Get the facts. Go see. Ask why. Involve everyone. Don't referee disputes among your staff. These are the things your team needs to expect from you. If you are consistent in your behavior, then your people will know what to expect and will be consistent in their behavior as well. They won't waste a lot of time trying to figure out where the boss is coming from or what is expected from them.

Be Accessible

Jerry: Art, I can make the time to be visible when it comes to supporting our Lean transformation. But you have to understand that we have a lot of employees. Do we really have the time to be accessible to all of them?

Art: Most of your people will be skeptical about the shift to Lean. They will be afraid of the changes, and most of all they will be asking, "Will I lose my job?" They need to be able to voice these types of concerns without fearing any repercussions. Jerry, this is less of an issue about managing your calendar than asking yourself: Are you approachable by everyone no matter what their job? As CEO, do you have an open door policy whereby anyone can come see you at any time? Do you listen well? Do you make sure that everyone understands that they can ask you any question or raise any issue? Do you have a reputation for being fair and treating everyone equally? All of these things are magnified in importance when you are asking your people to make major changes in the way they do things.

Take the Leaps of Faith

Jerry: That's a helpful way of thinking about being accessible. Now, Art, what do you mean by "leaps of faith"? As a manager I was always taught to eliminate risks, to know exactly what was likely to happen before taking any action. Are you saying that now we all need to become bigger risk takers? Isn't this dangerous?

Art: I don't see it as dangerous, Jerry. Implementing Lean is nothing if not a constant series of "leaps of faith" into the unknown. The moment the machines have to be moved or the office rearranged into a better flow, the question of "but what if it doesn't work?" will always be there. The fact that you thought this through quickly, say, during a one-week kaizen, only adds to the anxiety. But you have to take the leap. See Figure 5-3 for leap of faith examples. Sometimes everything works just great. More often it doesn't. Keep leaping. Figure out what went wrong, fix it, and keep moving forward. Many of the people on your team will want to stop and go back to the way we have always done it. Your job is to not let this happen. Never go backward.

Jerry: Art, I hear what you are saying. Even in our current state people are reluctant to change or take any risks. With Lean we are trying something totally new—taking what you call leaps of faith together. What should the leader do when problems pop up, as I'm sure they will?

Art: Well, as you suggest, a key role for the Lean leader is to push through problems as they pop up. Every business has numerous unexpected problems that seem to show up at the worst possible time. The reaction of most companies is to go backward. A traditional batch company will respond to customer service problems, for example, by building more inventory. The Lean leader in contrast wants to lower inventory. He will push hard to uncover the root causes for the customer service problems and put fixes in place as soon as possible. Only the leader can take this approach. It is a leap of faith that you can solve the problems quickly enough so you don't have to take a step backward and "build more inventory." You never want to do that. It is admitting defeat and a slippery slope in the wrong direction.

"Leap of Faith" Examples

Action	Issues/Risks
Moving Machines	Damage, Out of Alignment, Long Time to Hook Back UP, Customer Service Issues
Creating New Cells	Don't meet TAKT Time, Operators Unhappy, Customer Service Issues
Reduce Inventory	Vendor Problems, Customer Stockouts
Change Sales Terms to Help Level Production	Customers Unhappy, Sales Force Confused
Alter Equipment to Cut Set-Up Time	Doesn't Work, Lose Capacity, Stockouts

Figure 5-3. Leap of faith examples

The Lean leader also has to overcome the "lore" that exists in almost any company or industry. By "lore" I mean the beliefs that develop over time about the way something must be done and are then taken as gospel. For example, I was on the board of a jewelry company and showed them how to go from an eight-week lead time to two days to make a ring. The lore in the jewelry industry was that it takes eight weeks to make a ring. This type of lore would be perpetuated whenever anyone hired a new VP of operations because they would look for someone with "jewelry industry experience." Unfortunately, industry experience almost always comes with a fixed set of useless ideas about what has to be done. Every company or industry that I've encountered has its own "gospel." The thing is that you can't make much progress toward becoming a Lean enterprise unless you challenge these old beliefs head-on and get beyond them.

Respect and Support Your People

Judy: As VP of human resources, I am very interested in this notion of respecting and supporting your people. Also, I like to think that we *do* respect our people here.

But perhaps you're saying that doing so in a Lean context translates into different behaviors. I've read that "respect for people" is one of the key tenets of the Toyota Production System. Is that what you are talking about here?

Art: This is an important part of the Toyota approach . . . but Toyota or no, this just makes sense. The traditional companies will say that they respect their people, but it is a pretty abstract notion for them. They don't really listen to ideas from their employees or expect that they can do great things. With Lean the most important thing for you to do is support your people. The people doing the value-adding work will always have the best ideas of how to improve it. You have to set the ground rules of adhering to the Lean fundamentals but once that is established make sure you listen to your people. They will be reluctant at first because you never listened to them before, so you have to approach them. Ask what they think. How can we make this better? What problems do you have in doing your job? Make them understand that you are looking at the work and not at them personally. Help them understand that the changes will make their job easier and safer. Having 8 to 10 people with stopwatches looking at what you are doing for a whole week can be intimidating. My VP of operations, Frank Giannattasio, and I even went out on the floor and spent several shifts making the product ourselves. We gave stopwatches and observation sheets to the regular operators so they could observe and come up with recommendations on how to improve the work. We weren't very good (Frank claims he was better than I was), but our operators came up with a lot of good ideas.

If you are always in the gemba checking how things are going and stopping to look at the production control charts and talking to your operators, it will become normal and expected by everyone. People will seek you out to show you some cool new thing that they came up with or to explain a problem and ask for your help. Getting to that stage is all part of the "respect for people" that will determine your success.

Set Stretch Goals

Art: Another key thing is to make sure you always set stretch goals. Stretch goals to me are a sign of respect for your people. It tells them that you have tremendous faith in their ability to achieve great things. You have to use the Lean fundamentals and other Lean tools to help them get there, but there is no greater feeling for a leader than to give a team a goal that they all think is impossible and then watch how proud they are when they not only reach but surpass it. Traditional managers who argue against setting stretch goals are in effect saying, "I don't believe my people can achieve that." This, in my opinion, shows tremendous disrespect for your people. Don't do that. You will regret it.

Let's say, for example, that I ask my team for a 50 percent reduction in defects per year. My competitor, Mr. "I Don't Want to Set Stretch Goals," sets a goal of 5 percent reduction in defects. At the end of the year his team beats their goal by 50 percent and achieves a 7.5 percent reduction in defects. They are all very happy. My team, in contrast, missed its goal by 20 percent and only achieved a 40 percent reduction in defects. They are sad that they didn't hit the target but at the same time energized by the fact that they got a 40 percent reduction. The results are tangible. Quality is much better and is being noticed by the customer. Let's say this continues for several years. They beat their goal by a little and we miss ours by a little. What is really happening here? We are killing them in the market and taking market share from them. My people are proud and excited. His people can't understand how they can be beating their goals and losing market share.

Jerry: Art, thank you very much; that was very helpful. A lot for us to do and learn, but at least we know what is expected and why. I see that our time is up and we need to go into the kaizen kickoff meeting now.

Kaizen Kickoff Meeting

Jerry's management team now moves to the larger room where the kickoff meeting for this week's kaizen will be held. Also present is Mr. Kurosaki from Shingijutsu, who will be this week's outside consultant, and Jim Boots, who has recently joined the company as the head of UGH's Kaizen Promotion Office (KPO). Art and Jim Boots, along with Jerry York, Frank Gee, and Scott Smith, have preselected the first kaizen teams and set the objectives for each team. They chose the projects based on what would give UGH the biggest gains and set the goals for the week after analyzing the current state. Three of the teams will be focused on the shop floor. Two will be setup reduction teams, and one will be a flow team. All three will concentrate on product family team (value stream) A. The fourth team will be an office kaizen team focusing on order entry.

Jerry York: Good morning, everyone! How is everyone doing? I can't hear you—say it again!

Welcome to our first kaizen event here at UGH. This will be a completely new experience for us, and I have to tell you I am really excited about all the things we hope to achieve this week. We have placed all of you on teams. The teams are composed of both hourly and salaried employees, because this is really a companywide effort. Everyone on a kaizen team is equal. Titles mean nothing. We want you all to contribute your ideas on how to remove the waste from what we currently do so that we can better serve our customers.

We have picked a leader and coleader for each team to add some structure and help move things forward. Other than that there is no hierarchy. My staff and I will be full-time members of the various teams but only as members. I mean it when I say that you should treat us that way. The goals for the week are very aggressive. Art Byrne, our new chairman, and Mr. Kurosaki, our outside consultant for the week (please stand up), have assured me, however, that these stretch goals are achievable. In fact, other companies have done even better on similar types of kaizens. So, keep an open mind, work hard during the week, and I'm sure we can get our Lean journey off to a great start.

So let's start with team number one. Will the team leader introduce the team and give us an overview of the current state and the objectives for the week? Thank you.

Team One

Paul Rush: Good morning, I'm Paul Rush. I'm a manufacturing engineer here at UGH. Let me begin by introducing my team. (He then introduces the 10-member team, including Harry Gault, a district sales manager, who is the coleader.) As you can see from the overview sheet, Figure 5-4, we are setup reduction team number one. We will be working on press 43, which is a 150-ton, coil-fed press using progressive dies.

The current status is . . . I'm sorry, what? . . . OK, the current *state* is that it takes three hours to change this press from one product to the next. That in turn causes the following problems:

- The press can only be changed over about three times per week
- The run quantities average three to four months' worth of product
- We carry four months of WIP inventory
- We also carry from three to five months of finished product
- Frequent die problems cause product stock-outs
- Our lead times are six to eight weeks
- We carry three to four months of raw materials for this press
- The area around the press is very dirty and dangerous

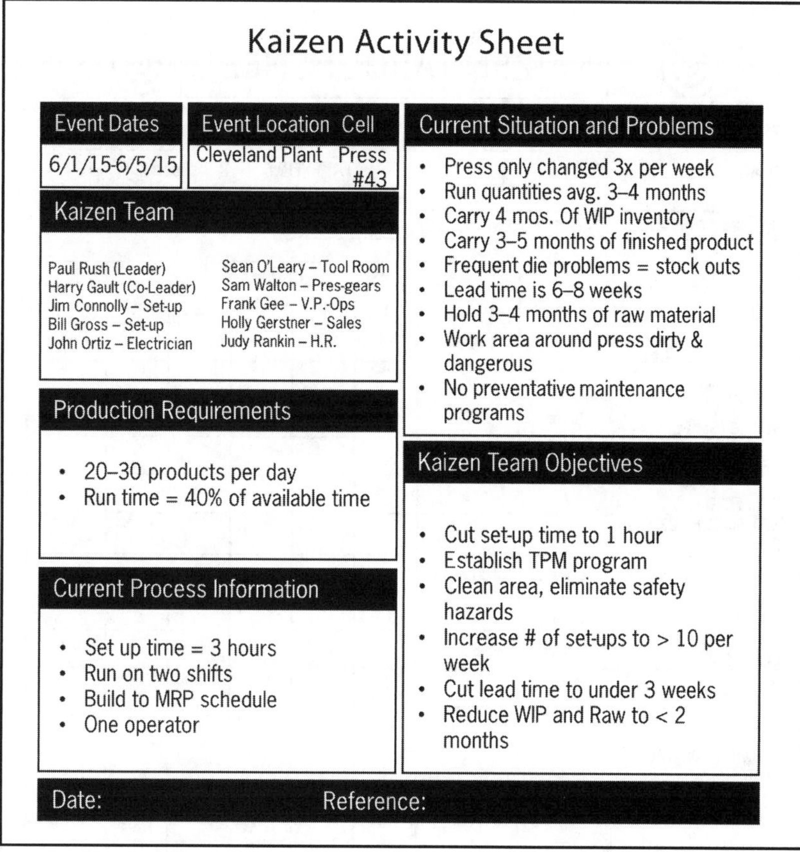

Kaizen Activity Sheet

Event Dates
6/1/15-6/5/15

Event Location Cell
Cleveland Plant Press #43

Kaizen Team
Paul Rush (Leader)
Harry Gault (Co-Leader)
Jim Connolly – Set-up
Bill Gross – Set-up
John Ortiz – Electrician
Sean O'Leary – Tool Room
Sam Walton – Pres-gears
Frank Gee – V.P.-Ops
Holly Gerstner – Sales
Judy Rankin – H.R.

Production Requirements
- 20–30 products per day
- Run time = 40% of available time

Current Process Information
- Set up time = 3 hours
- Run on two shifts
- Build to MRP schedule
- One operator

Current Situation and Problems
- Press only changed 3x per week
- Run quantities avg. 3–4 months
- Carry 4 mos. Of WIP inventory
- Carry 3–5 months of finished product
- Frequent die problems = stock outs
- Lead time is 6–8 weeks
- Hold 3–4 months of raw material
- Work area around press dirty & dangerous
- No preventative maintenance programs

Kaizen Team Objectives
- Cut set-up time to 1 hour
- Establish TPM program
- Clean area, eliminate safety hazards
- Increase # of set-ups to > 10 per week
- Cut lead time to under 3 weeks
- Reduce WIP and Raw to < 2 months

Date: Reference:

Figure 5-4. Kaizen activity sheet for team one

- We have no preventative maintenance program in place

Our targets for the week are:

- Cut the setup time to under one hour
- Establish an initial daily and monthly maintenance program
- Clean up the area and eliminate the safety hazards
- Increase the number of setups to more than 10 per week
- Cut the lead time to under three weeks
- Reduce WIP and raw material to less than two months

Figure 5-5 shows our targets and has space for the daily tracking of our progress during the week. Obviously it is blank at the moment.

Figure 5-5. Kaizen target sheet for team one

KAIZEN TARGET SHEET

PROJECT AREA	Press #43	DATE	6/1 - 6/5/15
TEAM #	ONE	TAKT TIME	2.5 seconds

FILL IN AREAS APPLICABLE TO THE KAIZEN PROJECT

			PROGRESS					
OBJECTIVES	TARGET	START	1	2	3	4	5	RESULT
INVENTORY W.I.P.	864 k	1.728 m						
CYCLE TIME	1.0"	1.0"						
SPACE (Sq. Ft.)	50 sf	90 sf						
PRODUCTIVITY								
STAFFING	1	1						
STANDARD WORK (1-5)								
SET-UP TIME	60 mins	180 mins						
5S SCORE								
LEAD TIME	3 wks	6-8 wks						
SAFETY (1-5)	5	2						
Q C DEFECTS								
VISUAL CONTROLS (1-5)	5	0						
PARTS TRAVEL	n.a.							
WALK DISTANCE								
TRAINING (1-5)								

Team Two

Jennifer Fazio: Good morning, everyone. My name is Jennifer Fazio, and I'm in charge of production planning for this plant. Let me begin by introducing my team. [*She introduces her nine-member team, including coleader Russ Adams, the foreman of the punch press shop at this plant, and UGH CFO Dick Conway—who tried so hard not to be on a kaizen team.*] As you can see from this overview sheet, Figure 5-6, we are setup team number two, and we are working on press 12. At 80 tons, this is an older and smaller press than team one's. Our press is also coil fed, but the material is much smaller and the dies are not progressive.

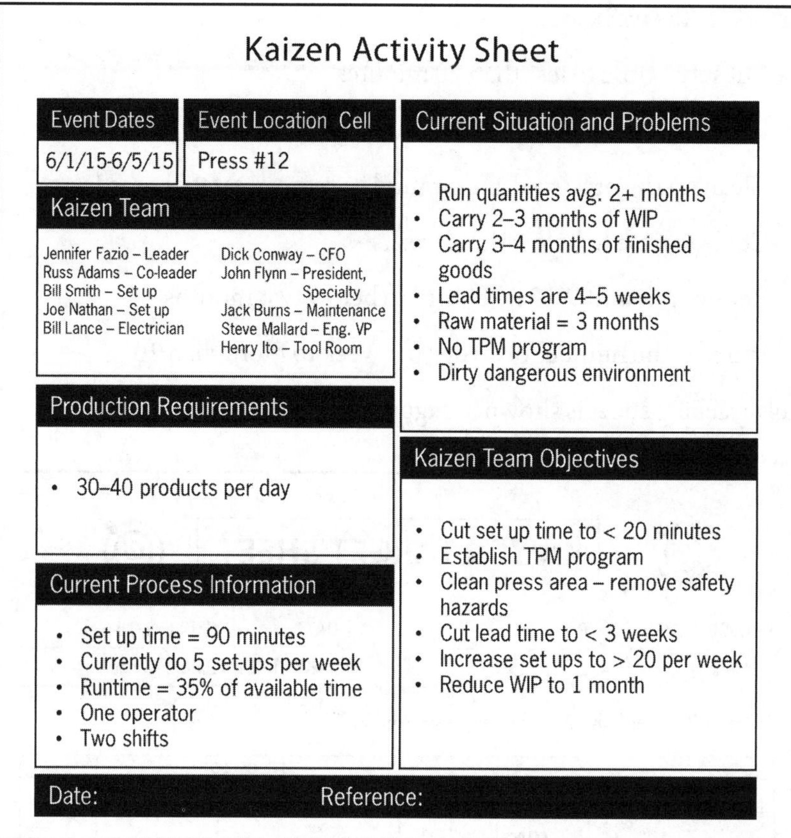

Kaizen Activity Sheet

Event Dates
6/1/15-6/5/15

Event Location Cell
Press #12

Kaizen Team
Jennifer Fazio – Leader
Russ Adams – Co-leader
Bill Smith – Set up
Joe Nathan – Set up
Bill Lance – Electrician
Dick Conway – CFO
John Flynn – President, Specialty
Jack Burns – Maintenance
Steve Mallard – Eng. VP
Henry Ito – Tool Room

Production Requirements
- 30–40 products per day

Current Process Information
- Set up time = 90 minutes
- Currently do 5 set-ups per week
- Runtime = 35% of available time
- One operator
- Two shifts

Current Situation and Problems
- Run quantities avg. 2+ months
- Carry 2–3 months of WIP
- Carry 3–4 months of finished goods
- Lead times are 4–5 weeks
- Raw material = 3 months
- No TPM program
- Dirty dangerous environment

Kaizen Team Objectives
- Cut set up time to < 20 minutes
- Establish TPM program
- Clean press area – remove safety hazards
- Cut lead time to < 3 weeks
- Increase set ups to > 20 per week
- Reduce WIP to 1 month

Date: Reference:

Figure 5-6. Kaizen activity sheet for team two

The, ahem, *current state* for this press is as follows:

- Setup time is 90 minutes
- Run quantities average two-plus months
- The number of setups per week is five
- We carry two to three months of WIP
- We carry three to four months of finished goods
- Lead times are four to five weeks
- Raw material is approximately three months
- There is no preventative maintenance program
- The area around the press is very dirty and dangerous

Our targets for the week are:

- Cut setup time to less than 20 minutes
- Establish a preventative maintenance program
- Clean up the press and area around it; remove safety hazards
- Cut lead time to below three weeks
- Reduce raw and WIP inventory to below two months
- Increase the number of setups per week to more than 20

Our daily tracking sheet is shown in Figure 5-7.

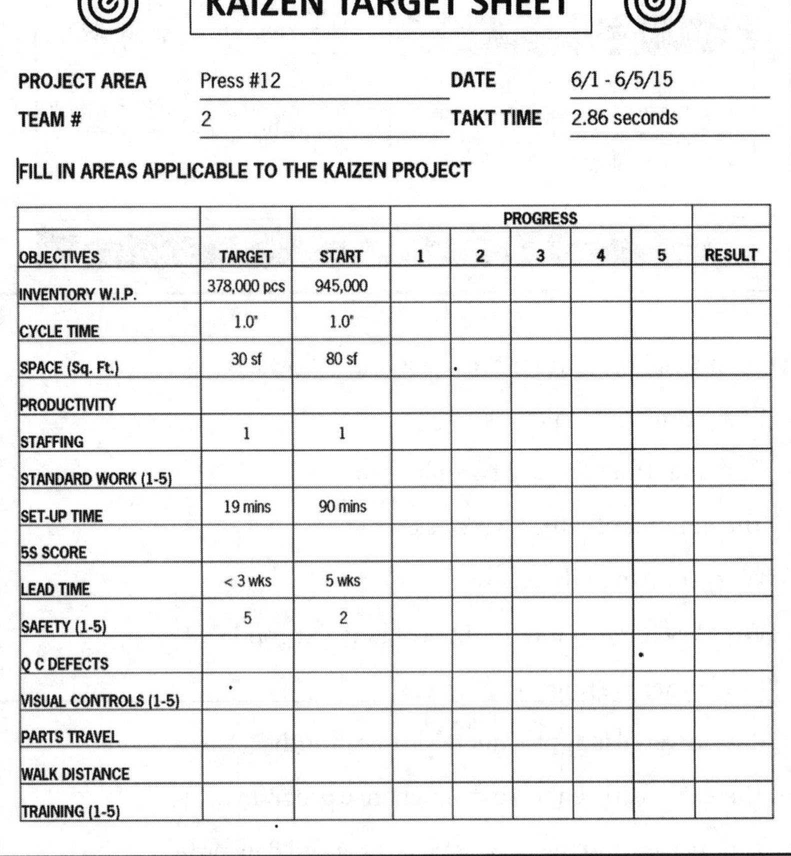

KAIZEN TARGET SHEET

PROJECT AREA: Press #12 — DATE: 6/1 - 6/5/15

TEAM #: 2 — TAKT TIME: 2.86 seconds

FILL IN AREAS APPLICABLE TO THE KAIZEN PROJECT

			PROGRESS					
OBJECTIVES	TARGET	START	1	2	3	4	5	RESULT
INVENTORY W.I.P.	378,000 pcs	945,000						
CYCLE TIME	1.0"	1.0"						
SPACE (Sq. Ft.)	30 sf	80 sf						
PRODUCTIVITY								
STAFFING	1	1						
STANDARD WORK (1-5)								
SET-UP TIME	19 mins	90 mins						
5S SCORE								
LEAD TIME	< 3 wks	5 wks						
SAFETY (1-5)	5	2						
Q C DEFECTS								
VISUAL CONTROLS (1-5)								
PARTS TRAVEL								
WALK DISTANCE								
TRAINING (1-5)								

Figure 5-7. Kaizen tracking sheet for team two

Team Three

John Rollins: Good morning, I'm John Rollins, manager of assembly operations at this plant. My coleader is Sally Lombardi, who is a product design engineer for the products we will be working on. The rest of the team includes some guy named Jerry York and [*introduces the other eight team members*]. We will be trying to create the first flow cell here at UGH, focusing on our highest-volume product family for this plant. The current state, just like all other products, is that the product is made in various functional departments, which are scattered around the plant. See Figure 5-8.

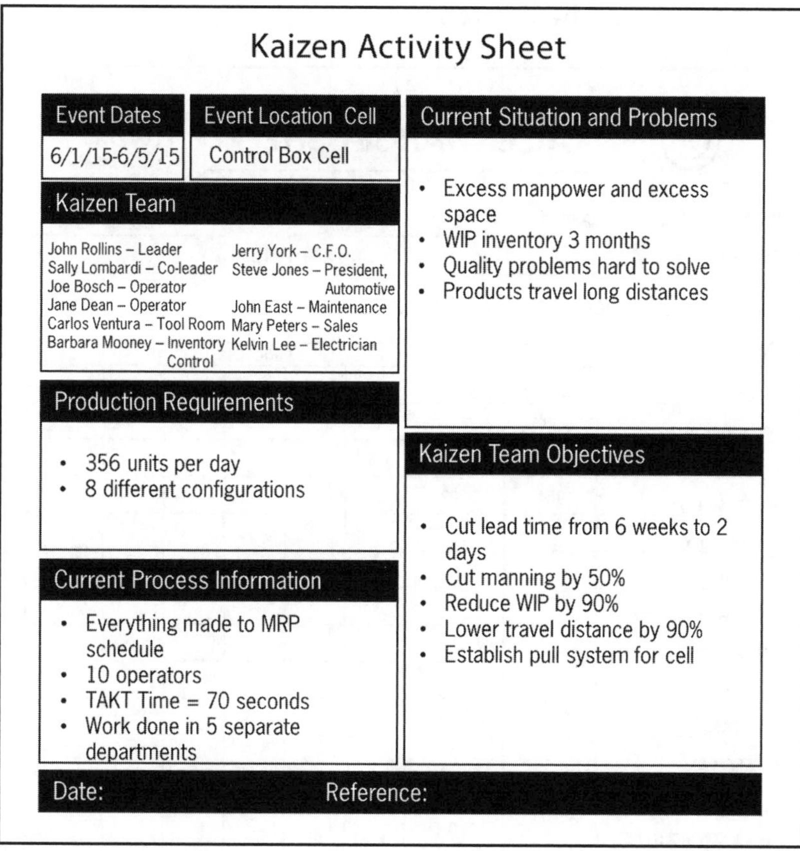
Kaizen Activity Sheet

Event Dates: 6/1/15-6/5/15

Event Location Cell: Control Box Cell

Kaizen Team

John Rollins – Leader
Sally Lombardi – Co-leader
Joe Bosch – Operator
Jane Dean – Operator
Carlos Ventura – Tool Room
Barbara Mooney – Inventory Control
Jerry York – C.F.O.
Steve Jones – President, Automotive
John East – Maintenance
Mary Peters – Sales
Kelvin Lee – Electrician

Production Requirements

- 356 units per day
- 8 different configurations

Current Process Information

- Everything made to MRP schedule
- 10 operators
- TAKT Time = 70 seconds
- Work done in 5 separate departments

Current Situation and Problems

- Excess manpower and excess space
- WIP inventory 3 months
- Quality problems hard to solve
- Products travel long distances

Kaizen Team Objectives

- Cut lead time from 6 weeks to 2 days
- Cut manning by 50%
- Reduce WIP by 90%
- Lower travel distance by 90%
- Establish pull system for cell

Date: Reference:

Figure 5-8. Kaizen activity sheet for team three

No one works on the whole product, just a part of it. The customer is not present in the manufacturing process as everything is made on an MRP schedule based on a sales forecast. This creates the following problems:

- Lead times average six weeks
- We have excess manpower and excess space
- WIP inventory varies between two and three months
- Quality problems are hard to solve due to the long lead times
- Products travel a long distance in order to get made
- The production approach is "push" by way of an MRP system

Our objectives for the week are as follows:

- Reduce the lead time from six weeks to one to two days
- Cut the manning by 50 percent

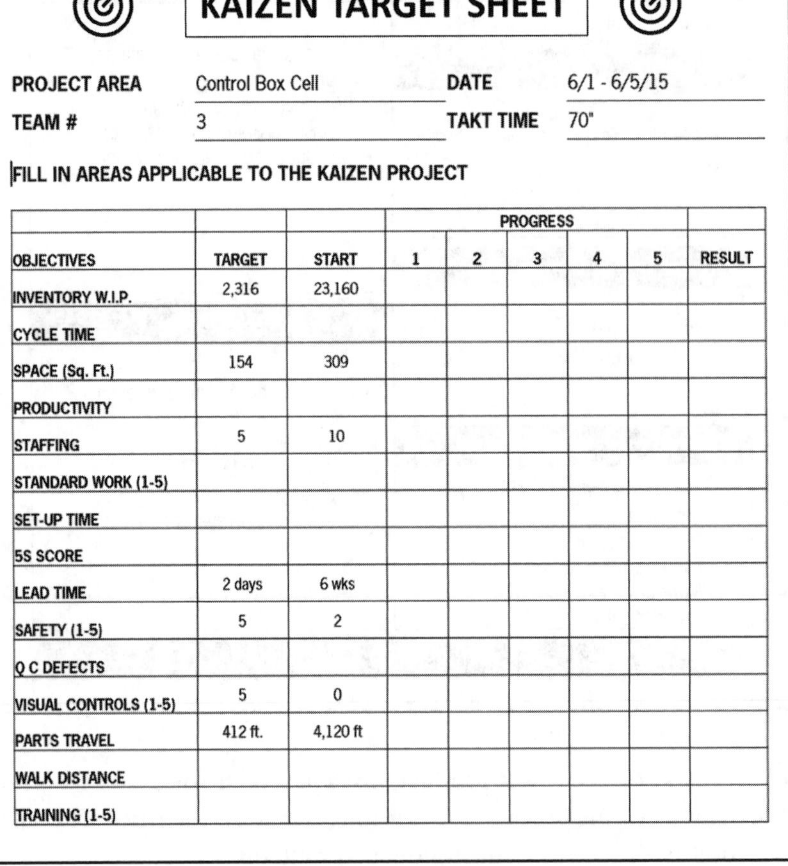

KAIZEN TARGET SHEET

PROJECT AREA: Control Box Cell | DATE: 6/1 - 6/5/15

TEAM #: 3 | TAKT TIME: 70"

FILL IN AREAS APPLICABLE TO THE KAIZEN PROJECT

			PROGRESS					
OBJECTIVES	TARGET	START	1	2	3	4	5	RESULT
INVENTORY W.I.P.	2,316	23,160						
CYCLE TIME								
SPACE (Sq. Ft.)	154	309						
PRODUCTIVITY								
STAFFING	5	10						
STANDARD WORK (1-5)								
SET-UP TIME								
5S SCORE								
LEAD TIME	2 days	6 wks						
SAFETY (1-5)	5	2						
Q C DEFECTS								
VISUAL CONTROLS (1-5)	5	0						
PARTS TRAVEL	412 ft.	4,120 ft						
WALK DISTANCE								
TRAINING (1-5)								

Figure 5-9. Kaizen target sheet for team three

- Lower WIP by 90 percent
- Reduce the space needed by 50 percent
- Reduce the products' travel distance by 90 percent
- Establish a "pull" system for manufacturing

Our daily tracking sheet is shown in Figure 5-9.

Team Four

Joe Rappaport: Good morning. My name is Joe Rappaport, and I'm a regional sales manager for UGH focusing on the northeast. My coleader is Betty Wagner, head of order entry/customer service. The other seven members of our team, please stand, are as follows [*he introduces the rest of the team*]. Order entry, as I'm sure you are all aware, is a critical function for the company as it is the key interface between our customers and our internal operations. Anything we get wrong in order entry tends to multiply itself throughout the organization and almost always results in some form of customer service issue.

The current state, as shown in Figure 5-10, is as follows:

- Order entry errors are in excess of 5 percent
- We feel we are overstaffed
- Product allocations to some customers create stock-outs for others
- Wrong quantity and wrong pricing are the biggest problems
- Large orders cause many manufacturing problems

Our targets for the week are:

- Cut order entry errors to below 2 percent
- Reduce manning by 20 percent
- Develop a solution for large orders
- Implement new rules for how product is allocated

Our activity and target sheets are shown in Figures 5-10 and 5-11.

Figure 5-10. Kaizen activity sheet for team four

Kaizen Activity Sheet

Event Dates

6/1/15-6/5/15

Event Location Cell

Order Entry / Customer Service

Kaizen Team

Joe Rappaport – Leader
Betty Wagner – Co-leader
Mariko Sato – Order Entry
Marcy Royster – Order Entry
Sharon Hennessy – Order Entry
Scott Smith – VP Sales
Ellen Minor – VP Mkt.
Gary Cook – VP Custom
Ned Collins – Maintenance
George Burke – Finance

Production Requirements

- Process all incoming orders daily
- Average order has 9 lines
- 120 orders per day
- 95% of orders by fax or email

Current Process Information

- Product allocations for some customers cause stock outs for others
- O/E clerks enter orders and take phone calls
- Time from order receipt to delivery t o customer is 3–6 days
- Time to acknowledge an order is 2–3 days

Current Situation and Problems

- Order entry errors > 5%
- Feel order entry is overstaffed
- Wrong quantity and wrong pricing are biggest problems
- Large orders causing manufacturing problems

Kaizen Team Objectives

- Cut order entry errors to < 2%
- Reduce manning by 20%
- Develop solution for large orders
- Implement new rules for how product is allocated

Date: **Reference:**

Art: Thank you very much for the overview. We have many exciting challenges ahead of us for this week. Remember that kaizen is your full-time job for the week. We need you all to be completely focused on the targets that your team has been given. Stay away from your phone and e-mails and focus on the task at hand. This focus is what makes kaizen such a powerful tool. Now before we get started I'd like Mr. Kurosaki to say a few words.

Mr. Kurosaki: [*through interpreter Michico-san*] Thank you, Art-san, nice to see you this week, I am most honored to be here. I know that you are just starting your kaizen efforts, but after a brief walk of the plant earlier this morning I can tell that you should be embarrassed. You have the most enormous opportunities ahead. You need to be humble and work fast this week. Some of your targets could also be more aggressive. The two setup teams, for example, should have targets for single-minute (i.e., under 10 minutes) setups. This is the only target that is acceptable. I will be working with each of the teams to help you reach your goals. Please

KAIZEN TARGET SHEET

PROJECT AREA Order Entry / Customer Service **DATE** 6/1 - 6/5/15

TEAM # 4 **TAKT TIME** 225 seconds

FILL IN AREAS APPLICABLE TO THE KAIZEN PROJECT

			PROGRESS					
OBJECTIVES	TARGET	START	1	2	3	4	5	RESULT
INVENTORY W.I.P.								
CYCLE TIME								
SPACE (Sq. Ft.)								
PRODUCTIVITY								
STAFFING	13	16						
STANDARD WORK (1-5)	5	0						
SET-UP TIME								
5S SCORE								
LEAD TIME								
SAFETY (1-5)								
Q C DEFECTS	< 2%	> 5%						
VISUAL CONTROLS (1-5)	5	0						
PARTS TRAVEL								
WALK DISTANCE								
TRAINING (1-5)								

Figure 5-11. Kaizen target sheet for team four

spend your time on the shop floor and not in the conference room. Kaizen is a "doing" activity, not a "planning" activity.

Also, when you first get to your work area, I want you to start by confirming the current state. Even though the data was given to you on your target sheets, each team should confirm that this is in fact true. You want to see it with your own eyes. You don't have a lot of time, so you should organize this right away. Kaizen is serious business.

Art: Before we start, I just want to make sure that you have cleared the way for the kaizens. During the week the needs of the kaizen teams take precedence over everything else—except of course the customer. If they need help from the tool room or maintenance or IT, they always have to go to the head of the line. We only have a week to make some major changes, so everyone has to pitch in. We may need alterations to the machines or the dies on the two setup teams done overnight or even right now. The flow team will have to move a lot of equipment in a very short period of time, starting today, and get it hooked back up. This will take maintenance support and maybe some outside resources like riggers or extra electricians. This is not business as usual. You can't be asking the kaizen teams to fill out "work orders" and get in line until someone gets around to it.

So let's get started! Remember that there will be a meeting at four this afternoon for the leaders and coleaders to update us on your progress and your plans for tonight and tomorrow. This will give us a chance to see where you are and determine what additional help you might need. It is also a great opportunity to set new (and more aggressive) targets if we need to. I expect this will be the case this week.

Mr. Kurosaki will start with the two setup teams. In fact, he would like to give them both an initial overview of how to look at setup reduction from a Lean approach, as opposed to the way you are doing it now. So, why don't the two setup teams just remain in this room for a few minutes so he can give you this overview. I will start with the one-piece flow team, team three, and Jim Boots will work with the order entry team, team four. So let's go. Work hard and have some fun this week.

Summary Points

- The Lean leader needs to be committed, consistent, accessible, and supportive of her people.
- The Lean leader needs to go see, be willing to take the necessary leaps of faith, and, above all, constantly drive the Lean fundamentals.
- Becoming a Lean enterprise requires you to create successful, motivated teams throughout the entire company: members of a strong Lean team support each other and are willing to give and accept criticism.
- The vision of the Lean leader starts with a clear understanding of value from the point of view of the customer.
- An effective Lean leader has a vision for growth and maintains a constant, visible presence in daily Lean practice. The leader demonstrates a commitment to Lean by spending time on the shop floor every day.
- Show respect for people by asking what they think about improving the work, setting stretch goals, and providing them with the means to improve.

6

Setup Reduction Kaizen

OVERVIEW

The sad fact is that most companies totally miss the strategic significance of setup reduction. They see it as a singular exercise and can't make the connection between what across-the-board reduced setups do for shorter lead times and the enormous competitive advantage this provides.

Like most traditional companies, UGH has always taken setup times as a given. Certainly with a setup time of 180 minutes for team one and 90 minutes for team two, it is a good bet that no one has ever taken the time to actually observe a full setup. In this case, after some training from the consultant on how to separate internal setup time (things that can be done only while the machine is shut off) from external setup time (things that can be done while the machine is still running), UGH's first step is to do exactly that. Observe the setups. The waste they discover is shocking to them. So, step by step, they go about eliminating it. They position the next die and coil of raw material next to where they will be used while the machine is running. They work to eliminate tools, cranes, and jogging the new dies into place. They make small alterations to the dies and presses and improve the coil feeders. They establish standard work for the operator and, where possible, use two operators for the setup instead of just one.

By the end of the week, team one has cut its setup time from 180 minutes to 25 minutes, and team two, which we will focus on, has cut its setup time by 93 percent from 90 minutes to 6 after spending just $332. Does the company understand the strategic nature of these results? If they do, then these two initial kaizens should set the direction of the company going forward. They point the clear path to delivering more value to the customers. Going from 90 minutes to 6 minutes means UGH can now do 75 setups per week (15 per day) instead of the 5 per week they had been doing. Customer response can be almost instantaneous. Lead times can drop from six weeks to one to two days. Cash can be freed up from inventory and reinvested in new products and innovations for the customer.

SMED Training

Mr. Kurosaki: Good morning again. Now that I have both setup teams here, I want to give you a brief overview of how I want you to go about the week before you go out on the floor. First of all, how many of you are familiar with the term *SMED*? Only three? OK, so what does it mean?

Team member: It means single minute exchange of die.

Mr. Kurosaki: That is correct, but can you take me further? Does it mean changing the die in 1 minute or in under 10 minutes?

Team member: I'm not sure, but I think it means to be under 10 minutes. When you addressed the whole group earlier, you said that a single minute, meaning under 10 minutes, was the only acceptable target for a setup team.

Mr. Kurosaki: Very good. You are correct, and despite the targets you have been given for the week, we will target single minute exchange of die this week. OK? Let me share a little background. The concept of SMED was created by Shigeo Shingo over 50 years ago. Shingo, working as an outside consultant, was instrumental in helping Taiichi Ohno develop the Toyota Production System or TPS. SMED will also be key for you here as you work to develop your version of TPS: UPS, or UGH Production System.

Setup reduction is a core activity in any shift from traditional manufacturing, which you are doing here at UGH, to Lean. Most companies batch in order to offset their long setup times by producing big batches every time a new setup is completed. As long as long setups persist, it is impossible to get to a state of flow. That means it is also impossible to achieve all the benefits that flow production brings.

Team member: Mr. Kurosaki, my name is Hank Brown, and I'm a setup operator. I've been here for 20 years, and although setup times have come down over that time, we all think that we are as low as we can go . . . so your "single minute" goal seems totally crazy to me. I don't mean to be disrespectful, but do you really think we can get to a state of, what is it you call it, flowing?

Kurosaki: Brown-san, you are right: setup reduction is a real barrier. If it takes three hours to change over a machine, then doing three changeovers a week means that you lose a whole day of production (assuming you are a one-shift operation). So, many companies will choose to change over only two times per week—or even one time per week. They would rather just live with the excess inventory. But as I'm sure Byrne-san already told you, excess inventory is "the root of all evil" because it is the single biggest waste of all. As Lean is all about finding and removing waste in order to deliver more value to your customers, then cutting our setup times will be key.

Our main thrust this week is to find the waste in the way we do setups now and remove it. I want you to do this by following the SMED principles of separating the internal setup steps—anything that can only be done while the machine is turned off—from the external steps that can be done while the machine is still running. In most cases just doing this will get you a 50 percent reduction (or more) in setup time right away for no money.

Team member: You've got to be kidding me. There is no way that this can happen. Especially with these two presses.

Mr. Kurosaki: Please calm down yourselves. Let's not be concrete heads before we even get started. Let's look at this a little closer. For most traditional companies, the first thing that happens in a setup is that the machine, in this case the press, is turned off. This makes everything that happens, from that point on, internal to the setup. This obviously adds a lot of time. If, in contrast, all the things that can be done while the press is running are done to get ready for the next setup, then the time it takes will come down dramatically.

So, as you start your kaizens, I want you to focus on doing as many things as you can external to the actual setup. Make sure the next die is in place at the press. All tools, lubricants, and other items that you will need for the next setup should also be present and stored at point of use. You should also establish a setup sequence that can serve as the standard work for how we will do the work. Step one, step two, and so forth.

Jennifer Fazio, team leader: Mr. Kurosaki, what other things should we be thinking about? We've got very big goals and only a week to accomplish them.

Mr. Kurosaki: Yes, Jennifer-san, as we proceed through the week, I want you to eliminate all cranes, forklifts, heavy lifting by the operator, and all tools. I want you to think about the setup like you would removing a CD from the radio in your car and replacing it with another. Easy out, easy in. This will require us to make small alterations to the press and the dies as we go through the week.

Team member: Did I hear you say spend money? You don't understand. They never let us do that here. And even if they did, we would have to file a work order to get anything done, and that takes forever.

Mr. Kurosaki: That may be your traditional approach, but during a kaizen everything is different. Kaizen teams get priority. Things have to be done right now, and all the support functions have been made aware of that. As for money, we shouldn't have to spend much, and if we do we have the company's CFO, Conway-san, on our team so we can get instant approval.

Dick Conway: Hey, wait a minute; Conway-san doesn't like to spend money, so let's not get carried away with this instant approval stuff.

Kurosaki: [*laughing*] Don't worry, Conway-san; we can't spend much money in just one week. OK, now I want you to go to your presses and do the first setup so that you can see and chart the current state. You will need to split your team into smaller groups to get all the data. Two people can be responsible for recording the setup. Two can be responsible for creating the spaghetti chart that traces all the movements of the operator. Two more can list and time each step so that we know what elements take the most time. Two more might start to look at and access all the dies that are used on this press. What is their size, height, length, and depth? Where are they stored? How are they maintained? Once you have this data, it will start to be clear what steps you need to take before you do the second setup this afternoon. I expect you to cut at least 50 percent of the time off the setup by the end of the day. OK, let's go.

The teams now go to their meeting areas near their presses. For the rest of this chapter, we will follow team two on the smaller press as one press should be enough to get an idea of what happens during the kaizen. The press operators who are on the teams, as well as the press room supervisors on the teams and a couple of team members from Jerry York's staff, start out with the attitude that this whole thing is a waste of time. These presses have always taken three hours (team one) and 90 minutes (team two), and nothing they have done over time has changed that.

Jennifer Fazio: Kurosaki-san outlined a lot of work that has to be done. If we are going to get the second setup done this afternoon, we need to get a fast start observing the first setup. Let's start by dividing into pairs for our observations. Russ Adams, our coleader and a foreman in the press shop, has the most experience with the dies, so I'll ask him to look into the die information on what runs on this press. I'll fill the filming, timing, spaghetti charts, and work sequence teams by asking for volunteers. Let's get organized then with your camera, stopwatches, paperwork, and all. Russ has the first setup for us to observe starting in 15 minutes. This should allow us to finish before lunch. Mr. Kurosaki will be here to observe the first setup with us.

The First Setup

At 10:00 a.m. team two begins its first setup. The team starts by explaining the objective and mechanics of the kaizen to the setup operator. There will be many people standing around observing, filming, and of course timing the various elements. Jennifer explains that they are not watching him but rather watching and trying to understand the work itself. The operator is asked to relax as best he can and just go about the setup in his normal way. Easier said than done, but very important to make sure that the operator is part of everything that goes on all week.

The observations are eye-opening for everyone. To begin with, the first thing the operator did, just as Mr. Kurosaki predicted, was to shut off the press, thus making everything internal to the setup. The next thing he did was to cut the coil of steel that was feeding the press. He then wound it back on its coil and taped it off. Next, he disappeared in search of an adjustable die cart, saying, "There is never one around when I need it." He had to go to the next building to find one that wasn't being used. When he came back, he dumped the die cart off to the side and started to remove the old die. This took a lot of effort as he had to walk around the press several times, use three different wrenches and a hammer, and manipulate the press up and down several times to remove the remaining piece of raw material and get the die in the right position.

While all of this was going on, Mr. Kurosaki was pointing things out to the team and telling them, "No good. No good. You should all be fired for letting this happen." At the same time he shared alternative ways to do the same things with much less effort and time. The team took copious notes. No one took offense as everyone welcomed Mr. Kurosaki's insight. His ideas represented a totally different way of looking at the setup. More important, they were simple changes that made sense to everyone.

Once the die was detached from the press, the operator slid it out of the press and onto the die cart. This was an awkward and potentially dangerous process. Once that step was complete, the operator headed over to the next building again.

Jennifer: Now where are you going?
Operator: I need to put this die away and find the new one.

Several team members followed the operator to record everything he was doing. This took a long time. He had to find the right spot to put the old die and then had to move several rows of die storage racks to find the new die. When he came back, he positioned the new die at the press and then slid it onto the bed of the press. He then spent quite a bit of time trying to position the new die in the right spot so it could be bolted to the press with the proper alignment. Mr. Kurosaki of course hated this and tried to explain to the team why it was so unnecessary.

Kurosaki: All no good. Change die like cassette from one side of press only.

Once this was done, the operator had to open the top of the press and spend quite a bit of time adjusting the ram of the press because this die had a different shut height than the one that had just come out of the press. In fact, all but two of the dies used in the press had different shut heights, as they were never designed with setup time in mind. Instead they were designed to minimize the cost of the die itself.

The next step was to change the material. This involved changing the coils of steel. The old coil had to be taken to the next room and put away. The new coil was then selected and brought to the press. The operator needed to unwrap and unband it as it was still in the condition in which it had come from the supplier.

Kurosaki: Jennifer-san, can you see much waste? Why do you allow this?

Jennifer: Yes, sir, there is a lot of waste. He is walking all over the place. You're right; we should be embarrassed.

Once the steel was mounted on the decoiler, which required a crane plus several different wrenches, the raw material was fed to the die. The operator then tried to make his first new part. Unfortunately, it was out of spec. It took a number of adjustments to the die, the ram, and the way the material fed to finally get a good piece. Total time elapsed was 88 minutes—which was very close to the 90-minute historical average that the team had been given. Mr. Kurosaki of course nearly fainted. He was ready to fire everyone. Not literally, but they got the message.

The Analysis

Jennifer: OK, that was ugly. Now that we are all back in the meeting room, let's start by reviewing the video of the setup. This should give us a better idea of what we just saw and help point out the major opportunities.

Dick Conway: Jennifer, we don't have time to watch the whole 88 minutes; we can fast-forward through it. Even so, we can see clearly that the operator spent more time away from the press than at it.

Steve Mallard: Even when he is at the press, look at all the time he spends looking for things and going back and forth to get tools.

Joe Nathan: I'm a setup operator, and I have to admit that I have been doing things this way for over 15 years and never even thought about any of this. It's just the way we have always done things here.

Kurosaki: But can't you now see why it is no good? In fact, who here has ever watched a full 90-minute setup before? . . . Just as I thought: no one.

Russ Adams: Well, Mr. Kurosaki, I'm the foreman of the punch press shop here, and I have to admit that I have never had the time to watch a full 90-minute setup before. But I have to defend my guys. They are all very good workers and know how to change over the presses.

Kurosaki: Russ-san, no one is making any comments about your people. We are just looking at the way the work is organized and seeing if there are ways to make improvements.

Jennifer: OK, now let's take a look at the spaghetti charts to examine the operator's movements.

The operator's movements are shown in Figure 6-1, which dramatically illustrates all the back-and-forth walking done by the operator. The total distance from

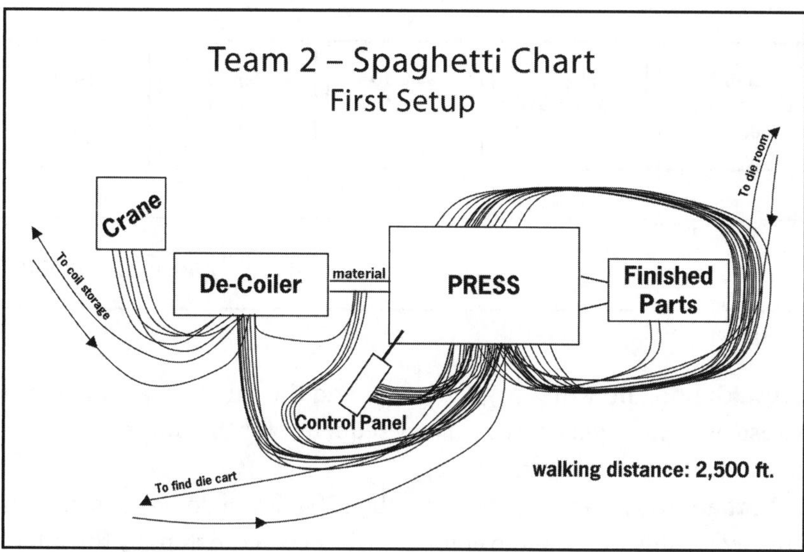

Figure 6-1. Spaghetti chart for first setup

the coil of raw material to the press is only 15 feet, yet the operator walked more than 2,500 feet during the setup.

Kurosaki: Now can you see how all of this walking is a form of waste? I want you to eliminate it by creating a sequence for the operator with the least number of steps.

Next they reviewed the rough value stream map that had been created (Figure 6-2). This broke the setup into major steps such as change the coil, remove the die, get the new die, install the die, and make adjustments to get a good piece. It included the time that each step took so the team had a good idea of which areas contained the most waste and should therefore be attacked first. Mr. Kurosaki told the team they should think in terms of completely eliminating as many steps as possible.

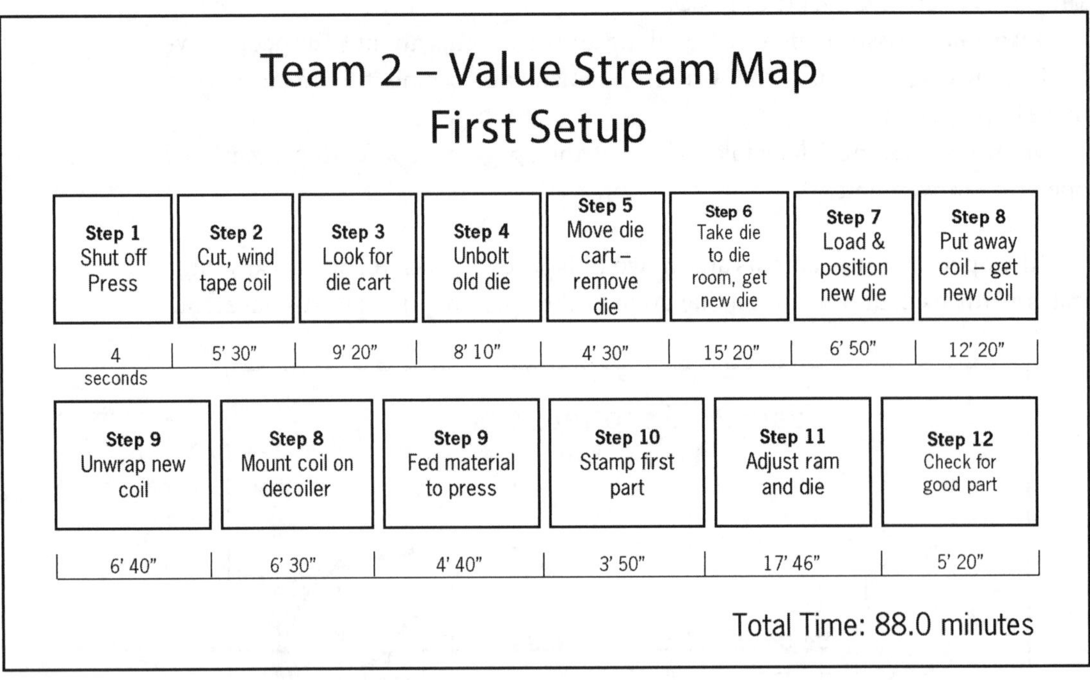

Figure 6-2. Value stream map for first setup

Kurosaki: Look how the spaghetti chart and the value stream map show you where waste is. I want you to create a new sequence for this afternoon's setup that eliminates completely a lot of these steps.

Joe Nathan: You mean that after more than 20 years of doing our setups the current way successfully, you want to eliminate a bunch of the steps by this afternoon?

Kurosaki: Joe-san, you're fired! Just kidding. Look, you watched the setup and the video of the setup. You can clearly see the waste, so remove it right away. Don't you want to make your fellow setup operators' job easier and safer?

Joe: [*mumbling*] Yeah, I guess so.

Next the team looked at the results from coleader Russ Adams's subteam studying the dies used in this press. As expected, he found that almost all the dies had different dimensions. By some miracle, two of the dies had the same height, but the other dimensions of these two dies were different. Russ also reported that there were no clear rules for how a die was treated after a run and no regular die maintenance program. This led to many dies being out of service and needing repairs, usually at the very time that the demand for the parts they made was the highest.

Mr. Kurosaki: You need a common shut height for all dies. Perhaps for this plant you need two common shut heights, one for all your secondary dies and one for your bigger progressive dies. This will eliminate the need to adjust the ram stroke on every setup. It will cut the setup time dramatically and make it easier for your operators.

Russ: But Mr. Kurosaki, we have over 1,500 dies here, and getting them all to a common shut height will take a lot of work. Why do we need to do this? It only takes two to five minutes to adjust the ram. Can't we just leave it as it is? I just don't get it.

Kurosaki: No, Russ-san, you cannot just leave it as it is. You miss the point. As the setup times come down, this two- to five-minute ram adjustment becomes a bigger part of each setup. Also as times come down the number of setups you do each day will go way up. A machine that you change 3 times a week now might be changed 20 to 30 times per day. Now multiply all these setups by the 2 to 5 minutes, and you will see just how much time will be wasted if you don't make this change. It will affect your ability to deliver value to your customers.

Russ: Well, OK, I get your point, but as I just said, we have over 1,500 dies here. Altering all these dies will take a long time.

Kurosaki: Yes, it will, so you should start soon. Begin with the highest volumes first. You can probably get 85 percent of the total impact after converting 20 percent of the dies. You can finish the rest over time. Your return on investment will be large.

Russ: If you say so, we will do it.

Kurosaki: Thank you, Russ-san. Now, just to help you see this for the rest of the week, I want you to use only the two dies that we have found that have the same shut height for all the rest of our setups. This will eliminate the need to adjust the ram.

Jennifer: Are there other things we should be thinking about while we are talking about dies? One of our big issues seems to be the number of dies we have out of service at any point in time.

Kurosaki: Ah, Jennifer-san, good point. Yes, you must eliminate this thing you call "dies out of service." This can never be allowed in a Lean company. You will shut down everything if this condition exists.

Russ: Oh, boy, you're really making my head hurt. We have always had a lot of dies out of service. I mean, you know, stuff happens. How do we stop this?

Kurosaki: Not so difficult, Russ-san. Set up a separate die maintenance area near the production area. Every time a die finishes a run or when it reaches a certain number of strokes, it should be taken into the die maintenance area and inspected. In most cases (say, 95 percent of the time), the die would simply be opened, checked, cleaned, and then returned ready for use. In the event of a problem with the die, this group would do the repair immediately and then return the die for use. This would require the building and maintenance of a set of spare parts (starting with the high runners) that could be kept in the die maintenance area.

Russ: Mr. Kurosaki, most of my die makers spend the bulk of their time making new dies. These have always had priority. Do you really want to change that? Where will I get the extra die makers?

Kurosaki: Russ-san, you already have too many die makers. They are doing inefficient things. Freeing up four or five of them to inspect dies and repair them if needed after every run will probably free up the rest of your die makers to concentrate on making new dies without being constantly interrupted with emergency orders to fix dies whose parts have gone "out of stock."

Russ: Makes sense; lots of our critical new product programs are delayed because our die makers get diverted repairing old dies that have broken. We have never carried spare parts for these dies because finance didn't want to make the investment.

Dick: Now wait a minute, we never said that per se; we just want to limit the amount of capital spending.

Kurosaki: Yes, Dick-san, but you should never do it at the expense of the customer, even if you don't understand that that is happening. Making this change is a longer-term fix and not something that we can do this week during the kaizen. Even so, I want you to come out of the kaizen with a new understanding that it will no longer be acceptable to have a die that is out of service. All dies have to be available for use instantly in order to satisfy the pull of the customer. The focus is always on satisfying the customer.

The Second Setup

The team spent the time after lunch getting ready for the second setup later that day. Mr. Kurosaki explained to them the importance of planning out the specific sequence of steps that the operator should take.

Kurosaki: For the next setup, I want you to use two operators if you can. This will shorten the time.

Joe Nathan: I like your idea, Mr. Kurosaki, but the setup has always been done by just one operator. We would all welcome some help.

Russ: Now wait a minute—where am I supposed to get these extra setup guys from? They don't grow on trees.

Kurosaki: No trees are needed Russ-san. You are not making trees. You already have good setup men here, but you are wasting them by having them spend most of their day watching automated machines make parts. It is also possible to use your material handlers, whom we call water spiders, to train them to help with the setup. Please don't worry so much.

They had a lot of opportunity, as the waste involved in the first setup was pretty clear. The issue was how to eliminate it. They went back to the principle of separating the internal steps from the external. Going off to find a die cart and going to put away the old die and get the new one, for example, were obvious things that could easily be moved to external from internal. In fact, the plant had a number of adjustable die carts that they could use. By positioning the new die on one cart and leaving another one empty and available to receive the old die they felt they could save about 24 minutes. They also looked at the time-consuming elements that could only be done internal to the setup, such as unbolting the old die, positioning and attaching the new die, and similar tasks.

Jennifer: Before we try this second setup, let's just go through everything one more time. We have the team divided into subteams just like the first time to do the observations. Is everyone clear on their assignment? [*They all nod approval.*] OK, great. And what about the operator—have we explained everything to him?

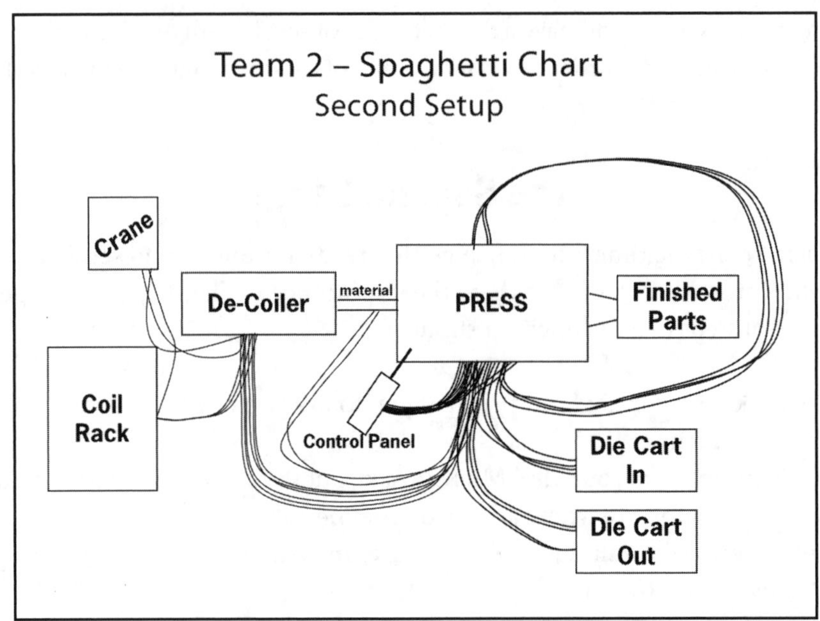

Figure 6-3. Spaghetti chart for second setup

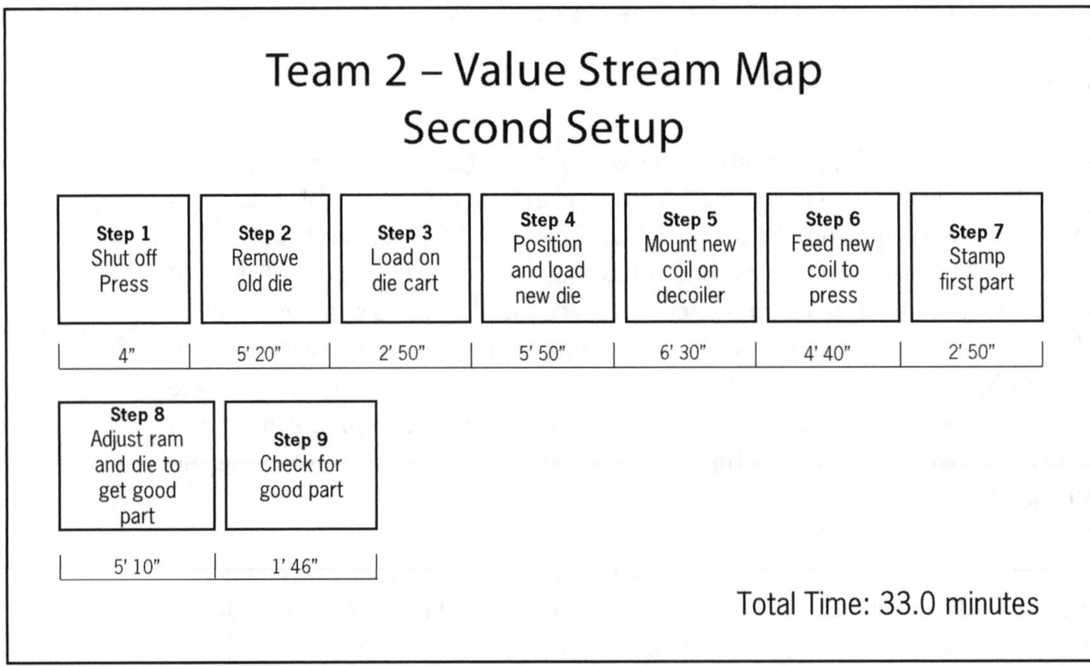

Figure 6-4. Value stream map for second setup

Russ: Yes we have walked him through the sequence of steps we want him to follow several times. We even went and numbered each step with large numbers and pictures so it would be easy to follow.

They filmed this setup as well, and the original subteams again created the spaghetti charts and value stream maps. In addition, before they began, they cleared the area of anything that was not required for this setup. This eliminated safety hazards that they found in the morning and made the operator's job safer. The second setup took 33 minutes. This was a 63 percent improvement from the first setup but still above their target of 20 minutes. Even so, the team was encouraged. The spaghetti chart (Figure 6-3) and the value stream map (Figure 6-4) from this second setup showed enormous opportunity to reduce the time further.

Preparing for the Third Setup

The spaghetti chart still showed lots of walking, with the operator having to get to both sides of the press, to and from the raw material coil, with a great deal of movement looking for tools and other items. The value stream map showed that these areas also were the most time consuming. In addition to the movement, which of course was all waste, the operator spent too much time trying to position the die and get it locked down as well as making adjustments trying to get a first good piece.

Kurosaki: Look, the operator has to be able to do the setup from just one side of the press. No more walking to the other side and back. I also want you to solve the problem the operator has locating the die on the press. Too much time is spent jogging it around to get it positioned over the bolt-holes. You need to make the die location absolute, like putting in a cassette. This way every die used in this press will always be located in the right position by simply pushing it into place. Look, here is a simple example (Figure 6-5) to illustrate this. By cutting a V shape in the baseplate of the die and installing a fixed backstop with a corresponding male V on the back bed of the press, the die will self-locate in the same position each time by simply pushing the die against the backstop. This eliminates the time-consuming process of jogging the die around to line up the bolt-holes in the press bed. It is not the only way to do this, but it is cheap and easy and you can make the alterations before the next setup.

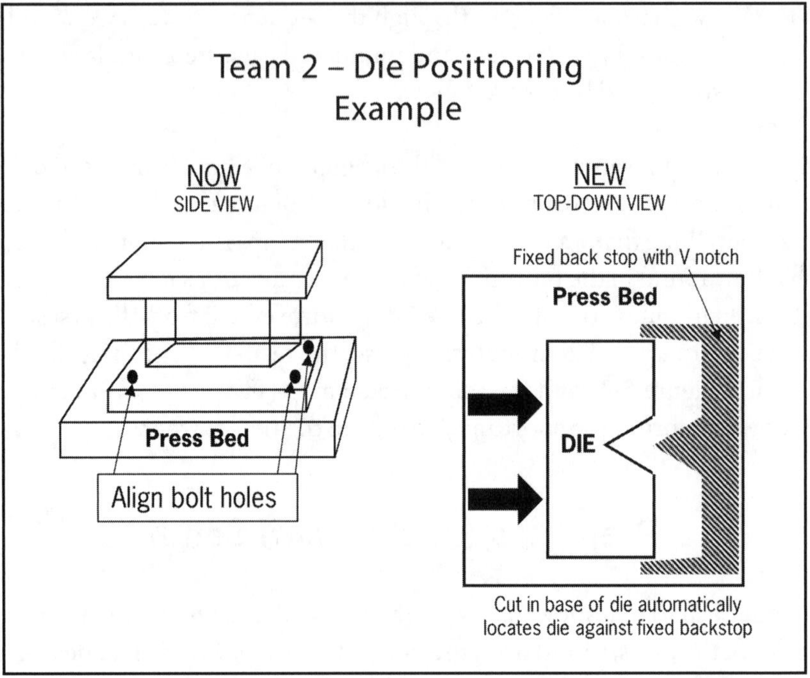

Figure 6-5. Die positioning example

Jennifer: Looking at the data and the film, we can see how much time is spent changing the coil. Anyone have an idea on how to improve this?

Russ: We have several old two-reel decoilers lying around somewhere. We could grab one of those and hook it up. That would allow us to change the coil as an external step while the machine is running.

Kurosaki: Good, Russ-san.

These were all good ideas and would remove much of the waste that still existed in the second setup. They all required slight alterations to the press, the tool, the coil feeder, and so on. These would take time. They broke up again into subteams to attack these problems. Kurosaki expected the work to get done tonight through a combination of the second-shift maintenance and tool rooms and some overtime from the first shift, especially all of the team members. This was going to be an order-in-pizza kind of night for team two.

The Third and Fourth Setups

The third setup was delayed until Wednesday afternoon because of all the work that needed to be done. The subteams were very busy. Those who weren't on them kept busy cleaning up the area and creating the standard work for the next setup. It was a little after 3 p.m. when they were ready (just before the 4 p.m. leader's meeting). Their work, however, paid off. This setup took 17 minutes—down 81 percent from the first setup and well under their 20-minute target. They were really excited about this, but they still had observed a lot of waste.

The team presented this 17-minute result at the 4 p.m. leader's meeting. Jerry York was excited and congratulated the team on their success in beating the 20-minute target.

Kurosaki: Yes, Jennifer-san and Russ-san, very good. But now you need a new target. So your target now will be 9 minutes.

It looked like another night of ordering in pizza was on tap. Even so this was no problem as the team was pretty excited by now. The operators were happy about how much hard work was being removed from their daily lives and had great ideas as to how to remove even more. Rather than being upset with Mr. Kurosaki for giving them a new goal, they were determined to beat it.

The team worked hard that night. They did two setups on Thursday and two more on Friday morning. Figure 6-6 documents their results. They ended with a final setup of six minutes, a decrease of 93 percent from their first try on Monday. Dick Conway, the CFO who had tried every excuse possible to stay in his office and not be on the team, was blown away by the results.

Dick: Well, I never would have believed it if I hadn't been on the team. Every other time we pushed for lower setup times, the engineers always came back with a big capital spending plan. As a result, I made it a point to keep track of how much we spent this week. It is a little simplistic, but it's in the ballpark.

Setup Reduction Spending

Hand clamps	$89.00
Self-locate adds to two dies	$102.00
New parts for old decoiler	$97.50
Miscellaneous	$43.00
TOTAL	$331.50

The results for the week from team one were also impressive. They cut their setup time from 180 minutes down to 25. Just like team two, they spent little

Figure 6-6. Completed kaizen target sheet

KAIZEN TARGET SHEET

PROJECT AREA	Press #12	DATE	6/1 - 6/5/15
TEAM #	2	TAKT TIME	2.86 seconds

FILL IN AREAS APPLICABLE TO THE KAIZEN PROJECT

			PROGRESS					
OBJECTIVES	TARGET	START	1	2	3	4	5	RESULT
INVENTORY W.I.P.	378,000 pcs	945,000	945,000	354,000	182,000	94,500		
CYCLE TIME	1.0"	1.0"				1.0"		
SPACE (Sq. Ft.)	30 sf	80 sf				27 sf		
PRODUCTIVITY								
STAFFING	1	1				1		
STANDARD WORK (1-5)								
SET-UP TIME	19 min	90 min	88 min	33 min	17 min	6 min		
5S SCORE								
LEAD TIME	<3 wks	5 wks	6 wks	3 wks	1.5 wks	3 days		
SAFETY (1-5)	5	2	2	3	4	4		
Q C DEFECTS								
VISUAL CONTROLS (1-5)	5	0	0	2	3	4		
PARTS TRAVEL								
WALK DISTANCE								
TRAINING (1-5)								

money during the week. In addition, the whole team was convinced that they could get the setup below 10 minutes with a few additional kaizens (which by the way they eventually did).

After the kaizen was over, Dick Conway, still very excited, was talking with John Flynn, president of UGH's Specialty Gears Division and also a member of team two.

Dick: You know, John, if I hadn't been on this team myself, I would never have believed the results that we got. If we can do this across the board, we can start to get to the kind of one- or two-day lead times Art has been talking about. Have you ever seen or heard of such results?

John Flynn: I'm with you, Dick. I would never believe we could do this at UGH. The way Mr. Kurosaki helped us see everything differently made the change easy. But to answer your question, I have seen something like it before. I'm on the board of my local hospital, and they have been going down the Lean path for several years. As a midsize city hospital, capital is very tight for them. One of the most capital-intensive parts of the hospital is the operating rooms. Over the past several years they have focused on setup reduction there and now can put 60 percent more cases through the same physical plant as they could before.

Dick Conway: Wow, that's a great story. I never thought it could work here, let alone in a hospital. I guess this crazy kaizen stuff can work in any kind of business.

John: Yeah, I'm sold, and I'm glad Jerry seems to be on board. It is only our first kaizen, but it is exciting to start to imagine what this approach can do for UGH. We need to keep Mr. Kurosaki around helping us for as long as we can.

Dick: Amen to that.

Summary Points

- Separating the work that can be done external to the setup (while the machine is still running) from the work that can only be done internal (while the machine is off) in most cases will cut the setup time in half.
- Standardization of things such as die heights can save much more time than you would think when accumulated across multiple setups.
- Setup reduction is very strategic as it drastically lowers lead time and allows you to deliver more value to your customers.
- In a Lean company you can never allow the condition where "dies are out of service waiting for repair." All dies must be available to respond to customer demand at all times.

7

Flow Kaizen

OVERVIEW

Most companies see kaizen as event-driven, a scheduled opportunity for one-time gains. This fits traditional thinking but misses the whole point that kaizen means *continuous* improvement. It has to be practiced every day and become the way you do business. That's why doing a flow kaizen early on is an important step on your Lean turnaround, providing early gains and serving as a learning exercise moving forward.

Once the initial flow is created, it is easy to see the opportunities for lowering lead times and responding to the customer. For example, the flow team working on creating a control box cell (team three) reduced staffing from 10 to 5 operators with a clear path for how to get to 4 in the first week. Space was reduced by 50 percent, WIP inventory was cut by 90 percent, and travel distance was reduced by 95 percent. Unfortunately, understanding what really happened is lost on most traditional companies. They will focus on the fact that head count was cut in half. The space, inventory, and travel distance reductions won't mean much to them. The tendency will also be to see kaizen as an interesting "one-off" event. There won't be any sense of urgency to run the next kaizen, maybe in six weeks or so, as no one will believe that this type of result could be repeated.

The key lesson here is that the real gains from this new cell are not "head count" reduction; they are strategic. Lead times can be cut from six weeks to one or two days. Quality will improve by a factor of 10, and cash freed from reduced inventory and space needed can be reinvested in new products. The value delivered to the customer will go up, and UGH will gain market share and grow. The cost reduction from needing fewer people is a nice side benefit, not the main event. Traditional companies have a hard time grasping this reality. After all, they started out thinking of Lean as a "cost reduction program," and reducing the number of people from 10 to 5 just reinforces this belief. It is sad but true.

Starting the Flow Kaizen

Art Byrne was working with the flow team for the week. Team leader John Rollins, the manager of the assembly department, and his coleader, Sally Lombardi, a product design engineer, had never been on a kaizen team before, so they were a little nervous. Having UGH's CEO, Jerry York, as one of their team members didn't make them any calmer. Their objective for the week was to create the company's first one-piece flow cell. They were working on UGH's highest selling control box. It sold in about eight different configurations, but much of the product (the box itself, for example) was pretty standardized.

Up until this kaizen the product was built using a batch approach in five different functional departments. These were all physically separated from each other and were controlled by an MRP system. No one worked on the whole product—only components. The customer was not present in that everything was built to a forecast. This created a six-week lead time. On the plus side, because this was the company's highest selling product, all of the equipment needed to make the product was already dedicated to just this product. In addition, because the team had already cleared an area where the new cell would go, they had been able to do some prework: they installed all the required services (electric, air, hydraulics, etc.) overhead to reduce the amount of time required to rehook up all the equipment they expected to move during the kaizen week. They also built a little excess inventory to cover the fact that not much would be built during the kaizen week, as all the machines would be moving around. Both of these "get ready" steps are good rules of thumb to follow.

Once they got to their team room, Art started asking questions and giving some guidance on how to go about the flow kaizen.

Art: As a first step, let's get a sample of each of the eight configurations and lay them out on the table so everyone can see what we will be making this week. (The configurations looked pretty similar, but each version had its own special features.) I want you to start with the highest volume product of the eight, which accounts for about 70 percent of sales. Next, I want you to lay out the step-by-step sequence by which the product is made. [*The results of this exercise are shown in Figure 7-1.*] This gives us a pretty broad outline of what will be involved.

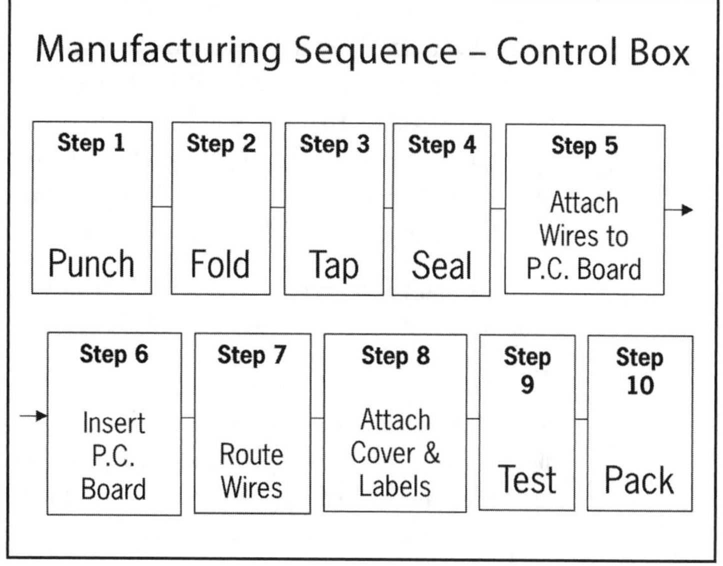

Figure 7-1. Manufacturing sequence for control box

John Rollins: But Art, this equipment is all over the plant, and it hasn't been moved in years.

Art: That's not surprising, and we can deal with that easily. We now have a good visual of what we are going to have to move this week to create the new cell. We have also lined up a little outside rigging help to move a couple of pieces of equipment that we can't move easily ourselves. The next step is to determine the takt time.

Sally Lombardi: Art, our project sheet for the week gives us the takt time. Can't we just use that?

Art: Yes, Sally, I know it does, but you shouldn't just blindly accept it. You need to confirm it for yourselves.

John: OK, then, I think we have already done that. We have looked at both historical and forecast sales along with the "time available" in the day to determine the takt time. The product is not very cyclical, so there is no need for a couple of different takt times. (For example, having one takt time for the eight months of the low season and another for the four months of high season.) Fortunately, our analysis shows a takt time that is very close to the takt time we were given. The takt time is 70 seconds.

Art: Great. Then you have confirmed the takt time. Now I want you to break into smaller groups and observe the various operations. I want you to use a time observation sheet and observe about 10 iterations of each of the work sequences. The main thing to focus on is the worker, but also check the cycle time of the equipment to make sure that it is all under the takt time so there will be no bottlenecks.

Barbara Mooney: Come on, Art, isn't that a bit harsh? I mean, what are the operators going to think when we descend on them with clipboards and stopwatches?

Art: Barbara, I don't want you to "descend" on anyone. I want you to have a discussion with the operators as soon as you get to the area to tell them about the kaizen and explain that the team will be doing time observations. The most important thing is to explain that you will be timing the work and not the operator and that the objective is to find the waste so it can be removed. The things you learn from observing the work should make the operators' jobs easier and safer. This should allay their fears.

The team then proceeded to the various functional departments to do their time observations.

Art: So what did you find?

John Rollins: Well, we observed the work and did the timing following the time observation sheet as shown in Figure 7-2. We then picked a time for each operation and displayed it on the percent loading chart shown in Figure 7-3. We

Team 3 – Control Box Cell

	Process for Observation	Control Box			TIME OBSERVATION FORM							Date: 6/1/15 Time:	Operator: Observer: Team 3
No.	**Component Task**	**1**	**2**	**3**	**4**	**5**	**6**	**7**	**8**	**9**	**10**	**Component Task Time**	**Points Observed**
1	Punch	12	13	9	10	11	10	10	8	14	10	10	Material feeding
2	Fold	20	25	20	27	19	20	17	20	22	20	20	
3	Tap	30	25	25	20	25	25	29	24	25	28	25	Aligning material
4	Seal	20	22	21	22	24	22	25	22	22	23	22	
5	Attach wires to PCB	90	75	80	80	83	80	78	80	84	81	80	Complicated process
6	Insert PCB	9	15	12	11	12	12	14	12	16	12	12	
7	Route wires	35	32	30	28	30	30	27	30	31	30	30	
8	Attach cover/labels	33	30	36	30	37	28	30	32	31	30	33	No fixturing
9	Test	15	13	15	16	15	15	14	15	15	16	15	
10	Pack	46	40	38	40	42	40	37	40	43	41	40	Poor material feeding
	TIME FOR 1 CYCLE												

Figure 7-2. Time observation for control box cell

used the lowest repeatable times that we observed—not an average of the times—to construct the percent loading chart. For example, if we did 10 observations and 4 of them took 35 seconds, another took 28 seconds, 3 were between 35 and 40 seconds, and 2 were between 40 and 50 seconds, then we used the 35-second time for the percent loading chart. Is that correct?

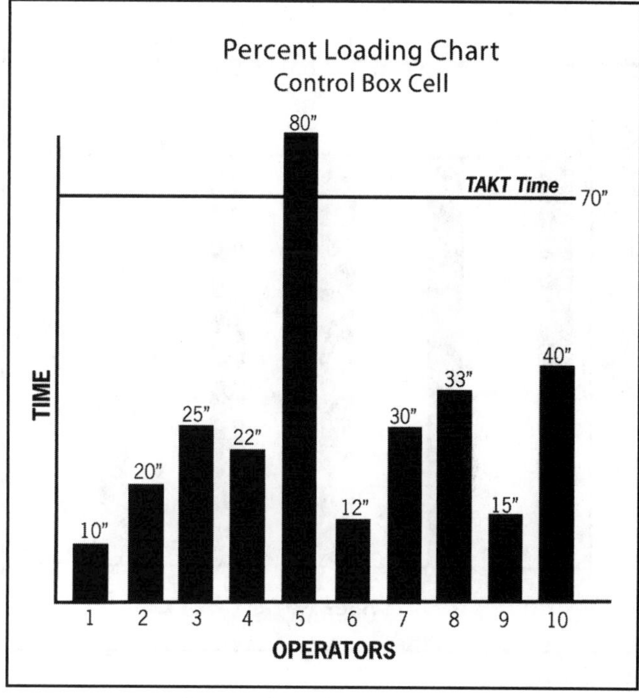

Figure 7-3. Percent loading chart for control box before kaizen

Art: Good work! You first confirmed the takt time, and now you are comparing that with the cycle times you observed. They may not be the lowest time you observed at each workstation, but you know they are repeatable. You also observed times that were longer, so you know there can be issues. You want to find and eliminate the waste that caused these longer times, not average them into your cycle time.

Barbara: Now that we know how long each task takes, it seems that it would be better to balance out the work so that every operator works the same amount of time.

Art: Barbara, I understand where you are coming from, but doing that would just institutionalize the waste. What we want to do is start with the first operator and bring him or her up to takt time, then the second operator, and so on. When the cycle time and takt time are equal, we know we have removed the waste—remember, that is our key goal here. In fact, we can easily calculate how many operators are needed by dividing the total observed work time, 297 seconds, by the takt time, which in this case is 70 seconds. The result is 4.2 people. So now I want you to draw the new percent loading chart, understanding that there is no such thing as 0.2 people, which means you will need to start with 5 operators.

They drew the new percent loading chart (Figure 7-4) with five people. This showed that operator 5 had only 17 seconds of work, while the other four operators had a full 70 seconds of work.

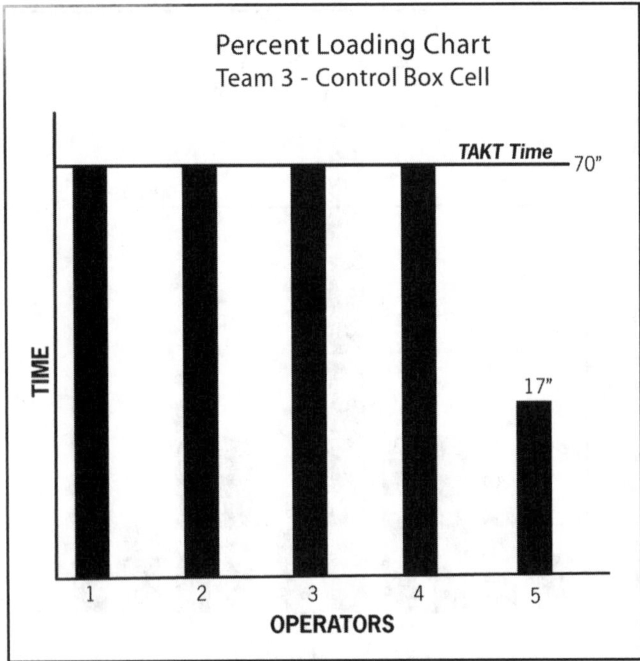

Figure 7-4. New percent loading chart

Barbara: Well, surely we can average out the work now. I mean, you can't have operator five with just 17 seconds of work and the other four with 70 seconds of work. You may cause a riot because, well, how is that even close to being fair?

Art: Remember that removing the waste is the objective here. One of the best ways to do that is to make the waste visible. "Make it ugly" is the way we like to say this. As a result of this, have operator five do nothing for the remaining 53 seconds of the cycle time. This will make the waste clear and force you to do another kaizen to eliminate the 17 seconds of work and get down to four operators. Once you get to four operators, you should look at what waste still exists that prevents you from getting to three operators, and so on.

The team then prepared a standard work combination sheet (Figure 7-5) to show that they could easily meet the takt time with five operators. Next Art had them draw a rough new layout (Figure 7-6) for the one-piece flow cell they were about to create.

John: Art, are you serious? You want us to start moving equipment after lunch based on this new cell layout? Why, it is barely a sketch! We need detailed blueprints before we move equipment. The finance department also insists that we do a full ROI analysis before any equipment can be moved.

Art: And how long does that take? More important, is there any value added in creating blueprints and doing ROI analysis just to move a few pieces of equipment?

Jerry York himself was skeptical, but to his credit he encouraged everyone to go ahead with the plan. After all, they were talking about a 50 percent reduction in manpower and an even bigger reduction in inventory and space needed to make the product as well as drastically reducing their lead time.

MODEL # AND NAME Control Box Cell	STANDARD WORK COMBINATION SHEET	DATE PREPARED 6/1/15	QTY/SHIFT	MANUAL ——— AUTOMATIC ······ WALKING - - - - WAITING ⟺ HOLDING
WORK SEQUENCE		DEPT.	TAKT TIME 70"	

STEP #	OPERATION NAME	TIME MAN	TIME AUTO	TIME WALK
1	Punch	10	2	2
2	Fold	20	3	2
3	Tap	25	5	2
4	Seal	22	10	2
5	Attach wires P.C.B.	80	-	2
6	Insert P.C.B.	12	-	2
7	Route wires	30	-	2
8	Attach cover/label	33	-	2
9	Test	15	60	2
10	Pack	40	-	-
11				
12				
13				
14				
15				
		Man	Auto	Walk

OPERATION TIME - sec. TAKT TIME

OPERATOR ONE

OPERATOR TWO

OPERATOR THREE

OPERATOR FOUR

OPERATOR FIVE

WAITING TIME 53" FOR OPERATOR FIVE OPERATOR # 5

UGH Corporation

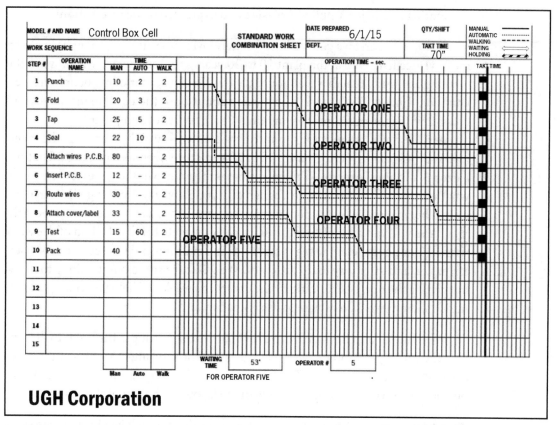

Figure 7-5. Standard work combination sheet

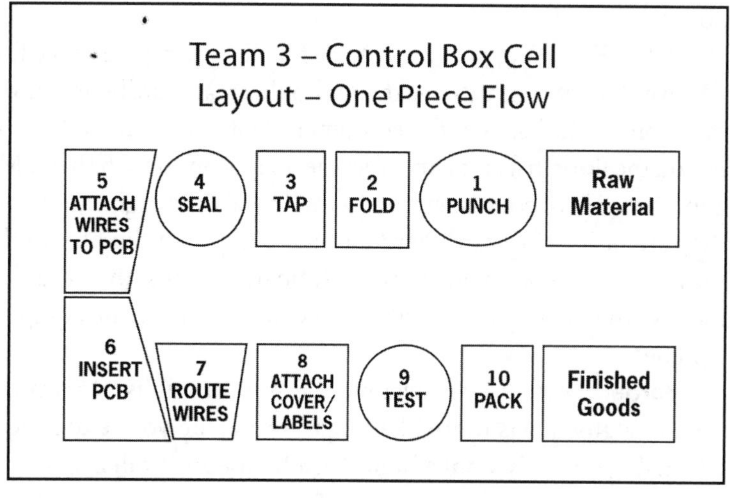

Figure 7-6. New one-piece flow layout

During lunch, Jerry pulled Art aside and expressed some reservations.

Jerry: Art, aren't we going a little fast here? Most of this equipment hasn't been moved since it arrived at the plant 10 to 20 years ago. I supported the move in the meeting as I really feel that we should try this. Even so, a lot of my people are nervous and think it won't work. They worry about both the equipment moves and cross-training the operators to work on different types of equipment.

Art: First of all, thanks for supporting the move—and the team—in the meeting. Your associates' concerns are all valid and quite normal. But as I said before, kaizen is a "doing" exercise. You need a breakthrough event to get everyone to see what is possible and to start to change everyone's way of thinking. This first cell should help you with that—but our time is short. That's why we need to move right away. You will win a lot of converts if we can complete this by the end of the week so that your people can (a) see that it is up and running and (b) see that it is a better, easier, and safer way to do the work. We will have some bumps along the way, but getting the new cell running by the end of the week will help you change a lot of minds and give you a template to use going forward.

After lunch John Rollins divided his team into subgroups. The order to disconnect the existing equipment was given just after the morning time observations, so it was already well under way. Part of the team under Sally Lombardi was responsible for transferring the rough drawing of the layout to the actual shop floor.

Sally: Art, my subteam is trying to transfer the new cell layout from the standard work sheet (Figure 7-6) to the shop floor. I could use some advice on how to do this.

Art: OK. First of all, you need to finish clearing the space for the new cell and remove all safety hazards. Next you should create cardboard cutouts in the exact dimensions of the bases of the equipment that will be moved into the cell. Lay them out on the floor in a circular cell shape. Play around with them. Make sure you have good flow. Have your operators actually walk through the sequence even though they are only using cardboard cutouts and pretending to do the work. Once all the adjustments are made to the cardboard cutouts, then draw chalk lines around them so the moving crews will know where to locate the equipment and assembly benches.

Barbara: Art, did you ever play with cutout dolls when you were a kid? I suppose as a guy it was more like Legos, or maybe you're too old for Legos. In any event, do you really want a bunch of adult people walking around with cardboard cutouts on the floor pretending to make parts? UGH usually uses engineers and CAD/CAM drawings to create a new work area.

Art: [*laughing*] I hate to admit it, Barbara, but yes, I am too old for Legos. I was more a wooden block and Erector Set kind of guy. But look, we are designing this new cell with a focus on the operator, not on what some engineer up in an office comes up with. One of the main reasons we need operators on the team is to get their input as to how the layout feels to them. What is the smoothest flow and the least amount of work for them? If we get this input before the machines are moved, it will shorten the time it takes us to complete the cell.

Barbara: But what if they don't like it once the machines are actually moved?

Art: Well, once the machines are in place we will have them run through the flow again before we actually hook the machines back up. I would expect that there will be several additional moves and adjustments at that point, based on the operators' input, before we reconnect the machines.

Barbara: You're really serious, aren't you? When you said before that you would listen to the operators' input, I was a little skeptical. You keep surprising me. Designing the layout with the operators' input, what a concept.

Art: Think about simple projects you do around the house. For example, if you're going to hang a picture, you probably have someone hold it up so you can see how it looks before you go and hammer a nail in the wall. That's really all we are doing here. I want you to get the machines as close as possible to each other and allow for only one piece of work in process except where there is a need for drying or cooling before the part can be moved. In addition, the height and orientation of the equipment should be adjusted to make it as easy as possible for the operator. The cell and work should flow from right to left because most people are right-handed and this configuration makes the work much easier for the operator when moving from station to station inside the cell. The emphasis always is on making the operator's job easier and safer.

John: We have the equipment being moved this afternoon and tonight, maybe into tomorrow. Shall we hook it up as it arrives to save time?

Art: No, as we just discussed, before you hook anything up you should make a dry run with the operators to see what feels good for them. Do things need to be adjusted to make their work flow smoother? This will probably cause a lot of small moves to the equipment and maybe some adjustments so they can work in the same plane without bending or reaching.

John: What about feeding the parts to the cell? We have the machines so close together that I can't see how we will feed the component parts.

Art: Yes, I want all parts fed from the outside of the cell to the point of use in as close to a one-piece flow as possible. They should also be fed in the proper orientation so the operator doesn't have to waste time turning parts. Think about the nurse handing the surgeon his instruments in an operating room. Remember that we are trying to optimize the value-adding operators and keep them steadily working at takt time.

This razorlike focus on the value-adding work as opposed to the traditional approach of making a certain number of parts each day or week is another thing that sets Lean apart. The value-added workers are the critical link to the customer in any business. Making what they do every day easier, faster, and more precise (think quality) will allow us to deliver the most value to the customer.

John: Art, all of our parts are delivered by forklift trucks in pallet quantities. This idea of feeding parts in a one-piece flow is a major shift. How are we going to handle this one?

Jerry: Good question. You're not suggesting that we have someone just stand there and hand the operator one part at a time, are you?

Art: No, of course not. Think about feeding parts from the outside of a cell, perhaps down a chute or slide. You can load this up every 15 minutes or so using an external water spider (I'll get to this shortly). The operator removes one, and the next one automatically slides down into place. For this week, we will just set up the one-piece flow of component parts and create a water spider route to deliver them. Later on you have to make the adjustments to your supply chain to get the parts to arrive naturally in the way you want them. Your current approach of dumping pallets of material near where it is used forces your value-added workers to do far too much non-value-added work getting parts, unwrapping the pallets, and the like. We want to eliminate that.

John: If you say so.

Despite all these challenges by the new chairman, the equipment started arriving and the cell started to take shape. It was clear that they weren't going to get everything in place before 5 p.m., so the team decided to stay late and order dinner in. The maintenance team was doing a great job. Even so, they got a little frustrated by the constant requests to move things a little more this way or that way to make it easier for the operator. They certainly were glad they had not tried to hook up the equipment yet. In fact, they had already determined that when they did hook it up, the connections would be flexible so it would be easy to move things when these crazy kaizen people decided to move things again—10 minutes later.

During dinner, with the cell about 80 percent complete, Jerry York said to Art, "I confess that I was skeptical that this would actually work, but now I'm impressed with what I see. Still, how are we going to accommodate the eight different products that are in this family?"

Art: Good question. In this case it will be pretty simple as they all use the same basic housing, and the eight products are created based on the different component parts and wiring. This work is done mostly at manual stations and only requires different assembly fixtures and standard work. The fixtures can easily be stored under the benches so that we can change quickly from one product to the next. Changing from one SKU to another should be able to be done within the takt time. That means there would be no stoppage of the line for changeover and the casual observer won't even notice that you changed from one product to the next.

Jerry: But Art, we are so used to making things in two- to three-month batches, and then supplying everything to the lines in pallet quantities, that it will be a big change for my people to think about making and supplying things in smaller amounts. Take this cell, for example. What kind of supply quantities are you thinking about?

Art: Well, I don't want to shock you too much this early; you have a long way to go to get everything into flow cells. And honestly, switching from batch to flow is the top priority. Over time, however, you will need to evolve to where you are supplying parts to the line in the "pack out" quantities built on each line. In the case of this line, we pack everything at the end in boxes of 12. That means that the "pack out" quantity is 12, and all parts and components should be supplied in quantities of 12 (or some multiple of that). This doesn't mean that you set up a big press and only run 12 at a time. The quantity will likely be higher than that as it is inherently a batch machine. It just means that you put the parts off the press into boxes or trays of 12 for delivery to the line.

Once you get to that point, all you have to do to change from Product A to Product B is to pull down the next box of 12 parts. No inventory has to be taken away, and therefore no setup time is involved to change the line. This change has to run back through both your internal and external supply chains. You are a long way from doing this right now, so don't worry. We may try to simulate it this week if we have a chance. It is way too advanced for this week's kaizen, but it is important for you as CEO to know where you are going and all the changes that will be required to get there.

Jerry: Thanks, I think. This really is taking on quite a lot, Art.

Art: Yes, I am aware of that, and I am not trying to scare you, just trying to help you see where UGH needs to go. After all, when Mr. Kurosaki and I are not here you have to provide the leadership and the push to keep going. Got it? Now let's get back on the floor and see how our new cell is coming along.

Flow Kaizen, Day Two

By the next morning, the cell was largely in place. The maintenance team worked overtime on the first shift, and the second shift spent the majority of their time on the move. One of the assembly benches was missing; one of the punch presses was already disconnected and being jacked up and ready to move in an hour. John Rollins once again split the team up to focus on the various to-do items such as creating standard work, training the operators, making sure the equipment was in the right position and easy for the operators to use, and creating a parts supply route and delivery mechanisms to deliver the parts to the operator. Art wandered by the parts supply subteam to see how they were doing.

John East: Art, just who we were looking for. I'm John East from the maintenance department, and we are trying to figure out the best way to supply parts to this new cell. You mentioned the need to create a "water spider" route. What the heck is a water spider?

Art: Ha, no problem. A water spider is in effect the material handler. The Japanese use the term *mizusumashi,* which means "water spider," as the motion is not unlike that of a water spider running on top of the water. Like most things in Lean, a mizusumashi differs from the traditional idea of a material handler as the job is busier and more intense. The water spider is responsible for supplying the right parts at the right time in the right quantity so that the line never runs out, yet honors the Lean principle of never carrying too much inventory. A typical water spider will supply two or more lines at a time depending on complexity. As a result, it requires a highly skilled person who can think ahead and take initiative. This is almost the exact opposite of our traditional definition of a material handler being a low-skill worker.

Barbara: Art, first you start with some Japanese word like *kaizen*. Next you switch to German with this *takt time* stuff. Then you want to put everyone in a jail cell and have people called water spiders bring them stuff. I hate spiders! They give me the creeps.

Art: [*laughing*] Barbara, this is your lucky day. You are on the subteam tasked with setting up the first water spider route. Don't worry; this spider will only have two legs and won't bite.

I want you to start by drawing the cell and determining where parts have to be supplied. Once you have this done, you can fill in the places where the parts will be stored. Next you need to determine the supply quantities and the frequency that the water spider has to visit the cell.

For example, if we want the water spider to visit every 20 minutes, then we calculate takt time (20 minutes × 60 seconds = 1,200 seconds/takt time of 70 seconds), meaning the water spider has to bring 17 parts/components every 20 minutes. If the water spider came every 30 minutes, he would have to bring 26 parts each time. Your "pack out" quantity (the number of units in the final shipping box) is 12, however, so try to create a sequence such that everything comes in sets of 12. That would mean the water spider would have to come every 14 minutes or, if you think it is easier to have less frequent visits to start with, you could have him come every 28 minutes.

The subteam went to work and came up with the water spider route shown in Figure 7-7. They decided to start with a 28-minute cycle. With a 450-minute workday, this was 16 trips per day. This was nice on paper. They were not sure if they got it right, so they asked Art what he thought.

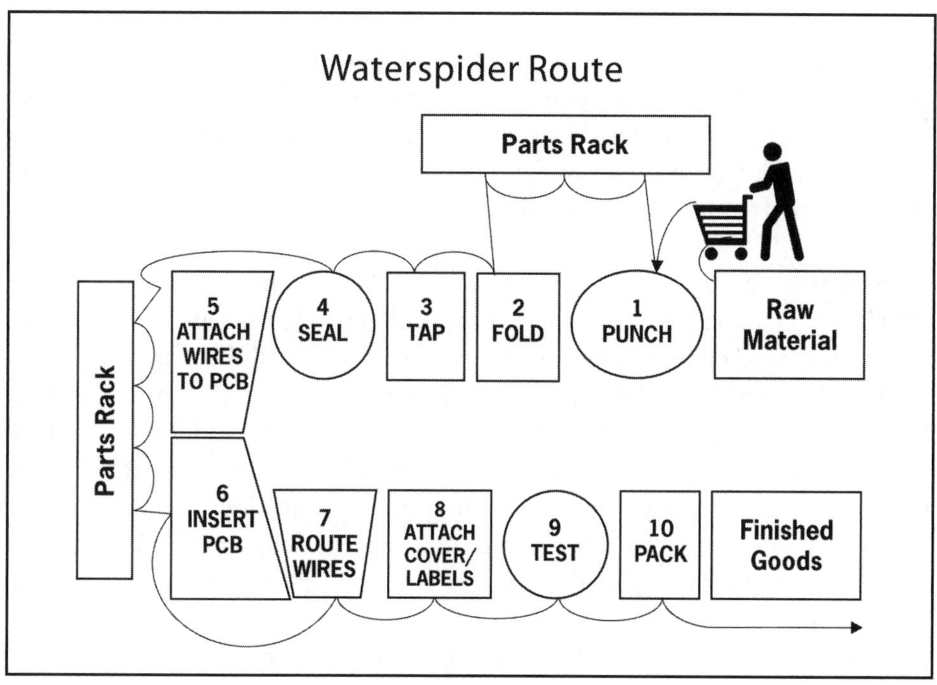

Figure 7-7. Water spider route

Art: This looks pretty good. Nice artwork—now you need to put it into action. I want you to make one of your subteam members the water spider and then follow and time her to make sure the work can get done in time. Once you determine this, then see how much extra time the water spider has so you can estimate how many more cells she might be able to handle.

Barbara: See, I told you guys he would just come up with more work for us to do. And how come you refer to the water spider as "her," Art? I'm the only female on this subteam, and I already told you I hate spiders.

John East: I think you would make a great spider, Barbara. What about the rest of you? [*Everyone was laughing, but they all agreed.*]

Barbara: OK, OK, I'll do it. You guys are a pain in the neck. If you try any spider jokes, I'm going to smack you.

Most of the rest of day two was spent getting the cell ready, creating the standard work, and getting the equipment rehooked up. This work went on all the way through second shift.

Flow Kaizen, Day Three

Day three took up where day two had left off. Getting the equipment hooked up was the major thrust. While this was happening, the team spent its time walking the operators through the process and getting their feedback and input on what worked and what was awkward for them. The operators also made suggestions on how to make the traditionally difficult parts of the process easier for them. The team then tried to implement all of the operators' suggestions.

Barbara: Wow, I'm glad I'm here to witness this with my own eyes. We are finally listening to the operators' suggestions and implementing all the little things that will make their jobs easier and safer. I might get to actually like this kaizen stuff.

John Rollins: I hate to admit that you are right, but when we look at the work itself through the lens of takt time, standard work, and value-added versus non-value-added, it makes the waste jump out at you. Now that we can see it, the operators' suggestions make all the sense in the world. But making headway on these targets only reveals what feels like an even longer list of things to do. We have to remove the excess inventory, build some simple devices, and clean up the whole area.

Jerry York was right in the thick of things, helping to move equipment, remove excess items, and even sweep things up.

Art wandered over to where he was doing some sweeping and asked, "So, Jerry, how's it going? Having fun yet?"

Jerry: Oh, hi, Art. Yes, I am having fun. This team of people is just great. Even so, I worry that they will think less of me for being out here doing this kind of work. I mean, it is not typical CEO behavior.

Art: It is not typical CEO behavior for a traditional batch, "make the month" company, for sure, but what you are doing is typical for a Lean CEO. The Lean leader leads by example, so being out here working with the team is one of the best things you could do. It is a very big deal. I'm sure that all the team members appreciate your involvement. One of the main thrusts of Lean is to get everyone participating in finding and eliminating the waste in order to deliver more value to customers. There should be no distinction between the CEO and the lowest-paid operator in this regard. So keep going; you're having a big impact.

Barbara: [*as an aside to Art during a brief team break*] Gee, it's great to see Jerry out here working side by side with everyone else. In all the years I've worked here, I can count on one hand the number of times our CEO was even on the shop floor. In just the past two days, 10 different people have told me how much they like to see this. But now, what about the rest of the managers around here? Now what?

Art: To be successful, these managers will have to change as well: to become problem solvers and teachers and not just issue orders. They need to "go see," ask why, why, why, and encourage their teams to look at things differently and come up with solutions. Everyone needs to feel that they are part of the team and that their suggestions to eliminate waste are taken seriously.

Barbara: And a kaizen is a good way to do this?

Art: Absolutely. A kaizen project is a great way to create this atmosphere. In this case we have Jerry York working on the shop floor all week as just a team member. He is learning a lot about all the problems that exist on the shop floor that never came to his attention before. He is also, along with everyone else on the team, learning completely new ways to look at the work itself and understand how to organize it better with far less waste. The same is true for all the other managers on these initial kaizen teams and for other managers on future teams. This is how they will learn and start to change their approach.

Barbara Mooney: I'll believe it when I see it, but I love the idea.

John Rollins: OK, we are hooked back up. At 2 p.m. we will start our first trial run. We have created the initial standard work and trained the first operators. I have split the team into subgroups to time and observe the operation.

Art: Great; let's start it up and see what happens.

After running the cell for 30 minutes, the best they could do was a cycle time in the 85- to 90-second range. The takt time was 70 seconds.

Sally Lombardi: That didn't work too well. What are we missing?

Kelvin Lee, electrician: Well, I can see three specific bottlenecks. There is also some awkward material handling going on.

Mary Peters, sales rep: That is probably why we are having a hard time getting each of the first four operators working to takt time.

John: One of the problems seems to be getting the right material in the right place at the right time. Let's create a subteam to develop a simple pull system using kanban cards to make sure that the material the operators need will be available when it is needed and in the amount needed. Also, I want to assign two people to operators one and two, two more to operators three and four, and another two to operator five and the water spider to observe them in more detail and try to solve the problems they are having.

They restarted the cell, and these subteams spent the rest of the day making small adjustments to make things easier for the operators and lower the time. The operators themselves contributed some of the best ideas.

Flow Team, Day Four

More adjustments and changes were made to the cell on the second shift of day three. When the team came in on Thursday morning, they were excited about what would happen next. They spent the first couple of hours going over the details, training the operators, and making sure the tools and raw material were in their proper places.

John: Now that we have taken corrective actions, let's run the cell again.

After a bumpy start, things were running pretty smoothly by the end of the first hour. They were still above the takt time at 75 seconds, but due to the one-piece flow, they could clearly see where the problems were. After lunch they made the needed changes, and by the 4 p.m. leader's meeting, they were consistently hitting the 70-second takt time. In fact, they still could see problems in the cell and were convinced they could get the cycle time down to 64 to 66 seconds, which would allow them to remove the fifth operator.

They asked Art what he thought about their progress.

Art: I hope that all of you feel good about what you have achieved this week. You have cut the staffing from 10 to 5 with a clear path for getting to 4. You have reduced the total space needed to make this product family by 80 percent. You cut the WIP inventory needed by over 90 percent, from several months to just two days. You cut the travel distance needed for the product to be made by 95 percent. The combination of these things should allow you to cut your lead time from six weeks down to one or two days. You also have the beginnings of a pull system in place to make sure the cell is supplied. We can work more on that in the morning.

Sally: I think I can speak for the whole team in saying that this has been an amazing week. We feel great about how far we have come, but I would expect that there is still more to be done.

Art: You are right, Sally, there are still more gains here. Much more. As you move from this initial cell to more of a chaku chaku (load load) line where the operators' main responsibility is loading parts and checking quality, and the bulk of the work is done by low-cost semiautomated machines, then the potential is there to go down to three or maybe even two operators. But what I think isn't important. The more important thing is, what do you think?

John: I don't know where to begin. I've been working here for 20 years, and we never even thought about doing something like this. I don't think we could have done it on our own. It really opened my eyes to what is possible.

Barbara: This has been a fun week. Thanks for letting me participate. Despite all the funny words you use like *cell* and *spider*, it is great to see everyone working together to make things better, safer, and easier. Or as you say, removing the waste. We sure have a lot of that. Getting down to only two or three operators at some point, however, still seems impossible to me.

Jerry: What about the pull system? How do we signal the cell what to make?

Art: Another good question. All we did this week was create a simple pull system that focuses on how to supply the cell. This is important, but the real objective is to produce to the pull of the customer. Right now you can't do that. You have in fact hardwired the customer out of the equation. You produce everything on an MRP system based on a forecast. So for now what you need to do is go into your MRP system and adjust the parameters so it can recognize the shorter lead times and increased flexibility of the new cell. There is no reason to schedule two- to three-month batches when this cell can turn things around in a day.

Longer term you want to create a pull system based on the demands of the customer. This can take many forms. One good way is to establish kanban quantities for each product. Once these are established, every time the incoming customer orders reach one kanban worth of a product, the kanban card for that product should print on the shop floor to tell the cell what to make next. This way you will have connected the customer directly to the shop floor and greatly reduced your lead times and need for inventory.

Jerry: This was a pretty straightforward product line. It is our biggest seller, so it should give us the most gains. What happens when we have much more complicated product lines?

Art: You're jumping ahead now. First make sure this cell works as designed. At the same time, you are correct to think about this. It won't be uncommon, for example, for you to run into cases where a set of 8 to 10 machines makes a product family of 20 to 30 different products. They all use the same machines, so they need to be made in this cell. Even so, not every product needs to use all the machines, and to complicate things a bit more, each product has a very different cycle time. You'll have a lot of fun figuring that out.

The principles remain the same, however. You still want one-piece-flow, and you want to make high variety in small quantities. We will help you when you get to the point of creating such cells. For now, the best way to think about this is to divide things into blocks of time. Each kanban card, for example, could be worth 10 minutes of production and should be clearly labeled as such. The amounts made in 10 minutes will vary from product to product. For example, you may be able to make 50 Product As in 10 minutes but only 10 Product Bs. This will help you load the cell and determine if you are working to takt time no matter what product you are making and in what sequence.

Sally: I feel very lucky to have been selected to be the coleader on this team. I'm of course impressed by what we achieved, but how do we sustain it and build on it? I'm worried that this will be a "one-off" kind of event that is not really sustainable.

Art: You are right to worry about that. It is all too common for traditional organizations to act just that way. To avoid falling back, start by following up on the unfinished items on your kaizen newspaper and make sure they are complete. Next, the value stream leader has to report to management every week at the weekly value stream (product family team) leader's meeting on how the gains are being sustained. You also need daily reviews by the cell team and its direct supervisor on their progress and further improvements (preferably having the value stream leader present). In addition, you have to work to get all of the products in this value stream into similar flow cells as soon as possible. Using kaizen as the main method

Kaizen "To Do" 30-Day Follow Up

AREA: Control Box Cell **Date:** 6/15

ITEM #	OPPORTUNITY	CORRECTIVE ACTION	PERSON RESPONSIBLE	DUE DATE	% COMPLETE
1	Go from 5 to 4 operators	Reduce cycle time to 65"	John Rollins	7/1/2015	
2	Improve visual controls	hour by hour production control and quality board	Cell Leader	6/20/2015	
3	Establish Kanban quantities	Determine Kanban amount for every product made in cell	John Rollins	8/1/2015	
4	Create simple pull system	Connect Kanban to order entry order system - link to customer	Frank Gee Scott Smith	9/1/2015	
5	Clean new cell area	Clean cell and surrounding area - remove safety hazards	John Rollins	6/25/2015	
6					
7					
8					
9					
10					
11					

Figure 7-8. "To do" follow-up list

to do this just as we did this week will speed it along. There is no free lunch here. You have to work at it and be determined.

For now, focus on implementing the "To Do" things on your 30-Day Follow Up list (Figure 7-8). Oh, and once again, congratulations. You worked hard, but you got great results. You should feel very proud.

Summary Points

- While tangible benefits such as head count reduction, WIP reduction, and lowered inventory come out of flow kaizen, the real benefits are strategic.
- Kaizen is not a one-time scheduled "event" but a continuous process that you practice every day: the way you do business.

- When doing a time observation, you are always checking the work and not the operators.
- Creating a breakthrough event or result early on with kaizen helps people understand what is possible and builds commitment and momentum for more.
- Flow conditions are supported by a water spider that supplies the right parts at the right time in the right quantity so that the line never runs out, while honoring the Lean principle of never carrying too much inventory.
- Lean leaders must lead by example with a visible presence. When it comes to delivering value to the customer, there is no distinction between the CEO and the lowest-paid operator.

8

Office Kaizen

OVERVIEW

Waste for any company can be found everywhere—not just in the factory. White-collar functions are made up of a series of processes as well, all of which can contain waste. It is important to kaizen these areas as well. UGH's office kaizen team (team four) had an excellent week working on the order entry process. It created a new approach to handling excess orders that were creating problems for their factories. The team also changed the way that product would be allocated for future delivery as well as the way they responded to customer inquiries about how much they had in stock. Order entry errors were reduced from 5 percent to less than 1 percent. Order acknowledgment was reduced from two to three days to same-day with the expected result of reducing incoming phone calls by 15 to 25 percent. In addition, they were able to lower head count by four people (or 25 percent). The fact that problems in order entry can send the rest of the organization in the wrong direction, causing rework and added cost, means that improvements would reduce cost further, but this could not be calculated.

Most traditional companies will see the headline of this kaizen as a 25 percent reduction in head count, which completely misses the more important strategic benefits. The factories, for example, can produce in a level fashion as excess orders are smoothed out, which lowers costs and improves quality. UGH can leverage its understanding of true customer needs by shifting from simply blindly trying to execute customer requests even when it is clearly not good for the customers and potentially terrible for UGH to helping solve customer problems at the source. Not only will the customer see you as easier to deal with, but the gains from lowering inventory and eliminating unnecessary space can be reinvested in new innovative products that will deliver even more value.

Kicking Off the Office Kaizen

Jim Boots, the newly hired head of UGH's Kaizen Promotion Office (KPO), was assigned to work with team four, the office kaizen team, for the week. Jim had conducted a number of office kaizens at his previous company and was familiar with the different challenges that exist in this environment.

First of all, Jim knew that in an office environment, unlike the shop floor, it is difficult to actually observe the work. Much of the work occurs on someone's desk or on the phone. In addition, determining the work flow is difficult, as it tends to go through in and out boxes and some form of internal mail system. Jim also knew from experience that the resistance to change was much higher in the office. Over time, people develop their own routines for how to do the work. There are few real standards, so everyone does the same job differently. People in the office are also more protective of their own space. They move in with all kinds of personal items, and if you want to move their desk or workspace even a couple of feet, you are in for a fight.

Once the team got to its meeting area, Joe Rappaport, a regional sales manager and team leader, reviewed the current state. Their goals for the week were:

- Cut order entry errors to less than 2 percent from more than 5 percent
- Reduce staffing by 20 percent
- Solve the problem of how to handle large orders
- Develop new rules for allocating product to customers

Joe: I've never been on a kaizen before, but I am very excited to be leader of this particular team. As a regional sales manager, I can tell you that I spend a disproportionate amount of time, up to 50 percent some months, just chasing down customer complaints that can be traced back to order entry. We did a study not long ago that determined that 60 percent of our customer complaints were not related to the factory but due to other errors, many of which come from this department, like wrong price, wrong ship-to address, wrong quantity, wrong product, and so forth. So I look forward to a successful week. Before we get started I'd like my co-leader, Betty Wagner, to give her perspective as head of customer service, and then Jim Boots can give us an overview to get us going.

Betty Wagner: Thanks, Joe. I'm excited to be a part of this team too. Although, as head of order entry, I have to say I'm a little apprehensive. I don't disagree with the fact that we make more than our share of errors. We all feel terrible about all the problems we seem to be causing! So anything that we can do this week to reduce those will be very welcome. As for our goals on changing how product is allocated, this is decided above our pay grade, and we just comply. At the moment the mantra is "We are customer driven," and so we do everything we can to satisfy the customer request whatever it is.

The issue of large orders (or I am hearing people call it excess demand) is another important objective to take on. It certainly creates a lot of problems and puts us between customers and the factory. Once again, this isn't policy that we can make in this department, but hopefully the team can make a recommendation that management will accept. The goal of reducing our head count by 20 percent, in contrast, seems impossible to me. If anything I think we need to add 20 percent more people.

Jim Boots: Good morning, and thanks for coming. I'm sure by now that you have heard our new chairman, Art Byrne, say that in order to become a Lean enterprise, "everything must change." What he means is that Lean is not just some manufacturing thing. What we do in sales, order entry, product development, IT, human resources, and finance has a huge impact on how we deliver value to our customers.

George Burke: Jim, I'm a manager in the finance department. What could we possibly have to do with Lean?

Jim: George, I think that you're going to be surprised to learn that one of the areas that Lean impacts the most is finance. Like most companies, UGH uses a standard cost accounting system. This not only provides bad or misleading information (all the so-called variances don't tell you much) but also incentivizes many of the behaviors—like building inventory—that Lean seeks to eliminate. You're going to have to change to Lean accounting, and it will be a big shift for the finance department.

Now, back to the task at hand: let's start by understanding in detail what order entry does. We want to go and see and find a way to get at the productivity and quality issues that are part of our goals for the week. Let's start by determining the takt time for order entry. What is the takt time? Can anyone tell me?

Betty: Jim, I don't see how you can apply takt time to order entry. It is just impossible. I mean we have orders with only 3 line items and orders with 300 line items and everything in between.

Jim: Betty, I hear you; now let's see what we can do. Remember our formula for calculating takt time?

Daily Work Time/Daily Customer Demand = Takt Time

Also remember that we can calculate takt time in any setting in any business. Takt is one of the most important fundamentals in Lean. It tells us how much time we have to respond to the customer's demand. It is like asking, "So, what are we trying to do here?" For example, what is the size of the average order that you get in terms of line items? Also, what is the number of orders that you receive each day?

Betty: Well, if you ask it that way, then the average order has nine line items. We keep track of that, and for some reason, it doesn't vary very much year to year. As for the number of orders per day, that varies a bit more, but 120 orders per day would be a good number to use. That might be on the high side but should be pretty accurate.

Jim: Great, that was kind of what I expected. So, let's do the math.

Line items per day = 120 orders × 9 lines per order = 1,080

Work time = 450 minutes × 60 seconds = 27,000 seconds per day

27,000 seconds per day / 1,080 lines = 25 seconds per line

This is the takt time for one person. If you had two people, they would each have 50 seconds to enter a line, and if you had three, they would each have 75 seconds. Are you with me?

Betty: Jim, this sounds like some form of black magic. Are you sure this makes sense? I mean we only look at how many orders we have.

Jim: Don't worry, Betty; you will get more comfortable with it as we go along. With that input, let's divide the team into two groups. I want the first group to complete a value stream map of the entire order entry process from the customer all the way to when we ship the product. This doesn't have to be fancy, but it should include all the steps and the time it takes for each step. I'd like the second part of the team to go to the floor and find 10 orders that each have nine lines on them. You can split them up between order entry associates if you want, or you can just use one. Then I want you to time how long it takes to enter the order when you remove all distractions—incoming phone calls, for example—and just focus all attention on entering the order.

Joe: Let's have Betty lead the value stream mapping team, and I'll head up the timing team. [*Joe then populates each team.*] Now, when you get out on the floor, make sure to explain to our associates what you are doing in terms of analyzing the work, emphasizing that you are not analyzing them personally. Helping people understand that this is the approach should help to overcome any fears. Let's plan to get back together here after lunch.

The groups gathered again after lunch to review what they learned.

Jim: So, how did your morning go? What did you learn? What surprised you? Let's start with the takt time team. Joe, I think you were in charge of that.

Joe: We found quite a few orders with nine lines on them, so we actually did 14 observations as opposed to the 10 you recommended. We split them between two of our more experienced order entry clerks to make sure that we didn't just pick the fastest or the slowest one. This turned out to be a good idea as they both took roughly the same amount of time to enter an order and because the places where they had trouble, like the faxed-in order not being printed clearly enough, also took about the same amount of time for each person.

We get about 95 percent of our orders by fax or e-mail. The other 5 percent come in over the phone. It took the two people we observed 7 minutes to enter a nine-line order. When they had trouble, this could rise to 9 minutes, but most of our observations were at 7 minutes, or 47 seconds per line, with a few even lower at 5.5 or 6 minutes. As Betty said, we get 120 orders on average per day in total. As a result, based on the takt time, if we isolated the order entry operators and had them only do order entry without any phone time or other duties, then two order entry clerks could easily handle all the orders every day. The actual math is:

120 orders per day × 9 lines per order = 1,080 lines

47 seconds per line × 1,080 lines = 50,760 seconds per day

50,760 seconds ÷ 60 seconds/minute = 846 minutes per day

846 minutes ÷ 450-minute day per person = 1.88 people

We assumed that the 5 percent of orders that come in by phone could be written down by the order entry clerks manning the phones and given to the two order entry clerks for the actual entering in the system. This was a pretty shocking result as we currently have 16 order entry people in the department. If two people can enter all the orders, then it certainly raises the question, what are the other 14 doing?

Jim: Yes, that is a good question, and your next task will be to observe and question the order entry clerks about their other tasks besides just entering the order. For the moment, let's stick with what you have observed so far. What impact do you think that isolating two order entry clerks on entering the orders will have on quality?

Joe: Besides observing and timing the operators, we spent a lot of time on the subject of order entry errors. We spoke with about half of the order entry operators about what they thought gave rise to so many order entry errors. Overwhelmingly, they felt that being distracted by other things, mainly incoming phone calls, created the most errors. They may be halfway done entering an order when the phone rings or someone comes to their desk with a question and they have to stop entering the order. By the time they get back to it, they may have lost their place or gotten one order confused with another and entered a wrong shipping address.

They pretty much all felt that if they could enter the orders without distractions, they could do it with almost no errors. They explained that the fax machine does not always print clearly (and in fact rarely does), so they often confuse the number 6 with the number 8—or makes similar types of errors. They said that if order entry was their only duty, in these cases they would have time to call the customer and clarify if it was a 6 or an 8 instead of just making their best guess. They were all pretty excited about this possibility as they hate to make errors and are embarrassed when they occur.

Jim: Nice discovery. Did you discuss how you would go about staffing this approach?

Joe: We haven't reached any conclusions yet, but no one seems to want to just enter orders all day with no customer interface. They all understand and support the reduction in errors, however. As a result, we felt that some form of scheduling where two different order entry clerks are rotated into the order entry job every day might be a good solution. This way we get the quality gains and no one has to do this job more than once every seven or eight days or so.

Jim: The job rotation sounds like a good idea. I would suggest that the next step for your team is to split in half. Have one part of the team set up the two-person order entry process tomorrow morning and then observe and document what happens. The other part of your team should observe what the rest of the order entry team does. What happens when the actual order entry part of their job is taken away from them? How do they spend their time? What is the most time-consuming part of the job? Where can we get efficiencies?

Jim now moves on to Betty's subteam.

Jim: OK, Betty, what did your team observe? We gave you some training in how to construct a value stream map in the prekaizen training session that all of this week's kaizen members attended on Friday afternoon. Was that helpful?

Betty: Wow, that was an interesting exercise. And yes, the brief training was helpful. We never heard of a value stream map before, but it was instructive to look at what we do in this way. Here is our value stream map (Figure 8-1).

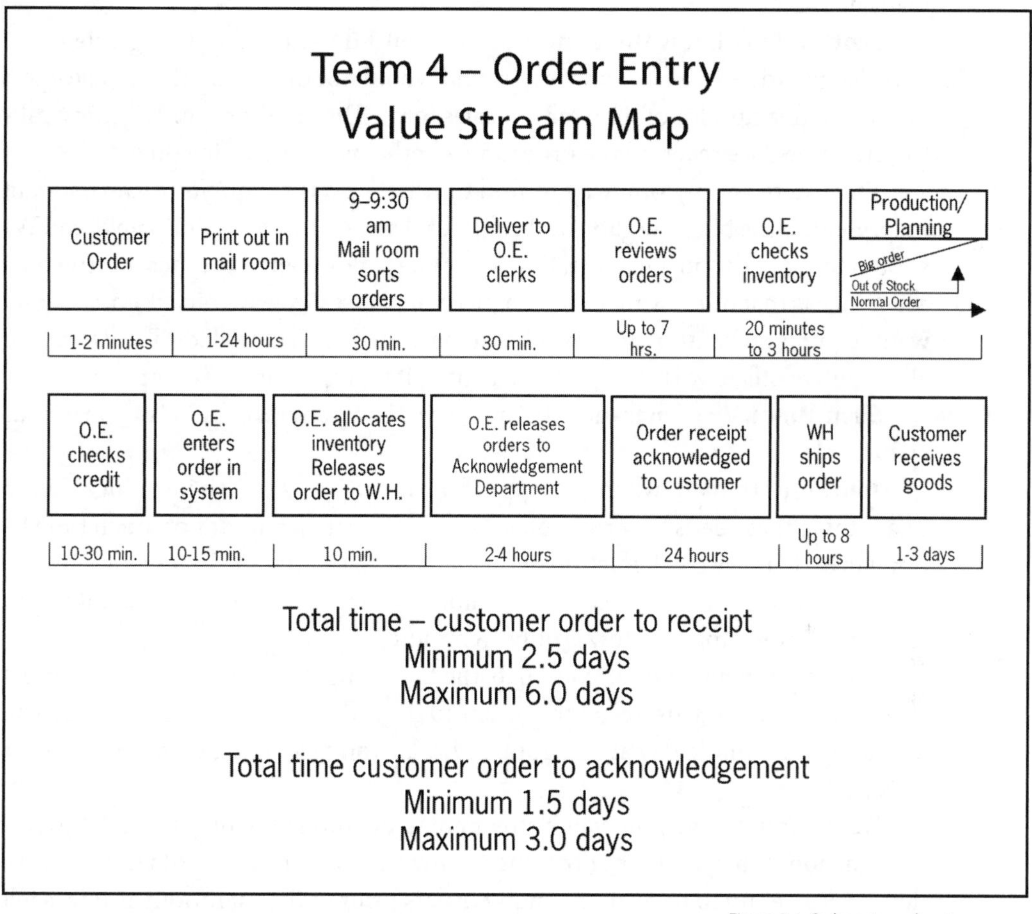

Figure 8-1. Order entry value stream map

You can see now that it takes a total of from three to six days from the time a customer enters an order until the goods are received. Some of that is transportation time and doesn't really have anything to do with our internal processes (some customers are just farther away from our warehouses than others). It takes us from two to three days just to acknowledge the customer's order; this is all internal time that we can do something about. It is a little hard to pin down, for example, but approximately 60 percent of our orders are acknowledged in two days, and 40 percent in three days. Reducing this to two days or less across the board would have a big impact on our customer relations.

Jim: Why not one day?

Betty: Sure, Jim, why not? And while we're at it, can you get me a date with Brad Pitt? Look, one day would be even better of course. But do you think we could really do that?

Scott: I don't know the answer to that, but I do know that being able to acknowledge orders in a one-day turnaround would not only delight our customers but would free up a lot of time for our sales force. They are constantly getting calls to determine if we received the order and whether we are working on it.

Jim: There is only one way to find out. Let's go through your value stream map, identify the big time gaps, and explore what we can do to eliminate them. We should think of this just like creating a one-piece flow cell in the factory: the only difference is that our raw material is a piece of paper. Once we pick it up, we don't want to put it down until whatever has to be done to it is complete. This is true for all repetitive office work, not just order entry. It will apply in any company.

Ellen Minor, VP of marketing: Any type of company? Really? Can you give us an example?

Jim: Sure. Think of when you apply for a mortgage, a health insurance policy, or anything that needs government approval. The actual amount of touch time labor it takes is a very small fraction of the time you have to wait. That's why you may have to wait two to three weeks to get a mortgage approved when the actual time it takes if you could make it flow is only 15 minutes.

Looking at your value stream map, the first thing that jumps out is the time it takes at the front end just to get the orders to the order entry team. It looks like you are eating up a whole day at the front end. Can you give us a little more detail on this?

Betty: You're right; the value stream map definitely uncovers this. We never thought about this in order entry since our work doesn't start until we get the orders. It was set up to have all incoming orders print in the mailroom as it was felt that this would be the most efficient way to get the paperwork to the order entry clerks. Over time with head count reductions and normal turnover it evolved that the orders are only delivered once per day to order entry. This occurs at around 9:30 a.m. So, any orders coming in after that (except the few that come in over the phone) aren't delivered till the next day. I guess we never gave much thought to the problems this creates for the customer.

Jim: Believe me, this type of thing is not unusual. It should be easy to solve, however, based on the observations done by Joe's team. They found that we could easily process all orders every day with only two people if we took them off the phones and removed the distractions. If we did that, wouldn't it make a lot of sense to just have the orders come directly to these two associates in whatever space we set them up in?

Joe: Based on our observations, it looks like these two clerks could also acknowledge the orders back to the customer instead of the current practice of sending them to a separate department to do the acknowledgment. This could save us probably 8 to 10 hours on average due to transportation time of the actual orders (the mail room again) and other factors—the acknowledgment team does other things such as customer contracts, for example, and can't always get to the orders right away. In the worst cases it could save up to 24 hours.

Jim: Those would be fantastic gains. What does everyone think about that? [*The team agrees that these are great objectives to work on.*] OK, then, for tomorrow we need to prove out our initial observations. Let's get an early start.

Day Two

Joe Rappaport: Let's get going. Based on what we learned yesterday, Jim has asked us to start to create the structure needed to reduce the order acknowledgment time and the number of people needed to enter orders without error. My time observation team will work on finding the proper space for the new dedicated order entry function, arranging the work flow, and getting the incoming orders printing in this space and not in the mail room. We will in effect be setting up the future state. Betty's team can spend the day timing and observing what else goes on in order entry and determining the best way to do that once we remove the actual entering of orders. This should point out opportunities for productivity gains.

It is important to remember, and in fact to communicate to every individual, that no one will lose their job as a result of any gains that we do find. We will simply shift them to other work and where possible make these promotion opportunities as well. So, let's get started.

The two sections of the team then split up and began their tasks. After the leader's meeting at the end of the day, Joe and Betty got back together with Jim Boots to review their progress.

Jim: So, what did we learn today?

Betty: Boy, this was confusing. Trying to sort out what the order entry team does, other than enter orders, was not easy. Everyone works differently and has slightly different habits and approaches. As head of order entry I was aware of some of this, but I was surprised to learn how little standardization actually exists.

We spoke with all the order entry clerks first to get their opinion. They outlined it like this:

Order Entry Daily Tasks

1. Answering incoming phone calls 40%
    - Product availability 40%
    - Order tracking 25%
    - Where's my stuff 20%
    - Other 15%
2. Chasing orders, shipments, and expediting 30%
3. Correcting errors, price, address, etc. 20%
4. Other 10%

Our actual observations, however, were quite different. We started out by following your suggestion to get a good feel for how much time is "value-added time" where the order entry clerk is actually doing work and how much is "non-value-added" work where they are doing something else. We assigned two members of our subteam just to observe this for the day. They observed four clerks in the morning and four different ones in the afternoon to give us a good cross section. The results were surprising:

Value-Added Work	Non-Value-Added Work
55%	45%

The non-value-added work broke down as follows;

- Walking 20%
- Waiting 30%
- Visiting 30%
- Searching 20%

Our phone system is set up to route calls to the next available operator. The clerks, however, have the ability to log out of the system if they have to leave their desks to file or find something or if they are on break. Our observations showed a number of cases where they log off the system for no valid reason. In addition, the incoming phone calls that generate most of their work don't come in at an even pace throughout the day. As a result, we have times when more than half of the department is not needed on the phone and other times when everyone is on the phone and we still have some customer wait times. We know when the busiest times are and have some existing rules about phone coverage during these times, but our observations suggest that these need to be reexamined and tightened up. We are not following our own rules, and this is hurting our customers.

Our observations on the actual work didn't vary much from what everyone told us as shown in the table (following). Even so we could see that most of the value-adding time could be improved upon. And we could see waste eliminated with a better layout and organization to reduce the walking and searching that goes on.

Order Entry Team's Observations

	OE Clerks	Kaizen Team
Answering the phone	40%	35%
Chasing orders, shipments, and expediting	30%	35%
Correcting errors, price, address, etc.	20%	25%
Other	10%	5%

Jim: Great work today. As I'm sure you found out, observing the actual work in an office environment is much harder than in a factory. The work occurs on individual people's desks, so you can't see the flow (if there even is any). More important, I'm sure by now you recognize that there is no standard work. Each individual goes about the work in whatever way he or she wants to.

Scott: Standard work? You can't establish standard work in an office, can you?

Jim: Absolutely you can. It may not be the same as for an assembly job in the factory, but you can establish standard work for everything that goes on in order entry. Remember that standard work is one of the four Lean fundamentals. It forms the foundation on which improvements are made. It creates and lays out the sequence, the time, and the methods required to do any work in the "least-waste way." It has to be owned by the local manager and all the team members. Their task is to first standardize the work and then remove more waste so the standard work can be constantly improved.

For order entry, Betty already mentioned some areas, such as rules about when you can log off the system, how long you can spend on the phone with any customer, the best way to correct errors, and the standard way to track an order or shipment. We won't be able to create standard work for all of these this week, but we can get a good start. You can put follow-up steps on your "kaizen newspaper" at the end of the week that will lead to the next kaizen and the next.

Joe: Well, our day wasn't as exciting as Betty's. First we focused on locating space for the order entry function and then creating a tentative layout. We want this to be within the overall order entry space so that these order entry clerks have easy access to the rest of the team who will be handling the "where's my stuff" inquiries that come in every day. It looks like we will have to install a couple of glass walls to give the quiet atmosphere that we need to remove all distractions from the order entry process. Maintenance says they will be in place by noon tomorrow. The transfer of the fax machines and printers, on which most of the orders come in, from the mail room will also be completed by noon tomorrow. We had the two order entry clerks who will start up this operation give us a lot of input on how they would like to see the space arranged. With their input, and the ideas of the rest of the team, we think we have a good initial layout. We should begin to actually operate it after lunch tomorrow.

Jim: Good work, Joe. Tomorrow your team should just continue to focus on setting up your area so you can start to enter orders. Once you do that, I'm sure you will see opportunities in both the layout and the way orders are entered. When you do, go ahead and make the improvements immediately.

Betty, you have a big task ahead of you as well. I'm sure that it will result in some rearranging of the space as well to make things more efficient. Just as I told Joe, when you see opportunities, go ahead and make the changes. Don't plan for moves to be made later. Maintenance can work on this all through the second shift. Also, for your team I would like to add the other two targets we have on our list as something to discuss tomorrow: (1) a policy for how to deal with large orders and (2) new rules for how we answer customer inquiries and how we allocate product to customers.

Day Three

Jim spent the first part of his day with Betty's team, with half of them continuing the observations of the remaining order entry work (the "where's my stuff" portion) and the other half starting to lay out the issues that arise from large orders and from the way product is allocated. He spent much of the morning with Joe's team watching the new space get put together and making suggestions. As he had expected, the layout they came up with was very much a reflection of how they had always worked and didn't reflect much Lean thinking at all. No surprise there.

Jim: Remember the four Lean principles that were part of your training for this kaizen? You know, work to takt time, one-piece flow, standard work, and pull? Well, I need you to reflect more of those in your layout. Having the two operators isolated in their own private spaces some distance from each other doesn't allow for any flow, nor does it allow for them to help each other out. You should think more about having them sit at the same table or at least right next to each other, for example. After all, no one will have this as a permanent job. They will just rotate in here for a day once every seven or eight days or so. As a result, they have no need to store any of their personal "stuff" here. Your current layout allows for just that.

Also, let's do what we can to eliminate them moving across the room to get orders from the printer or fax machine. There's no reason for this. I'd also like you to make the movement of orders and the status of where we stand at any time visual. I would suggest a series of simple open mail slots, for example, that orders could move through until complete instead of just piling them up on top of each other. That's my suggestion, but you are welcome to come up with your own. Also, you need an hour-by-hour visual control board so that you can write down the target and actual number of orders processed that hour, along with a simple explanation of why the target was missed or beaten. For example:

Order Entry Production Control Chart

Time	Plan	Actual	Comments
7–8	16	12	Fax machine down
8–9	16	15	Slow start
10–11	16	17	No comments
11–12	16	10	Concentration of big orders
12–1	8	10	Lunch
1–2	16	18	More small orders
2–3	16	9	E-mail system down for 25 minutes
3–4	16	16	No comments

Sorry to ruin your day, but I need you to start to see things from a Lean perspective. Kaizen is for doing, but it is also the best approach you can have for training all your people to see the waste and improve the work by eliminating it. Kaizen has to be done every day by everyone—not just during a weeklong event like this.

Jim then moved on to Betty's subteam.

Betty: Jim, your timing is great. We just completed a discussion about excess orders and product allocation. Let me first give you a summary of our discussion so far.

Excess Orders

1. Our traditional batch system loves big batch orders. It lets us have long production runs, and the finance department loves that. We are even willing to give price discounts for big orders.
2. At the same time, this causes havoc in the factory. Lots of expediting and tying up our equipment, not to mention the material supply issues that it creates.
3. And the worst problem of all is the problems this creates for our customers. Tying up equipment for one customer's big order pushes out lead times for everyone else. Trying to work around this causes us to carry substantial excess inventory.

Product Allocations

1. Every time an order entry clerk goes into inventory and allocates product for a particular customer, it removes that product from the system. If the customer doesn't want it for three weeks, then it just sits there. In the meantime, we might be back-ordering many other customers.
2. Our "we are customer driven" mantra forces order entry to do whatever the customer requests. This includes releasing all of our inventory to satisfy that customer even when it results in back-orders for others.

Jim: Excellent. Not, of course, that these are what you want! But I am pleased that you were able to uncover and agree upon these problems. Believe me, these are common—your list is similar to the problems of pretty much all traditional batch companies. They cover up these problems by carrying excess inventory. Our goal at UGH is to take our inventory turns from 3 to 20. That means we have to figure out how to solve these problems while lowering our inventory.

Let's start by talking about the "we are customer driven" part. This is a nice sentiment to be sure, but it sounds like it isn't always producing the intended results. Again, I can share from experience that this is fairly common. First of all, customers don't always do what is best for them. They order way too much inventory. Second, as you point out, doing what is good for one customer can often hurt other customers, which means the net result is not very customer friendly.

Scott, I can see that you are still skeptical, so let me give you an example. Let's imagine that a customer calls up and says, "I want to buy control box 102. How many do you have?" Our "we are customer driven" order entry rep goes into the computer dutifully and comes back with the answer, "We have 800 in stock." Well, right there we are already in a lot of trouble. The customer replies, "Gee, that is disappointing. I need 1,000, so ship me the 800 now and get back to me as soon as you can about when I can get the other 200." There's not much the order entry clerk can do at this point. So, what just happened? We didn't satisfy the first customer—he wanted 1,000—and at the same time we back-ordered the next 100 customers who each wanted 5 to 20 control box 102s as part of a bigger order.

Scott: But Jim, couldn't you also say that this shows that we need to increase the amount of control box 102 inventory that we carry? If we had more, we could have satisfied all the customers. I realize we want to reduce inventory. But how do we do that and still satisfy all the customers?

Jim: Well, we can't use inventory. Other successful Lean companies have trained order entry workers never to tell the customer how much we have in stock. Instead we should answer the customer's question of "How many control box 102s do you have?" with a question of our own: "How many do you want, and when do you want them?" This gets us out of the box we put ourselves in before. In addition, we should forbid order entry from ever releasing more than say 75 to 80 percent of our inventory to any single customer. These two changes will go a long way toward satisfying our customers and eliminating unnecessary back-orders. We know that the first guy who wants 1,000 right away can't install them all immediately. He is just building his own inventory. We can ship him some now and work out future delivery dates with him that satisfy his needs without hurting all our other customers. And without having to build inventory.

Now let's take a look at excess orders. The best solution here is to not allow them to automatically go through the system. First you will have to designate a level for each product that qualifies as "excess." Then, whenever you get an order that qualifies, it should be kicked out of the normal order entry process. Instead, it should require a conversation between order entry, production, sales, and the buyer-planner to come up with a plan that might satisfy the customer. You already know that he can't install or utilize all of the product on the day he is asking for it to be delivered. It probably represents three to four months' worth of stock to him. As a result, if you propose something like giving him 20 percent of what he needs now and 20 percent more every other week until the order is complete, I can almost guarantee you that he will happily accept and the disruption to your operations will be minimized.

The same thing holds true for allocating product to orders that are not scheduled to ship for several weeks. As your setup times and lead times come down, you can easily make this product before the due date. As a result, you free up existing product that can be shipped to customers who want it now and will still be able to satisfy the guy who wants it in three weeks. Your current allocation process prevents perfectly good inventory that is sitting on the shelf from being shipped and can result in you back-ordering customers who want it now. That is not very customer friendly.

Scott: Well, this is obviously a new way of thinking for us. It all makes sense, however, and I will concede that taking away our ability to solve problems by simply building more inventory reframes the discussion. It forces us to use the Lean principles to see this differently. We certainly should implement these recommendations as part of this kaizen.

Jim: Thank you, Scott. Remember that you will find some bumps along the way. You will have to work them out, but this is the right approach. Remember, as Art says, that "inventory is the root of all evil because it hides the waste." If we don't let you build inventory, you have to remove the waste.

Day Four

The two subteams spent the day getting the two parts of order entry up and running with the new methods they had developed. Joe's team made the rearrangements that Jim had suggested to their layout and got the hour-by-hour production control chart in place. They also made a number of other small adjustments as they observed the two order entry clerks throughout the day. Most of the suggestions came from the clerks themselves.

Betty's team made a number of physical rearrangements that brought the things that clerks needed closer to them as a way to eliminate the unnecessary walking. They also spent time creating new instructions for how to respond to customer questions such as "How many control box 102s do you have?" how to deal with product allocations, and how to handle excess orders. At the end of the day they summarized for Jim where they stood and outlined the actions they planned for Friday morning before the final report came out. Joe and Betty also presented this same progress report at the Thursday 4 p.m. leader's meeting.

Joe: Our focus today was to test how well the new layout allows us to enter orders as they come in, using the new format that we came up with. We made changes and adjustments along the way, but in general this worked very well. Our current results are as follows:

1. Two clerks can easily enter and acknowledge all the incoming orders every day. Today was a pretty average incoming order day, and they still had about 20 percent excess time on their hands.
2. Most of the orders could be entered in even less time than our original observations due to the layout changes we made. That allowed them extra time to double-check orders that didn't print well by calling the customer to be certain they had it correct. It also provided them time to call the customer to check when an order didn't look right (such as ordering 800 bases but only 300 covers). As a result, we expect that order entry errors will fall from the current 5 percent rate to less than the 2 percent target. In fact, we all believe that less than 1 percent is already happening.
3. The clerks like the new approach and are focused on getting the error rate down and getting all the orders entered and acknowledged to the customer on the day they come in.
4. Cutting the mail room out of the loop should save us 12 to 24 hours on the front end of the process. Eliminating the separate order acknowledgment function at the end of the process and having the order entry clerks do the acknowledgment as their last step will save another 12 to 24 hours on the back end. This should allow us to acknowledge the customer's order on the same day we receive it versus the current two- to three-day time frame. This should also reduce the number of incoming phone calls, many of which are following up to make sure we received the order, by 15 to 25 percent. This frees up a lot of time for the "where's my stuff" part of the team.

Betty: We also had good results, but it is harder for us to be as specific as Joe in every case. I'll do my best to summarize.

1. We have established the new rules for answering customer inquiries about how much product we currently have. We have also changed the procedures for allocating product for future shipment. We have the outline of how to deal with excess orders, but it will take more time to fully develop this policy and approach as we need much more input from production and the new buyer-planners.

   - Never tell a customer how much product we have in inventory.
   - Ask, "How much do you need, and when do you need it?"
   - Don't allocate product for future shipment beyond two days.
   - Don't let excess orders automatically be entered in the system.

2. We have established new standard work rules for many of our current procedures and have a follow-up list for other changes for our kaizen newspaper on Friday.
3. Our new layout makes things much more visual for everyone and reduces a lot of walking and searching for things. Between these changes and the new standard work, plus other insights based on our initial observations of up to 45 percent non-value-adding time currently, we are confident that we can reduce staffing by four heads, or 25 percent, versus our goal of 20 percent at the beginning of the week—while providing better customer service. So I think I have earned my date with Brad Pitt now.

Jim: Wow, great work by everyone this week. I'm sure Brad Pitt will be just as impressed as I am when he stops by to pick you up. You met or beat all of your goals. And you will provide better customer service. Not only that, but the improvements you make in order entry will in turn have a huge impact on the rest of the organization. You heard Scott say that fewer errors in order entry coupled with faster order acknowledgment will free up approximately 25 percent of his salespeople's time. That time can be better spent getting new customers and growing the business. Fewer errors and smoother incoming orders as a result of the changes to allocations and excess orders will also have a big productivity impact on the factory. Lead times will come down, as will product costs, and quality will be much better. We will gain market share and grow.

So, you still have some things to follow up on in the morning before your report comes out. But you should feel very good about what you have accomplished.

Summary Points

- Lean can be more challenging in white-collar settings because it's harder to see the work flow and because the physical elements may create further barriers.
- Ultimately the potential benefits from Lean applied to office and service work are far higher than those on the shop floor.
- Standard work plays a foundational role in office kaizen as well. It creates and lays out the sequence, the time, and the methods required to do any work in the "least-waste way." It has to be owned by the local manager and all the team members.

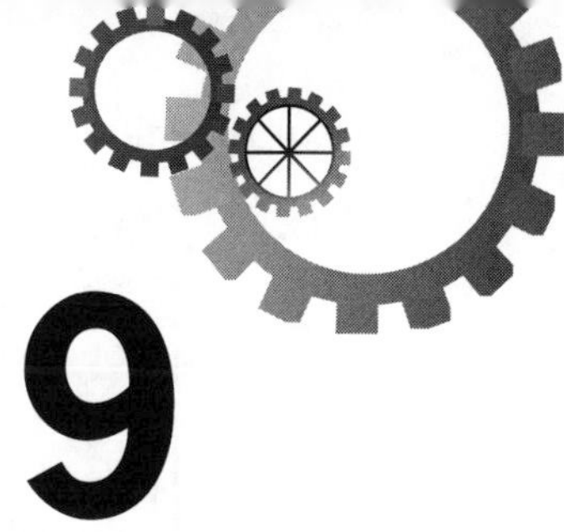

9

UGH'S Lean Journey, Year One

OVERVIEW

The fact that UGH's first kaizens were successful was not unusual. Any well-organized and well-run kaizen will produce dramatic results by the end of one week. The real challenge is building momentum and starting to change the way everyone thinks—which will change the future results. Pace, intensity, and follow-up are all important here. If you run one kaizen every six weeks going forward, you won't see much improvement in the bottom line and you won't convert many people. They will think of Lean as just another "program of the month" and do their best to ignore it. Think about two kaizens per week per facility. And the management pressure from the CEO and senior staff has to be intense. Changes won't always work the first time. Problems will pop up. The leaders need to solve them and move forward. Bit by bit you will convert your people and be able to get to a Lean culture.

UGH built on its early gains by rolling out an aggressive kaizen approach meant to get as many associates as possible on a kaizen team in the first year. It focused its early kaizen activity on the biggest value stream in its largest factory in Cleveland, Ohio. The plant managers from the other six factories joined kaizen teams at this location every six weeks and were asked to implement what they had learned in this model factory back in their own plants when they got home. As they stepped up their Lean work, the problems they faced and the customer service issues they caused went up exponentially at first. Machines they had never maintained well historically broke down frequently when they moved them into one-piece flow cells, shutting the entire cell down. The setup reductions and new flow cells didn't work as expected and caused late shipments to customers. To Jerry York's credit, UGH never wavered in its commitment. People dealt with and fixed the problems as they came up. To further build on the kaizen work and demonstrate UGH's commitment to its people, Jerry and his management team established UGH's first profit-sharing plan, which helped get all employees on board with the Lean turnaround.

Results in the first year were good compared to their original plan. Sales grew slightly, while EBIT was up $2.5 million (5 percent more than their original plan) and gross margin increased by half a point from 30.0 percent to 30.5. The biggest gain was a large reduction in inventory, which dropped by $37.7 million from their original plan. This in turn freed up about 30 percent of their floor space for future growth.

Getting Started with Focused Efforts

The first kaizens gave Jerry York and his team a good idea of the major improvements that were possible within UGH. Even Dick Conway, the CFO who fought so hard not to be on the kaizen team, became one of the company's most passionate advocates of Lean as a strategic approach and a key ally for Jerry York in his mission to convert UGH to a Lean enterprise.

Unfortunately, Dick Conway's new perspective was not widely shared among UGH employees. Even among Jerry's direct staff, only about 40 percent were excited about the potential of Lean and wanted to move forward. Most of the skeptics felt that Lean might be OK for others but couldn't see how it could apply to their department.

While normal, this type of behavior can't be tolerated. People's beliefs have to change before you will see a change in behavior. For UGH to be successful and for every person working at the company to see the commitment to Lean, the entire senior management group had to be on board and functioning as a single team. Without this visible commitment, it would be very difficult to deploy Lean down throughout the organization.

Fortunately, the most important person in making this happen, UGH's CEO, Jerry York, was very much on board. Jerry understood Lean as a strategy—not as a bunch of tools, a cost reduction program, or a series of events but as something to be deployed across the entire organization. It wasn't just "some manufacturing thing" that could be delegated down while everyone else stayed in their traditional batch approach. Jerry found that he still had his work cut out dealing with skeptical staff members from the next couple of management layers down. People at UGH had worked in a certain way for many years and were having trouble changing their ways. Jerry wasn't going to be dissuaded, but he knew he had a big task ahead, so he sought some advice when Art was in the Cleveland plant a month after the first kaizens. They were sitting in the lunchroom.

Jerry: Art, you don't have to persuade me anymore that we are doing the right thing. I am fully convinced that Lean is the right strategy for UGH—or anyone, for that matter. I really need help with one question: What is the best way to go about this moving forward? Now that we've enjoyed some success, it's becoming clear to me that making the Lean conversion is all about the people. But transforming this many people to a totally new way of thinking sometimes feels a little overwhelming. I still hear "this will never work here" and "but we are different from other companies" all the time. What do you suggest?

Art: Jerry, I have never seen a successful Lean turnaround that wasn't driven by the CEO. You have to be the Lean zealot and continually push forward no matter what setbacks you face along the way. And believe me . . . you will have setbacks. I'm thrilled that you understand that Lean has to be the strategy and that implementing this is all about people. At the same time, you have to keep your eye on the objective of delivering more value to your customers than your competitors consistently over time: this really applies to leveraging people as your resource. Let's take an example: you and I are competitors, and we both have 1,000 employees. You use only the top 35 to 50 of those employees to come up with all the improvement ideas, while I have every one of my 1,000 employees finding ways to eliminate the waste every day. I'm confident that over time I will crush you as a competitor.

Jerry: Yes, that makes enormous sense in theory. But how do I get all of my employees to be constantly looking for ways to remove the waste every day?

Art: Start with the fact that you need to create an atmosphere where there is consistent pressure to continuously improve. You don't want to be ruthless here. You just want to make sure everyone understands the urgency to improve and why. Setting stretch goals and making everyone aware that you are serious about reaching them goes a long way to change the conversation and attitude within the company. These aggressive goals need to be backed up, however, by a management system that supports and encourages improvement and learning every day. You can't become Lean without creating a learning organization. By this I mean putting people in roles where they have to become problem solvers. Removing the excess inventory step by step, for example, forces people to come up with new ways of working that remove the waste so they can live without the inventory.

Your structure, the way you are organized, is important, but finding ways to support the learning is far more important. We talked about creating a value stream (product family) structure with production cells formed by teams of five to seven operators, supported by cell leaders, with a supervisor layer above that. You have already created the value stream organizations; the rest will fall in place as you move everything from functional departments (batch) to production cells within a value stream (flow). Teams tend to naturally function better than individuals when it comes to solving problems and removing waste. Team members will support and encourage each other to reach goals, using a certain amount of social pressure and team rules to keep everyone focused.

Jerry York: What about kaizen events? I was impressed by the results we got from our first four teams. Shouldn't continuing these be a big part of how I convert people?

Art: Yes, you certainly want to make sure you continue doing them frequently. A pace of two kaizens per week per facility would be a good target to shoot for. Kaizen events are a great way to get momentum in the physical transformation from batch to flow. You are going to have to move almost all of your equipment—much of it multiple times—in order to do away with your functional departments and get to where everything is done in flow cells. Organized correctly, with the proper stretch goals, doing numerous kaizens is the best approach to both speed the conversion and impart learning—it's too confusing and in fact impossible to stay part batch and part flow for very long. As I told you before, Lean is a "learn by doing" methodology, and being on a kaizen team delivers a lot of learning in a short period of time.

Because of this, it is important that you and your management team continue to be on as many weeklong kaizens as you can each year. My suggestion would be four to six per year on an ongoing basis, but more in the first year. I would like to see you personally on a kaizen team for one week each month for the first year. I realize you are busy and have lots of "stuff" to do, but it is a question of priorities.

Jerry: It's a big commitment for sure, but it does make a lot of sense. So the main thrust should be kaizen, right?

Art: You have to be careful here, however. Kaizen events are great, but they are not the ultimate objective. You want to get to the point where everybody is doing kaizen every day. You need an environment where everyone can distinguish normal from abnormal and take immediate action to correct and permanently eliminate the problems as they are revealed. Think about the difference between Toyota and the other auto companies. The mantra at the non-Toyota companies was based upon line speed and "don't stop the line." Toyota, in contrast, focused first on quality. And a "stop the line" approach was developed as a way to ensure quality and build it into the product. The exact opposites. One seems to be pushing productivity, and the other quality. The problem of course is that you can't separate quality from productivity.

Jerry York: Thanks for making that distinction—I guess that I never really thought about it that way before. Most of my key managers and I were taught the U.S. auto companies' approach instead of Toyota's way. People just naturally want to push productivity first. I guess we never gave much thought to the fact that you can't separate quality from productivity.

Art: Well, it is actually even a little more sophisticated than that. In fact, what Toyota's line stop approach is really pushing is learning. Every time the line stops, the supervisor rushes to the spot of the problem. There is a conversation with the operator to determine what went wrong. A solution is implemented, and the line starts back up. The operator and the supervisor both learn something, and if the problem is big enough the engineers get involved. They are constantly coming up with solutions. Everyone, especially the operators, is asked to use the 5 Whys [asking "Why?" five times] to get at the root cause of the stoppages. Instead of "correcting" the defect after it occurs, they discover what made it happen and make the adjustment so that it never recurs. By doing this they are permanently solving a lot of problems every day. The line might stop over 100 times a day. Each time, problems are being solved and eliminated and everyone involved is learning. The line starts to run much smoother. It requires fewer people. Quality improves and productivity goes up. Everyone is becoming a problem solver. Operators are asked to come up with ideas that will improve quality and make their jobs easier. Waste is being eliminated through learning.

Jerry: What other approaches are really designed for learning?

Art: Well, asking the teams to constantly remove inventory is one of the best ways to promote learning. Inventory hides waste. Removing inventory forces every person to be involved. There's a positive tension now, because problems are no longer hidden, forcing people to deal with them as they occur. It is like the old saying of "lowering the water to see the rocks." The same with pull systems. A batch company likes to deliver a day's worth of inventory at a time (or at least a whole shift) to the line under the theory that this is less work for the material handler. This is false logic. The extra inventory just forces the value-adding operators to do more material handling, clutters up the shop floor, and, if something changes, results in shutting down the line while the old inventory is removed and new material is brought in. All waste. The Lean company, in contrast, schedules frequent deliveries of, say, every half hour or 15 minutes. This pace forces the operators and supervisors to solve problems to make the flow easy to accomplish. Another learning experience.

The same is true for adding inspection steps in an operation to ensure quality. The traditional company will set up a process to "inspect" quality into the product. The quality manager will be separate from the production manager, setting up some internal conflicts and adding another layer of costs without actually ensuring the quality. In a Lean company the idea is to never pass on a defective part to the next operator. In fact, you want a 100 percent quality inspection after every step to ensure that no bad product moves down the line. As problems are solved at the operator level, quality improves and so does productivity. You build in the quality, not inspect it in, and you don't need the extra overhead cost of a large quality bureaucracy.

Jerry: So frequent deliveries, 100 percent quality, and ever-decreasing inventories aren't just about operational goals—but a form of pressure to keep learning new ways to remove the waste. Are there other things I should be aware of?

Art: Tell you what, let's create a simple checklist for you to follow (see box).

Lean Implementation Checklist

- Create a value stream (product family) structure.
- Start with multiple kaizen events to shift from batch to flow physically.
- Use the kaizen events as a great source of hands-on training.
- Have the KPO and team leaders do weekly gemba walks to follow up on kaizen results and to-do lists.
- Establish visual control and daily management as each cell gets created.
- Provide shop floor supervisors and cell leaders with problem-solving training in 5 Whys and other tools.
- Provide operators with problem-solving training as well; the best way is "learn by doing."
- Have senior management participate on four to six full-week kaizen teams per year.

- When not on a team, senior staff should attend the kaizen kickoff, daily leader's meetings, and wrap-up presentations of kaizens that are under way.
- Create a suggestion program on ways to eliminate waste for all employees.
- Ask each cell leader to come up with one waste-eliminating idea per week.
- Make sure hour-by-hour production control charts are being kept up to date and countermeasures are in place to get back on track.
- Hold weekly update meetings for the value stream leaders to present their progress on UGH's five or six key operational excellence measurements to CEO and staff.
- You, your staff, and the team leaders need to constantly be on the shop floor checking the production control charts, observing the work, talking to people, and understanding how you can help and support them.
- Insist that the standard work be constantly improved upon.
- Set stretch targets that challenge people and make them think and learn.
- Take the leaps of faith required to get better.
- Never blame anyone for failure; in fact, encourage failure as a means of learning to get better.
- Get everyone on as many kaizen events as possible as soon as possible.
- Establish profit sharing so everyone can share in the gains.
- Conduct an annual employee survey and follow up on it with every team.
- Provide quality circle time for each cell team to discuss improvements.
- Screen new hires with a personality test that highlights teamwork skills.
- Never retreat—solve the problems and move forward.
- Constantly raise the targets to foster more learning and waste elimination.

Jerry: OK, OK, I get it. There is a lot to do! This is quite a list, and very helpful. Now, obviously we can't do all of this at once. Any ideas on that?

Art: Yes, focus your efforts. Start like we just did with the biggest value stream in the biggest plant. Create model lines and then a model factory. This will impact your financial results in a bigger way, and much faster, than if you spread the kaizens around. Instead, have the other plant managers attend one kaizen week, say every six weeks, in the model factory. Assign them to teams that are working on something similar to the work done in their plants. Then ask them to go home and implement something they learned in their own plant. Have them send you a video with their results. Go and see it. Congratulate them and then raise the bar.

The Board Meeting

A few weeks after UGH's initial kaizens, the board of directors held an executive session of all the outside directors. Jerry York was asked to leave the room. The board wanted Art's input on how things were going so far. They were especially interested in how Jerry York was responding as he had very little background in Lean.

Art: Well, as you know, the first four kaizens were very successful. All four teams beat their goals for the week. The more important thing is that with the help of an outside expert, we got the first 40 UGH employees (10 per team) engaged in Lean with a week of hands-on training. These first 40 kaizen participants included Jerry York and all of his direct reports along with the new value stream team leaders and a number of key thought leaders in the hourly workforce.

I was pleased to see how much progress the team made dealing with the inevitable skepticism that comes with this work. CFO Dick Conway, for example, really resisted being on a team doing kaizen at first, but once he went through it his eyes were really opened. He understood the strategic implications of setup reduction right away. Having him as a convert will be a big help to Jerry York going forward.

Board member: It is nice to hear that Dick seems to be an early convert. I always worry about the finance guys. They tend to be the biggest concrete heads. But what's your take on Jerry? Is he on board? Do you think he can lead the Lean conversion?

Art: I do. Jerry knows that we are going to convert UGH to Lean no matter what, so that may be a motivator. But more important, I truly believe that Jerry grasps the strategic aspects of Lean—not all CEOs see this at first, if ever. Jerry was hesitant at first, but after the first kaizen week he got fully on board.

Board member: What about the "respect for people" aspects of Lean?

Art: Actually, the bigger win for us is the fact that Jerry inherently understands that converting UGH from its traditional batch approach to Lean is all about people. He sees the real challenge not as running a bunch of kaizen events but converting every employee to the Lean way of seeing the work and trying to remove the waste every day. He also knows that he has to be hands-on and lead the conversion by his own example and that it won't happen overnight.

The best thing of all is that Jerry is just naturally good with people. He is not insecure or autocratic. He doesn't treat people differently because of their title or level of education. And so his employees feel comfortable around him. They can make suggestions and point out problems without fear of retribution. He will listen to everyone's input on ways to get better and take action to implement the good ideas. People know that he sees every associate as an equal member of the team. This allows him to point out problems or hand out stretch targets without anyone taking offense. This is a skill that is very hard to teach, so we are lucky that Jerry is a people person and leader, not a traditional top-down manager.

I will continue to work closely with Jerry to both guide him and keep the pressure on. Based on what I have seen so far, however, I think he and UGH will be very successful, and as a result so will we.

The First Six Months

Jerry followed Art's advice and set an aggressive kaizen schedule for the first year of UGH's Lean journey. UGH contracted with the external Lean consultant to do 20 weeks of kaizen consulting. As each consultant could mentor four teams per week, that meant that UGH could get 800 of its people on a consultant-led 10-member kaizen team during the first year. If each plant did 40 in-house kaizens per year, they could get another 2,800 people on a kaizen team during the first year (7 plants × 40 kaizens per plant). This would help UGH make the physical switch from batch to flow in as compressed a time frame as possible. The more important goal was to change the culture by teaching people how to look at the work differently.

UGH focused first on creating a model factory at its biggest facility in Cleveland, Ohio. Almost all of the kaizen work was done there for the first six months. The plant managers from the other six plants attended weeklong kaizens at the model plant every six weeks. They then ran kaizens in their own plants based on what they learned. The senior management team and the sales force participated in many of these early kaizens. Jerry York managed to free up his schedule enough so that he was on a weeklong kaizen every month for the first six months. He was learning so much so fast, he couldn't believe it. At the same time, he was starting to understand just how big an improvement opportunity there was for UGH. This knowledge helped him a great deal when things didn't go quite as planned. Instead of being cautious and slowing down the Lean implementation when problems arose, as many of his team members wanted him to do, his increasing understanding of the opportunity made him want to push ahead and go faster. And problems certainly did come up.

The Only Easy Day Was Yesterday

"The only easy day was yesterday" is a saying used by the Navy SEALs. Given what they do and the intensity of their training, it is easy to understand why this fits them so well. At the same time, it fits most businesses, especially manufacturing businesses where new challenges pop up every day. When you add in the rapid physical shift from batch to flow, the number of problems coming at you every day just multiplies. Machines that broke down frequently were hidden in the past by the batch nature of production and the excess amounts of inventory that covered up the problems. Move those same machines into one-piece flow lines and lower the inventory levels, and now you have a real problem. Everything stops. No Product A can get made. If one machine in a 10-machine cell stops, then the other 9 machines in the cell also stop. You have a crisis. Customers are yelling. Your traditional management team wants to stop this and go back to what they did before. Build more inventory! Lots of pressure.

The first six months were the hardest for Jerry as he encountered all of this and more. Things broke down all the time. People didn't follow the standard work. Suppliers didn't deliver on time or sent bad quality. Operators complained about the new one-piece flow cells and the fact that they had to work standing up. They also complained about having to run more than one machine and just about anything else you can think of. Sometimes when moving a machine from one place to another they broke something and had to send out for parts. This created more back-orders. You name it, it probably happened to UGH more than once during the first six months.

Jerry York was great. He wouldn't back off, choosing instead to focus on each problem as it came up. He organized the effort to get problems fixed and then moved on to the next issue. If machines were breaking down, manufacturing VP Frank Gee's team established total productive maintenance (TPM) programs to make sure that never happened again. If UGH had supply problems, both external and internal, Frank's team worked with the vendors to fix them. Management, Jerry included, spent a lot of time establishing standard work in the new cells and making sure the managers and operators were working together to establish and then improve it. Production control charts were put up at every cell that showed how the cell was doing compared to takt time on an hour-by-hour basis, with a list of reasons why the cell team was ahead or behind. Daily management meetings started the day at each cell to determine how the cell could get back on track. UGH was especially rigorous in its pursuit of 5S at each new cell. Progress was often slow. Customer service issues kept coming up. Some were just the result of all the machines being moved around and not enough safety stock being put in place. Others came from machine breakdowns or the new cells not being able to consistently meet their production goals.

One of the other key things UGH did during the first six months was to establish a profit-sharing program for all employees. Everyone in the company participated on the same basis, which greatly helped the sense of teamwork needed to implement and sustain Lean. It also was a big morale booster for everyone. They selected 12 percent of the pretax profit every month as the amount that would be shared with employees (see box). At Art's urging, Jerry York told all employees that he would like to get to the point where profit sharing was equal to 20 percent of everyone's normal pay. This was a significant amount and got everyone's attention.

The Profit-Sharing Discussion

Participants: Art Byrne, Jerry York, Judy Rankin, and Dick Conway

Art: As part of your Lean conversion, I want you to establish a profit-sharing plan for all employees. As you transition to Lean and someone who used to run one machine now runs eight different machines in a cell, it won't be long before they start asking "Hey, where's mine?"

Judy: Couldn't we just increase their base pay?

Art: You could, but that is a fixed cost, whereas profit sharing is variable. More important, profit sharing focuses everyone in the company on increasing profitability.

Dick Conway: What do you have in mind in terms of amount?

Art: Well, at Wiremold we shared 15 percent of the pretax profit.

Jerry: That seems like a lot. We only made $50 million EBIT last year. That would mean giving $7.5 million back to employees.

Art: It may seem high if you look at it that way. But if you look at it from where we are trying to go, you get a different view. We are trying to add $50 million in earnings. From that perspective, when UGH gets to $100 million in earnings, if it shares 15 percent, or $15 million, it still gets a gain of $35 million from where you are now plus an additional $60 to $70 million in cash freed up from inventory. So if it costs you $15 million to get about $100 million in extra earnings and cash flow and the money goes to the people who made it possible, isn't that a good deal all around?

Dick: It still seems pretty rich to me.

Art: Well then, do 10 or 12 percent. You can always increase the percentage, but you can never reduce it.

Dick: Well, it should be based on making or exceeding the budget.

Art: No, Dick, that would be a moving target, and people will just think you are playing games with them. Profit sharing should be very simple and always be from dollar one. If UGH makes a dollar, you share the dollar.

Dick: But Art, what if we make money in each of the first three quarters of the year and then lose more than what we made in the first three quarters in the last quarter? We shouldn't pay profit sharing then, should we?

Art: Dick, this is a "profit-sharing" program. It is not a "profit and loss sharing" program. You can't claw back money from your employees. Make it simple. People understand simple and will respond. If you make a dollar, share it.

Jerry: I think we get your point, but 15 percent still seems too rich. How about 12?

Judy: That sounds OK to me.

Dick: Well, I like 8 percent better, but I guess it is just because I'm the finance guy. If 12 percent is OK with Jerry and Judy, it's OK with me, too.

Art: Twelve percent going once, going twice, sold. We have a deal at 12 percent.

First Year Results

The results from the first year of Lean compared to the original forecast using the traditional management approach are shown below.

	2016 Traditional ($ millions)	2016 Lean ($ millions)
Sales	$568.0	$570.0
Gross profit	$170.4	$173.9
G.P. %	30.0%	30.5%

	2016 Traditional ($ millions)	2016 Lean ($ millions)
SG&A	$120.0	$121.0
EBIT	$50.4	$52.9
EBIT %	8.9%	9.3%
Inventory $	$116.9	$79.2
Inventory turns	3.4x	5.0x
Head count	6,242	6,000
Sales/head count	$91k	$95k

Sales grew slightly toward the end of the year as improved customer service and faster response times more than offset the customer service struggles UGH had early in the year as equipment was moving all over the place. In addition, having the entire sales force participate in weeklong kaizens early on sent them back to the field excited about what UGH was doing and what it would mean to their customers. Being salespeople, of course, they couldn't wait to tell their customers about their experiences on the kaizen and what the future held for them as loyal customers of UGH. We can't trace the slight sales rise just to this, but it certainly didn't hurt.

Increased productivity helped boost gross margins from 30.0 percent to 30.5 percent, and the dollars rose by $3.5 million. This would have been higher except for the absorption losses caused by the rapid drop in inventory. SG&A actually increased by $1 million. This was the result of a conscious effort on the part of management to prepare for faster sales growth as customer service and quality improved. It also reflected the outside kaizen consulting costs that were booked into these accounts. EBIT rose $2.5 million, or 5 percent, above the original forecast.

The biggest first-year gain came in inventory reduction, which fell from $116.9 million in the original forecast to $79.2 million actual, a decline of 32 percent ($37.7 million). This gain really helped Jerry York overcome the internal naysayers who were complaining about spending $1 million in outside consulting on kaizen. After all, cash on cash, he pointed out that spending $1 million and getting $37.7 million back in one year was a pretty good return on investment.

The bigger gains from Lean, however, were less obvious. First of all, the model factory freed up almost 50 percent of its floor space in the first year as the inventory was removed. This provided space for future growth at no cost. It also lowered the damage done to product as it was constantly moved in and out of inventory. The manpower needed to move it also went down, as did the carrying costs to have it. Lowering the inventory also got the factory much more in touch with the customer as opposed to the prior approach of just making a forecast that was based solely on an internal estimate. Above all, while the inventory reduction was valuable, the learning gained by the employees removing the waste was priceless.

Sales per employee rose slightly, from $91,000 to $95,000, on the productivity gains, and head count was lowered by 242 from the prior year, all through natural attrition.

In addition,, after six months of running both Lean and standard cost accounting, UGH made the complete switch to Lean accounting toward the end of the first year (see box).

Lean Accounting Discussion

The original discussion to make the change sparked resistance, but the argument to do so won everyone over and proved effective.

Dick Conway: Art, you can't be serious. Every manufacturing company I know uses standard cost accounting. Why should we change to something new that we don't really understand?

Jerry York: Well, I don't know how Art will respond, but I have to tell you that I don't understand the standard cost accounting that we have been using. There are all these variances that in the end don't tell you very much about what is happening. I'm not alone in this, by the way. It seems the only ones that understand all these variances are you guys in finance, and even then I'm not certain that you really do either.

Dick: But this is very straightforward. The variances are just differences from the assumptions we made when we put the budget together. The standard costs are figured out in detail for each product. Without these standard costs, how would we price our products?

Art: Dick, first of all, with the exception of finance, no one believes that your product costing is accurate. Listen to what you just said about "assumptions" and having a cost for each product "in detail." Your products costs "in detail" are actually based on assumptions. And it's even worse than that. Every element that goes into the calculation of the standard cost for each product contains estimates. As a result, your "detailed" standard product costs are nothing more than a series of compounded estimates, even though you calculate them out to four decimal places.

So the effort and cost to do this is all a waste. After all, the price for any product is set in the marketplace. Just blindly taking product costs that no one thinks are correct and marking them up by some percentage to arrive at product price will get you in nothing but trouble. Think about it this way: when you calculate that suggested selling price, you generally get one of two answers from marketing. The first might be "We can't sell it for that," which means they understand the market and what the customer is willing to pay. The second might be "Thanks," which means you gave them an answer that is lower than the number they had in mind and you left money on the table.

Dick: But you guys need to understand that there are IRS requirements as to how we have to report overhead into inventory. I don't think we can change that. Also, I'm sure our auditors will never let us switch away from standard cost accounting.

Art: Dick, congratulations, you managed to come up with all of the main excuses that every finance guy uses to hold on to his standard cost system. I have run into this many times before, and I can assure you that every one of your objections can be overcome. First, as you know, standard cost accounting is a management accounting system. It does not comply with either generally accepted accounting principles (GAAP) or the IRS regulations. The only thing that complies with both of those is actual cost. The way that you get from standard cost to actual cost is by capitalizing variances using a calculation based on inventory turns. As we continue to improve our turns of WIP and FG (finished goods) inventory, there is less labor and overhead to capitalize. And when we get to 12 turns or more, the amount to capitalize is one month of cost or less—and our current month's financial statements will tell us what that is. We have done this in many companies before, and neither the auditors or the IRS has had a problem with it. You will change the mechanics of how you meet the financial and tax rules but not the principle.

Dick: If we don't have detailed product costing for every SKU, I worry that we will lose control and not be able to see where the problems are.

Jerry: I have to admit this part scares me as well. We have always had product-by-product costing. Won't we lose some visibility?

Art: No, in fact you will gain visibility; it just will be at a higher level. As you move things into cells you will develop a clear idea of the material and labor for the products being made in each cell. And then at the product family or value stream level, you will also see the overhead for all of the products in the family. It will only be down to the gross margin line, as trying to allocate all your overhead cost on a product-by-product basis is an exercise in futility. Even so it will be a more accurate view of profitability than you have now. You can set your prices based on the market.

Jerry: Sounds like another of those "leaps of faith" you have been telling me about. So how do you suggest we go about this?

Art: The best approach is to introduce the new Lean accounting P&L, also referred to as the Plain English P&L, in parallel with your standard cost statements. Run them together for six months or so until you are comfortable that they both report the same revenue and profit and therefore are using the same accounting principles. The difference will be in how the costs are being reported in a simple manner that anyone can understand. I think you will find that by then no one will be looking at the standard cost statements anymore because the Lean statements will provide a much clearer picture of what is going on.

One last thing. The standard cost P&L shows an increase in gross profit, but it doesn't show the full results of all of the improvements you have made. This is because as you reduced WIP and FG inventory you had to reduce the amount of capitalized inventory on the balance sheet and, in accordance with GAAP, this was charged to income. In the standard cost P&L this is buried in the variances and is offsetting much of the benefit that you have achieved. In the Lean P&L the effects of this accounting rule are shown separately so that you can see the real benefits of your Lean work.

Converting to Lean accounting was a big hurdle—and a major accomplishment—for Dick Conway and his staff. The fact that no one outside of finance felt that their individual product costs were accurate helped, but once the Lean numbers started to run in parallel, no one wanted to look at the "variance" reporting anymore. Getting off of a system that rewarded the building of inventory, when one of UGH's major thrusts was to lower inventory and use the cash to grow the business, was a major step forward.

This was a good solid first year for UGH on its Lean journey. The main story was the inventory reduction and the number of associates who were able to participate in a kaizen and start to learn a new way to think about work, waste, and how to serve the customer better. The board was happy, and Jerry York was ecstatic.

He felt that he learned more in one year by being on 11 kaizen teams than he had in the past 25 years. He could really start to see the potential that still lay ahead for UGH and couldn't wait to get after it. Art felt that the results were just OK but the learning that was taking place from Jerry on down was a good sign for the future.

Summary Points

- You can't become Lean without creating a learning organization. By this I mean putting people in roles where they have to become problem solvers.
- Kaizen events are great, but they are not the ultimate objective. You want to get to the point where everybody is doing kaizen every day. You need an environment where everyone can distinguish normal from abnormal and take immediate action to correct and permanently eliminate the problems as they are revealed.
- The real purpose of Toyota's line stop approach is learning: instead of "correcting" the defect after it occurs, discovering its root cause and making the adjustment so that it never recurs.
- As problems are solved at the operator level, quality improves and so does productivity.
- While tangible results are invaluable, the learning that occurs through spotting and removing waste is priceless.

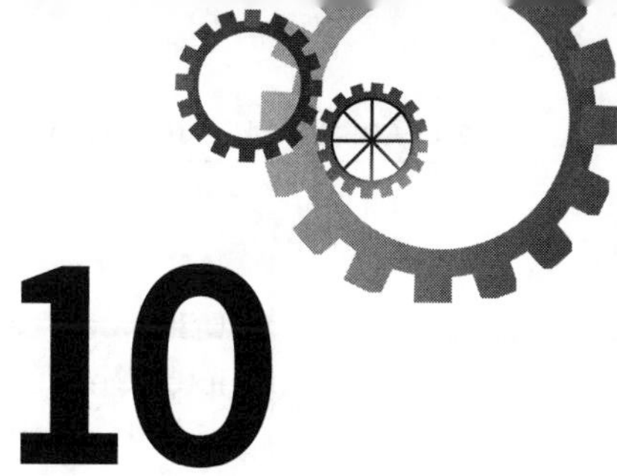

10

UGH'S Lean Journey, Years Two Through Five

OVERVIEW

Becoming a Lean enterprise takes time. It is a step-by-step process requiring change in the way everyone sees waste and thinks about work. Fortunately, UGH was quite successful, and the more the company accomplished, the more its leadership realized that they were only scratching the surface of what was possible.

Jerry York and his team continued their aggressive kaizen approach in years two through five. The problem of "out of service" tools was solved by setting up a secondary tool room to inspect each die after every run and make any repairs on the spot. Visual controls were established everywhere, office and factory. Job classifications were reduced from 60 to 6, providing the needed flexibility in the new cellular value stream structure. By the end of year two, inventory had been reduced by $55 million and earnings increased by $13 million. This generated the cash necessary to consider an acquisition, and in the middle of year three UGH purchased a smaller competitor with sales of $50 million. This strategic acquisition added new products and distribution channels that UGH could leverage with its existing distribution. The kaizen effort for this new acquisition began on the first day of UGH's ownership, and as a result it was quickly returning cash and enhancing UGH's ability to add other acquisitions in the future. UGH also took on the difficult issue of changing its sales terms to deliver more value to its customers. It also began delivering to its larger distributors on a weekly schedule, using dedicated UGH trucks. This was seen as valuable to the distributors, and, once established, UGH was able to get them to stop ordering in batches and just tell UGH what they sold every day.

UGH would convert this to an order and replenish it on the next truck. This allowed it to give a lot of cash back to its distributors (delivering customer value) by dropping the distributors' UGH inventory from four months to about three weeks.

At the end of five years, UGH's enterprise value using Lean was 2.4 times the value it would have achieved sticking with its traditional batch approach. The gains it got on the people and employee morale side of the equation were even more impressive. The people gains set UGH up to deliver even more value over the next five years.

Year Two

In year two, UGH continued down the same basic path. It increased the level of Lean consulting from 20 to 24 weeks. The initial Cleveland plant was still far from a model factory, so UGH continued to use outside consultants to help lead 12 weeks of kaizen in that plant. It added 8 weeks of this training in its second largest plant and 4 more in the third biggest facility. In addition, as each facility got more experienced at kaizen, it established a strong Kaizen Promotion Office (KPO) that enabled it to increase the number of internal kaizens that it ran.

One of the most encouraging trends over time was that a critical mass of practicing Lean believers was emerging. The leadership team went from "Gee, do I have to be on another kaizen?" to not wanting to miss them. The learning curve was steep for this group, especially when it came to learning how to think and act as a team. Jerry helped with the "learn by doing" aspect of this by encouraging input from his entire staff on every subject, whether it was in their area of expertise or not. Over time his team got used to discussing things this way. This led to better decisions and a stronger sense of teamwork.

Scott Smith: Now that we are all together in our staff meeting, I have a confession to make. When Jerry and Art first told us that we all had to be on kaizen teams, I thought it would be a waste of time. I couldn't understand how I could use this "manufacturing thing" in the sales force; I had no interest in what I might learn working in the plants for a week. Wow, was I wrong. Today we are using Lean in both the sales and inside sales departments to great effect. More important, every time I'm on a factory kaizen I learn more about our business and why we have to work together as a team.

Jerry York: Scott, these words are tremendously encouraging—thank you for sticking with this. What about the rest of you?

Judy Rankin: I think I can speak for the rest of the team on this, Jerry. At one time or another, pretty much each person has confided in me about how much they have been learning. The most important part, however, is how this has brought us together as a much stronger and more unified team. And this is not just among our management team. I spend much more time on the floor today than ever, and I know that throughout the entire organization, people are encouraged to see us working closely together and no longer pointing fingers at each other.

Jerry's leadership team realized early on that setup reduction and 5S are the foundational core of Lean. As a result and because UGH was largely a machine-based operation, they ran two setup kaizens, a flow kaizen, and an office kaizen each time they had an outside consultant. They kept this type of balance for their internal kaizens. Kurosaki made it clear to them that without reducing setup times there could be no flow and no pull. It also became clear that if people didn't have the basic discipline to do 5S, then it would be almost impossible to have the discipline to do kaizen. In fact, UGH's small gear factory was in such disarray that leaders were told they had to spend six to eight months just implementing 5S before the plant would be allowed to do any kaizen. Jerry said he was too embarrassed to even let the outside consultants into their factory until it was cleaned up. They got the message.

Jerry: [*to Sam Watson, president of UGH Small Gears*] Sam, there's no other way to say this: your plant is a mess. Before we started our Lean journey, I would never really have thought about this, but now it just jumps out at me. You have inventory everywhere; there is no organization; there are safety hazards galore; the floors, walls, and equipment are dirty; and it looks like a cave in here. I know you want to get the outside consultants in here to help, but quite frankly, I'm embarrassed to let them see this mess. I want you to spend the next six to eight months just implementing 5S here and getting this place cleaned up. If you don't have enough discipline to do 5S, then you will never be able to do kaizen. Do you understand?

Sam: Yes, boss, I get it. I guess I just accepted the way the factory has always looked because I've always been focused on getting the product out the door. I never thought that *how* you get it out the door is just as important. I promise you that you won't even recognize this plant on your next visit.

The hoshin planning that was introduced in year one became more formal and detailed in year two. Updates from the hoshin teams were incorporated in the weekly value stream leader's report-out meetings. This helped with the allocation of resources and, more important, kept everyone on top of where UGH stood on achieving the key objectives. The value stream leaders still reported weekly on the five key value drivers:

- 100% on-time customer service
- 20% productivity gain each year
- 50% reduction in defects each year
- 20x inventory turns
- Establishing visual controls and 5S everywhere

These goals kept everyone focused on delivering value to the customer while at the same time improving internal results. It oriented the entire UGH team to look forward not backward (as they once did in their "make the month" management days). This may seem simple, but it had a profound effect.

At the weekly value stream team leader's meeting, Jerry York reviewed UGH's current state.

Jerry: OK, this was a pretty good meeting, but we have many follow-up items. Product family teams two and five are falling behind on their inventory turns, and team one is having quality and productivity problems. In addition, it sounds like hoshin team three is running behind on its new product development. What are we going to do to help them?

Ellen Minor (VP of marketing): Team three needs a few more resources; we are addressing this by switching people over from a couple of teams that are ahead. We have scheduled a detailed review for early next week to get back on track.

Frank Gee: We have a full kaizen planned for team one next week to address the productivity and quality issues. We know the key problem areas, so I think this kaizen should be able to eliminate them. The KPO leader Jim Boots and I will be working with the other two teams on their inventory problems.

Jerry: Sounds good. I expect to see better results at next week's meeting.

As part of UGH's setup reduction program it established a secondary tool room in close proximity to the production floor. Each tool coming off a production run would pass through this tool room and be opened, inspected, and, if necessary, repaired. This took some time to establish but eventually eliminated any excuses that UGH couldn't respond to a customer need because a die was broken and waiting in a queue to be fixed. UGH also established a couple of full-time die makers to do nothing but rebuild existing dies to get them to a common shut height in order to facilitate quick changeovers.

Visual controls were set up everywhere, office and factory, which revealed to the team leaders, supervisors, cell leaders, and associates how important they were for problem solving. Senior and middle management learned that they had to stop and look at the visual control boards as they walked through the factory or office. The cell teams were proud of their ability to make takt time; the fact that senior management could look at the visual control boards and immediately recognize their good work was both appreciated and motivational.

Transform the People

Throughout all the equipment moves and the calculation of takt time and shifts in virtually everything UGH did, Art kept reminding Jerry and his team that Lean was "all about people." To beat the other guy, then, you had to hire, train, retain, and grow the best people. You had to in effect create a learning environment in which your people could constantly grow.

It took a little while, but Jerry York and his team embraced the principle of putting people first in thinking about Lean. An annual top-10, bottom-10 review for all of their people was implemented. Each member of Jerry's staff had to present to the other staff members the top and bottom 10 percent of the people in his or her organization on an annual basis. The top 10 percent had to have a growth plan in place to move them onward and upward in the company. The bottom 10 percent were asked to create an improvement plan to get them out of the bottom 10 percent. Just becoming aware of their status motivated almost everyone in the bottom 10 percent to improve. They got better, and the whole workforce spiraled upward in value and capabilities. UGH almost never had to fire anyone. Those who didn't want to improve tended to leave on their own. UGH's people asset kept appreciating at a rapid pace.

Jerry and Judy made sure there was a high level of communication about what the company was doing. They shared results and challenges with the workforce at the quarterly profit-sharing meetings. Kaizen results were publicized and celebrated. When a kaizen freed up people, the best people from that area would be reassigned to other jobs, as a promotion where possible. An annual employee survey was initiated and followed up on with face-to-face meetings with each team.

Judy: Jerry, I've got the results from our first employee survey. There are many questions and issues to be addressed. We need to do this team by team, so I have set up a tentative schedule that I think matches your availability. I know it is a lot of meetings and time on your part, but the survey will be useless unless we address every issue.

Jerry: No problem, I fully agree. Everyone deserves an honest answer to every question they have raised. I see this as a high priority. While we are discussing people, how are we doing on selecting team leaders and coleaders for the next set of kaizens? I see this as a key learning experience for our associates, and it seems like we keep uncovering a lot of hidden talent each time we pick these leaders.

Judy: Yes, we have had many positive surprises. Our whole staff team is pitching in with suggestions on potential leaders and making sure they free them up when we need them. I believe that we have a backlog of potential leaders and coleaders at this point.

Jerry York: Great; having good leaders and coleaders really helps us achieve our kaizen stretch goals.

UGH used the kaizens to provide leadership opportunities for people to be leader or coleader of the kaizen team. This exposed talent that might otherwise have been missed. Setting and maintaining stretch goals helped greatly in facilitating the learning environment. People had to learn, for example, how to lower inventory and still increase customer service. Many learned new skills through cross-training when they were moved into different jobs. Quality circles and daily management meetings were all learning experiences, as was responding to the problems shown on the hour-by-hour production control charts. Rotating people in and out of the KPO, team leader, or even cell leader roles created other learning opportunities. Everyone in the company came to see their core job to be learning the fundamentals of Lean and waste removal.

As production was reconfigured to one-piece flow cells and away from functional batch departments, associates learned to operate multiple machines instead of the single type of equipment they were responsible for in their functional areas. This of course created problems due to the prior job classification system. Before kaizen, UGH had approximately 60 job classifications. It became apparent very quickly that only 5 or 6 were needed with the new approach. Cell workers needed to be able to do every job in the cell, so flexibility became more important than rigid job classifications. People approached this step by step and slowly brought the job classifications in line with the new way of working. They were careful along the way to not reduce anyone's pay even if people were asked to work in jobs that formally carried a lower classification and pay rate. Over time this tended to increase associates' pay, but it was more than offset by their greater flexibility and productivity. All associates gained new skills and thus became more valuable.

The results for year two versus the prior traditional management approach are shown below:

	2017 Traditional ($ millions)	2017 Lean ($ millions)
Sales	$588.0	$592.8
Gross profit	$178.2	$192.7
Gross profit %	30.3%	32.5%
SG&A $	$124.2	$125.8
EBIT	$54.0	$66.9
Inventory	$124.2	$61.6
Inventory turns	3.3x	6.5x
Head count	6,323	5,646
Sales/employee	$93k	$105k

These results were much more dramatic than in the first year, particularly in earnings. Sales were $4.8 million (1 percent) higher than the traditional forecast, but gross profit was up 8 percent from the original forecast due to the productivity gains that were being achieved everywhere. Gross margin went from 30.3 percent to 32.5. This was helped by the fact that the absorption drag from inventory reduction was much less.

SG&A spending was again higher than the traditional forecast by $1.6 million due to the Lean consulting and to more sales and marketing to help grow the top line. The higher gross margins allowed for this increase in sales and marketing spending. EBIT rose 24 percent from $54.0 in the traditional forecast to $66.9 in the actual Lean results.

Despite the earnings gain, inventory was still the star of the show in year two. It declined by only $17.6 million, or 22 percent, but ended up being less than half of the inventory level forecast in the traditional approach. In fact, it was $62.6 million lower ($124.2 versus $61.6). And of course this came with the usual array of hidden cost benefits of less space, lower carrying costs, lower costs to move and track the inventory, lower inventory obsolescence costs, and more.

These productivity gains led to a 6 percent reduction in staffing from the prior year—all of which was achieved through normal attrition (no layoffs). The difference in head count versus the traditional forecast was much more dramatic. The drop here was 11 percent, or 677 people, which was a big factor in the 13 percent gain in sales per employee from $93,000 in the traditional case to $105,000.

Years Three Through Five

UGH continued to run an aggressive kaizen program over the next three years. It continued to employ a steady 24 weeks per year of outside consulting but greatly increased the number of internal kaizens run by its various KPOs. Senior management still participated on five or six kaizens per year and was active in leading the charge.

Management understood, however, that while kaizen events were helpful to make rapid change and expose everyone to a new way of thinking, they weren't the real objective. The real goal was to get every employee working to remove waste every day. The suggestion program that was launched toward the end of the first year was starting to pay dividends. More and more employees were submitting their ideas, and projects were being implemented. People spent an enormous amount of time teaching the supervisors and cell leaders problem-solving skills and helping them understand their roles as supporters and facilitators for the hourly workforce to encourage their waste removal efforts. Daily management meetings were conducted in every area to discuss problems and implement solutions. Quality circles were initiated in the cell teams to eliminate more waste. The hoshin planning process overlaid the whole thing and made sure that (a) everyone was on the same page and (b) UGH's limited resources were being properly allocated and only the projects it could properly resource were on the "must-do can't-fail" list.

The Acquisition

A couple of months into year three an acquisition opportunity came up. This was a company, AB Housings Inc., that competed with UGH in some product lines and had other products and distribution channels that would fit well with UGH strategically. The company had $50 million in sales on an annual basis. It had similar margins and inventory turns to UGH, with a faster top-line growth rate. It was a family-owned company that had put itself up for sale after the founder retired. That meant that it would be an auction and UGH would have to compete against a couple of its biggest competitors.

Jerry York, Scott Smith, Ellen Minor, and Dick Conway met to discuss the opportunity.

Jerry: We have an opportunity to buy this company, but it will be an auction. We will be up against our two largest competitors, plus one or two financial sponsors. That means that to win we will have to pay a higher price than anyone else. What do you all think?

Scott Smith: Strategically this would be a great fit for us. It has great products and would get us into a couple of new distribution channels that we could leverage with our existing products.

Dick Conway: A few years ago I would probably vote no . . . but our new Lean approach gives us a tremendous advantage here. We know that we can recoup a major portion of our cash in just a few years by simply improving its inventory turns. In addition, we should be able to significantly improve its quality and productivity. That in turn will lead to higher sales growth and better margins. Our competitors, well, they can't do this. So we can safely bid higher than they do without putting ourselves at risk. Besides, we have already freed up enough cash to easily handle the purchase price.

Jerry: I agree. Without Lean, this would have been a hard one for us, but given where we are today, this is almost a no-brainer. Besides, I already have backing from Art and his partners.

After two years of Lean, UGH had freed up $55 million in cash and added another $13 million in earnings, providing the financial wherewithal for the auction. The leaders also knew that Lean provided the cash and lowered the risk, giving them a clear game plan for how to proceed once the acquisition was complete. All of this allowed them to bid higher without adding extra risk. In the middle of year three, UGH paid $40 million to acquire this competitor. This was a great way to put its "sleeping money" previously tied up lying around in excess inventory to a more productive use.

At Art's urging, UGH leaders moved quickly once the acquisition was complete. It closed late on a Friday afternoon. On Monday morning Jerry York, Dick Conway, Frank Gee, and Judy Rankin were at the new company bright and early. They first met with the management team to get acquainted and explain their plan for the week. By 9 a.m. they called in the entire workforce and held a meeting to introduce themselves and UGH. This was fairly brief and was followed by a two-and-a-half-hour introductory training session on Lean conducted by Jerry York.

Jerry: That completes your brief introduction to Lean. I tried to give you the basics, but Lean is something that you can only learn by doing. As a result, we will start our first kaizens here right after lunch. I will lead one team, and Frank Gee, our VP of operations, will lead the other. I have put the names of the team members up here on the board, including a leader and coleader for each team.

By late that afternoon they were moving equipment and creating new, more efficient work flows. By the end of the week they had created a couple of model lines with half the number of people required (the extra workers were redeployed to other tasks), 50 percent less space, 90 percent less inventory, and 85 percent shorter lead times. Before they left they scheduled the next kaizens for one month later. More important, they left with everyone at the new acquisition having a clear understanding of their new direction and a taste of what it might be like. Lean was providing a clear game plan for everyone.

Pull

During this period UGH had to address the challenge of creating a uniform pull system for the company.

Jerry: Scott, we seem to be having some issues with our customers regarding deliveries. Can you give us some more detail?

Scott: Our customers want to place one order and get it all in one delivery. With seven factories in different parts of the country, the only way to do this is to consolidate product into our two warehouses and ship it complete from there. The only way we can do this currently is to carry excess inventory, as our factories don't seem to be keeping up in a uniform way and we are having a lot of stock-outs.

Jerry: Yes, I hear this from our distributors all the time. Frank, what is the problem, and what should we do about it?

Frank: Well, the factories see the orders in a different way. They have each developed rudimentary pull systems, but we don't have a uniform system for the whole company. We need to develop one if we want to be able to increase inventory turns and improve customer service at the same time.

Jerry: Sounds like we need to put a hoshin team together to make this happen. Where should we take the pull signal from?

Frank: The best place would be to take it directly from the order entry system. This way we can drop the orders directly on the production cells as they come in throughout the day. This should give us the quickest turnaround time and the best customer service.

Developing a uniform kanban card was the easy part. Next they had to determine how many kanban cards needed to be in the system for each SKU and to develop a methodology for how to update the number of cards on a regular basis. They chose a bimonthly review to start with. Once they determined how much product made up each kanban card (it varied from a whole pallet's worth to partial pallets down to 12 to 48 boxes worth), they had to determine where the signal to build the product would come from.

After much debate and trial and error, they settled on Frank Gee's original suggestion and utilized the incoming order system to generate the kanban cards and print them at the cell throughout the day. Once the orders for a given product reached the kanban quantity for that product, the kanban card would print at the cell. This would trigger the product being made shortly thereafter and sent on its way to the warehouse. The warehouse would also see the incoming order and use it to pull product from the shelves and send it on the way to the customer. In this way they were able to introduce the customer directly to the plant floor and stop building to a forecast. This allowed the workers in every cell to feel the pull of the customer on an hour-by-hour basis throughout the day. It put the customer front and center in everything they did. They still needed to do production planning, but it was more of a capacity planning function, including frequent adjustment of the number of kanban in the system and how to deal with large orders, than it was the traditional approach of creating a set production plan based on an internal forecast.

Delivering Customer Value

The UGH team learned in the initial order entry kaizen that being customer-driven didn't mean just doing whatever the customer wanted and then patting yourself on the back and saying, "We are customer driven." But what did it mean? They had a large number of small-volume products, not the traditional 80-20 type of mix. As they got better and better at creating flow and responding to the pull of the customer, they learned that the customer, or more specifically the way the customer ordered, was creating most of their problems. In effect, the customer was an obstacle to their ability to deliver more value to the customer.

Jerry: Well, getting a uniform pull system in place will certainly help us deliver more customer value. But it seems to me that the way customers order is an even bigger problem. They all order at the end of the month, so we wind up shipping 45 to 50 percent of our monthly shipments in the last week. That completely negates our Lean thrust to level load the factories. Why do they do that? It can't be good for them, either.

Scott: The problem is our sales terms. We offer a 2 percent cash discount for goods ordered by the twenty-fifth of the month if you pay by the tenth of the following month. This in effect gives the distributor 45 days dating but forces most of his orders into the last week of the month.

Jerry: Why don't we just change the sales terms and have them pay us twice per month? That would help to level out the incoming orders and in turn allow us to provide much better customer service.

Scott: That makes a lot of sense, Jerry, but these are pretty much industry sales terms. Our distributors will scream bloody murder if we force this on them.

Jerry: OK, then, let's give them a choice. They can have a 5 percent cash discount if they pay us twice per month, or they can choose to stay with their current 2 percent discount.

Dick: This sounds expensive. But if we can do a simultaneous price increase of 5 percent, the extra discount won't hurt us. Can we package that together, Scott?

Scott: Yes, I think so. There still will be a lot of complaining, but my guess is that they will all pick the higher discount terms.

Jerry: Let's go with that. That said, make it clear that we are making this move to increase our ability to deliver more value to them going forward. In order to do that we need to level out the incoming demand, and then we can give it back to them in inventory reduction.

The distributors did complain about this, but when forced to choose, they all took the new sales terms and paid twice per month. This flattened out the incoming order rate dramatically and allowed UGH to provide much better customer service.

While the new sales terms got rid of the big month-end shipping spike, incoming demand was still uneven. This was because the distributors all ordered from their own MRP systems and tended to order three to four months' worth of product at a time. With many low-volume products, this still created lumpy demand for UGH. The first step in addressing this was to create a delivery system for the bigger distributors that was reliable and predictable. Here UGH followed a more traditional pattern where 20 percent of the distributors accounted for about 80 percent of the volume. UGH therefore was able to create a series of truck routes so that each of these large distributors received delivery on a specific day and time each week, such as between 10:30 a.m. and noon on Tuesday. For some of the biggest distributors they had delivery scheduled for two days per week. The truck routes differed every day.

To ensure full truckloads, there were a number of additional distributors on each route that were easy to reach and could be added on if need be to get a full truck without disrupting the delivery windows of the bigger distributors. The distributors on these routes were told that everything they ordered by noon on Tuesday would be on their regular Thursday delivery (or everything they ordered by noon on Monday would be on the truck on Wednesday, etc.). It took a while to work this all out, but UGH was able to hit the delivery windows 100 percent of the time (except in severe blizzard conditions). Once the distributors got used to this, they loved it and gave UGH lots of compliments. This was delivering more value.

Jerry: Well, changing our sales terms really helped to flatten out our incoming orders and improve our efficiency. This helped us in implementing the new weekly delivery routes. I'm getting a lot of great feedback from our distributors about that. They love the reliability. But we need to take the next step.

Scott: Well, of course we do. What exactly do you have in mind?

Frank: All of our distributors order off their own MRP systems, and when they do they tend to order three to four months' worth of any given SKU at a time. This causes lumpy demand for us. It also results in high inventory for our distributors.

Jerry: I bet most of them carry three to four months' worth of our product in inventory.

Scott: It is probably closer to four months than three months.

Jerry: This doesn't have to be this way. We can deliver reliably to them every week at a set time, and they love that. So what we need to do is to get them to stop ordering on their MRP system. Instead they can just tell us what they sold every day so that we can convert that to an order and put it on their next truck. This will allow us to deliver a ton of value to them in the form of cash—they should be able to reduce the amount of our inventory they hold from three to four months to, say, three weeks. If we can get them to invest a portion of this cash into carrying more of our SKUs, then we can probably help them increase sales and profitability as well. They would become known as the best UGH distributor in their market.

While the reasons for giving up their MRP systems made sense to the owners of the distributorships, it was still a difficult transition. Even after a successful switch the distributor would often revert, as someone in the organization would suddenly order four months' worth of everything. UGH would reject the order and then have to go back to the owner and get it back on track. For those which did convert, the results were outstanding. Not only did they pocket significant cash and free up space from the inventory reduction but the expanded line of UGH's products allowed them to increase sales by an average of 8 percent each year and expand their profitability by 17 percent.

As part of the customer focus, UGH's people kept going back to the same machines and cells to do kaizen over and over. The first setup reduction kaizen may have gotten them from 2 hours down to 15 minutes. The next kaizen took them to 8 minutes. They went back again and got it to 4 minutes and finally settled out at around 2 minutes. The same was true for the flow cells, where they kept returning for more kaizen, going from, say, seven operators to five and then down to two—with the same output but better quality and almost no inventory. This was all just part of the Lean journey. The better they got internally, the more value they could deliver to the customer externally.

Starting in the middle of year three, UGH started serious kaizen activity in both of its warehouses. The main thrust was to change from the traditional method of picking by order to picking by size and time. For example, leadership divided the warehouse into sections based on product size and then determined how many picks an operator could do in a 10-minute time cycle in each of these areas. The work was then handed out by area in 10-minute time intervals. It of course required a consolidation step at the end to get the product back together by customer. This step allowed for a 200 percent quality check (the picker and the consolidator). Even after adding this consolidation step, picking this way was 30 to 40 percent more efficient and shipping errors dropped by over 90 percent.

The Results

When considering results, we have to think of it in two distinct buckets: the financial results and the more important people results. After all, the people are the ones who will determine the future results. So, while the financial results after five years might look good, the growth in the people is the truer measure of success.

Financial Results

At the end of the first five years UGH had made dramatic progress. The original forecast as a traditional batch company is shown in Figure 10-1 and reflects a forecast of steady improvement. Sales grew at a compound rate of 3.6 percent, gross margin increased by almost a full point from 30.1 to 31.0 percent, EBIT increased by 27 percent to $64.1 from $50.4, inventory turns rose from 3.3 to

United Gear and Housing Corporation
Traditional Batch Version
$ millions

	A 2013	A 2014	A 2015	F 2016	F 2017	F 2018	F 2019	F 2020	2015–20 AAGR%
Sales	$512.0	$532.0	$550.0	$568.0	$588.0	$609.0	$632.0	$657.0	3.62%
Gross Profit	152.6	159.6	165.6	170.4	178.2	185.1	193.4	203.7	
Percentage	29.8%	30.0%	30.1%	30.0%	30.3%	30.4%	30.6%	31.0%	
SG&A	106.5	110.8	115.2	120.0	124.2	128.5	133.6	139.6	3.9%
	-	-	-	-	-	-	-	-	
EBIT	$46.1	$48.8	$50.4	$50.4	$54.0	$56.6	$59.8	$64.1	4.9%
%	9.0%	9.2%	9.2%	8.9%	9.2%	9.3%	9.5%	9.8%	
Inventory	$108.9	$116.4	$116.5	$116.9	$124.2	$124.7	$129.0	$129.5	
Inv Turns	3.3	3.2	3.3	3.4	3.3	3.4	3.4	3.5	
Headcount	5,689	5,911	6,111	6,242	6,323	6,344	6,449	6,257	3.1%
Sales/Employee	90k	90k	90k	91k	93k	96k	98k	105k	

Figure 10-1. Traditional batch forecast

United Gear and Housing Corporation
Lean Results
$ millions

	A 2013	A 2014	A 2015	A 2016	A 2017	A 2018	A 2019	A 2020	2015–20 AAGR%
Sales	$512.0	$532.0	$550.0	$570.0	$592.8	$622.4	$659.8	$706.0	5.1%
Acquired Sales	-	-	-	-	-	25.0	55.0	60.5	-
Total Sales	$512.0	$532.0	$550.0	$570.0	$592.8	$647.4	$714.8	$766.5	6.7%
Gross Profit	152.6	159.6	165.6	173.9	192.7	216.9	246.6	272.1	
G.P. %	29.8%	30.0%	30.1%	30.5%	32.5%	33.5%	34.5%	35.5%	
SG&A	106.5	110.8	115.2	121.0	125.8	137.1	149.2	157.3	6.4%
	-	-	-	-	-	-	-	-	
EBIT	$46.1	$48.8	$50.4	$52.9	$66.9	$79.8	$97.4	$114.8	17.9%
EBIT %	9.0%	9.2%	8.9%	9.3%	11.3%	12.0%	14.0%	15.0%	
Inventory	$108.9	$116.4	$116.5	$79.2	$61.6	$61.2	$50.6	$44.9	
Inv Turns	3.3x	3.2x	3.3x	5.0x	6.5x	7.0x	9.3x	11.0x	
Headcount	5,689	5,911	6,111	6,000	5,646	5,912	5,736	5,845	
Sales/Employee	90k	90k	90k	95k	105k	110k	125k	131k	

Figure 10-2. Lean results

3.5, and sales per employee increased by 17 percent from $90,000 to $105,000. Not blowing the doors off, but a pretty solid performance by traditional batch standards.

The actual Lean results are shown in Figure 10-2. As you might expect, these are significantly different. Sales grew by a compound annual rate of 5.1 percent before the acquisition and 6.7 percent after the acquisition. Not an earth-shattering increase over the traditional case, but by year five, UGH's actual sales, thanks in part to the acquisition, were $109.5 million higher. Gross margin increased from 30.1 to 35.5 percent, and EBIT was up 128 percent from $50.4 to $114.8. This was despite the fact that in year five UGH could afford to spend $17.7 million more in SG&A, most of which was in sales and marketing, to drive the top-line sales. This was starting to show by year five as UGH's actual sales increased by 7.2 percent that year versus their original forecast of 4 percent. Inventory turns increased to 11x in year five vs. the 3.5x in the original forecast. This meant that UGH carried $84.6 million less in inventory in year five than the original forecast ($94.1 million less on an apples-to-apples basis to allow for the $9.5 million in inventory that came with the acquisition). Sales per employee rose from $90,000 to $131,000. This meant that UGH required 412 fewer heads at the end of five years than the original plan (912 fewer heads when adjusting for the 500 heads that came with the new acquisition).

Other key measurements improved dramatically as well. On-time customer service rose from its historical levels of 89 percent to 98 percent. The defect rate as measured by customer returns or complaints was cut from 2.3 percent to 0.5 percent. More important, lead times dropped from the prior six-week levels to two to three days. This gave UGH a great advantage in the marketplace as it became known as the industry's most reliable supplier, the go-to supplier whenever the competitors had a slight hiccup. In addition, it was able to use some of the freed-up cash and higher earnings to invest in better and more rapid new product development. This helped establish UGH as the industry leader in new products. UGH was poised for much faster sales growth from year six onward as it started to take more and more market share. It was benefiting from managing forward using Lean versus the managing backward of its old "make the month" days.

Valuation

As shown, UGH's faster growth rate and higher margins, along with its strong cash flow characteristics due to its higher inventory turns, allowed it to command a higher exit multiple (8.0 times versus 6.5 times) than it would have under its traditional batch approach.

Valuation

2020 EBIT × 6.5 multiple, traditional case = \$64.1 × 6.5 =	\$416.7 million
2020 EBIT × 8.0 multiple, Lean case = \$114.8 × 8.0 =	\$918.4 million
Plus cash freed up from inventory = \$129.5 – \$44.9 =	\$84.6 million
TOTAL Lean case =	\$1,003.0 million

In addition UGH freed up \$84.6 million in cash from inventory, which has to be added to the total. As a result, the actual UGH results using Lean were 2.4 times higher—or \$586.3 million more than would have been realized under the traditional approach. More important, UGH was poised for much faster growth and even better results over the next five years due to the people growth it created.

People Results

Art Byrne: Jerry, at the five-year point you have good financial results, but I am more interested in where you think you are in terms of what we could call people results. After all, five years is still the early stages for most Lean turnarounds. Where you go from here will be determined by how far you have come in developing your people. That's why I wanted to have a brief in-person review with you on this subject.

Jerry: Thanks for taking the time to come to Cleveland to meet with us on this subject. We think we have a good story to tell, but as always we value your opinion. To give you as broad a perspective on this as possible, I've asked Judy Rankin and Barbara Mooney to join me. Judy, can you get us started?

Judy: Thanks, Jerry, and welcome, Art. It is nice to see you. Let's start with training:

Lean Training to Date

- Run 1,120 kaizen events so far.
- Every employee has been on at least one kaizen.
- Every midlevel manager or higher has been on 10 or more kaizens.

- Jerry's staff members have all been on at least 25 kaizens.
- Every employee has received problem-solving training.
- All new hires get a three-day course in Lean principles.
- We have initiated an employee suggestion program.
- We have regular quality circles at the cell level and in the office.
- We have a biweekly 5S inspection team with rotating members.

People Advancement / Skills Enhancement

- Reduced 60 job classifications to 6 while broadening the skill base of everyone.
- Top 10/bottom 10 annual review creates development plans for all.
- Personality test for new hires and promotions avoids misplacement.
- When workers are freed up through kaizen, select the best for retraining.
- Cycled 80 individuals through KPOs and out with promotions.
- Promoted 20 people into team leader roles.
- 30 cross-training promotions, e.g., sales to manufacturing or vice versa.
- 40 people have had hoshin leader opportunities.
- 820 people have had kaizen leader/coleader opportunities.
- 90 people have had a weeklong training trip to Japan.
- 55 hourly employees promoted to salary or supervisor roles.
- We have lost almost no one we didn't want to lose.
- 92 percent of our people own UGH stock through our 401(k) stock matching.

Culture and Morale

Jerry: I'm going to let Barbara Mooney talk about this one as she has been with UGH for over 30 years and knows just about everyone here in our two Cleveland plants, which are our largest ones. By the way, Barbara was recently promoted to a salaried position in our Kaizen Promotion Office.

Art: Well, congratulations, Barbara, I think that is great and well deserved. So now when you find something that you don't like or want to complain about, you're in a position to initiate a kaizen and solve the problem.

Barbara: Thanks, Art, but it was a bit easier when all I had to do was complain. Getting rid of the waste is more fun but much harder. I have to admit I wasn't too sure about this Lean stuff at first. Like when you took away all the chairs in the factory and made all the jobs standing jobs, or outlawing food, drinks, and music in the plant as part of the 5S program. That certainly created some early griping. But that is all behind us now, and we can all see that the pluses far outweigh the negatives. In fact, I have never seen the morale at UGH higher than it is right now, and I think it is still going up. Let me give you a short list of the reasons why:

- Establishment of a simple, easy-to-understand profit-sharing program
- Honest communication at quarterly profit-sharing meetings
- Starting the employee suggestion program
- Including hourly employees on every kaizen team
- Training every employee in problem solving
- Actually listening to and implementing our ideas
- Creating the employee association and giving us space to build a gym
- Turning UGH into a place where everyone can learn every day
- Holding daily management meetings and quality circles
- Initiating the annual employee survey

All of these have combined to make a big difference. UGH is now a place where people enjoy coming to work every day. They tell their relatives and friends as well, so we always have a ready list of replacements should someone quit or retire.

Management Changes

Judy: Thanks, Barbara. Now I'm going to turn it over to Jerry to talk about management changes that we have made.

Jerry: This is a shorter list, but I think the changes are significant.

- Run the company based on weekly team leader/senior staff reviews of progress of our key operational excellence goals.
- All key goals are stretch goals.
- Hoshin planning sets the direction and is deployed down to every level.
- Daily management and visual controls are established everywhere.
- Senior management functions as one single team.
- CEO and all senior leaders have an open-door policy.
- High level of openness and communication to all employees.
- Management approach is "Go see."

Art: Wow, that was a great review. You seem to be making progress in all the right areas. I guess you were really listening when I told you that a Lean turnaround is all about people. Congratulations, and thanks for all the great work. With these people results, I'm sure your performance over the next five years will be even stronger than the past five.

Summary Points

- ➤ Being customer-driven doesn't always mean doing exactly what the customer is asking for (such as overordering inventory).
- ➤ Lean applies to every aspect of the work in every department at every company.
- ➤ While the financial benefits from a successful Lean turnaround are dramatic, the people benefits are even greater.
- ➤ Continuous improvement means that using Lean to find and remove waste to deliver even more value to the customer never stops.

Summary

So now we will leave UGH and sum up what we learned from the first five years of its Lean turnaround. I hope you enjoyed the story. UGH Corporation is of course a fictional company, as are all of the people you've met. While I created UGH as a manufacturer, it could have been any type of company or organization: a hospital, a bank, a distributor, a headhunter, or a state crime lab. It doesn't matter. Every company would have to go through the same steps that UGH did to become Lean. The Lean fundamentals, the respect for people, and the leadership approach that are needed are all the same. Just look at Virginia Mason Medical Center in Seattle, Washington, or ThedaCare in Appleton, Wisconsin. While they are hospitals that have excelled at Lean, they learned from visiting and adapting the best Lean practices of manufacturing companies. As a result, I thought a manufacturing company could serve as a universal example.

This was a fun book to write because it allowed me to draw from my own experience to share the many forms of resistance that you will face during a Lean turnaround. The pushback from UGH's people is common in any company when you challenge the conventional wisdom (if you can call it that) of how things are done. Think about your own company. What are the accepted norms or "sacred cows" that many people believe are causing problems for the customers (both internal and external), the traditions that no one has been able to change? I'm sure you have quite a few. What would you say if I sent Mr. Kurosaki to your company and he started out by saying, "Look, everything here is no good; what do you want to do about it?"

What would you do? Say you are running a company and your job is to provide better outcomes for all your stakeholders. You might not know much about Lean at all. But take to heart the fact that neither did I, nor did George Koenigsaecker, nor for that matter did Gary Kaplan, CEO of Virginia Mason. Neither did Jerry York and the rest of the UGH team. We all learned by doing. We failed a lot along the way but kept on going. Jerry York's path was littered with customer service problems early on, from machine breakdowns to cell teams not meeting standard work, supplier problems, and many other issues. Customers were screaming at him. His new chairman kept pushing him forward, although to his credit, he didn't need much pushing. He could tell from the results of the first four kaizens that there was a huge opportunity to remove waste and get better at UGH. He wanted to be part of that. He wanted to lead it. What about you?

Jerry knew he would face resistance from a majority of his associates in UGH, especially from the more senior leaders and managers. So will you. It is easy for everyone to agree with the simple concept that companies, any company, are nothing but a collection of people and processes trying to deliver value to a group of customers. Easy, that is, until we start talking about your company. Of course your company is so different from any other company! Things are so complex and difficult, you just won't believe it. We are a delicate snowflake with nothing quite like it in the world. Blah, blah, blah. Every excuse in the book will come your way, as well as a few that aren't even in the book. Can you push through this the way Jerry did? How do you think UGH's story would have turned out if he hadn't? You can say that Jerry got help from his chairman, but similar help is available to you in the form of good Lean consultants or experienced Lean hands you could bring in to start a strong Kaizen Promotion Office. No excuses, please.

I have tried to make the UGH story instructive by sharing all the steps you need to take to be successful with your own Lean turnaround. I also tried to have a little fun. I'm sure that you have a Barbara Mooney in your company. You know, a longtime employee who is a great worker and completely loyal to the company and is not afraid to speak up when she (or he) sees something wrong, or as we called it at UGH, waste. You love her, but there is so much waste that she is always making noise about some problem or another. As most traditional batch companies are adept at hiding any waste or problems, no one wants to listen to a Barbara. She is seen as a problem, when in reality she is doing you a big favor by pointing out the waste that needs to be eliminated. Can you begin to listen to her and fix the problems and eventually turn her into a positive force by putting her in the KPO to remove the waste as UGH did?

Despite the fun that I've had writing this, I am retiring from book writing for good after this book is published. I wrote *The Lean Turnaround* to pass on what I have learned over the past 30 years about implementing Lean. I wrote this sequel in response to all the requests I got from people saying, "We loved *The Lean Turnaround*, but how do you really do this?" That is how UGH got created. I can't think of a better way to explain how to do this than to just do it. Everything that UGH experienced I have experienced many times. UGH's initial five-year forecast of financial results, for example, represents the type of projections we saw from the 21 companies we bought at Wiremold and in nearly every company we try to buy for our private equity portfolio. However, the financial results from UGH after five years of Lean are quite conservative. I didn't want to put something out there that no one would believe. My own experience suggests that any company that copies UGH's approach will in fact beat UGH's results.

Putting in a five-year forecast as a batch company and comparing it to the same five years following Lean was done primarily to get the attention of business owners and CEOs. Of all the issues holding back the spread of Lean as a strategy, the number one hurdle is getting the top leaders involved. Every time I give a presentation, the first question I get is, "How do I get my CEO to do this?" or a slight variation like, "Can you come to my company and talk my CEO and senior management team into doing Lean?" I believe that if a CEO could see a side-by-side comparison of what his company looks like in both a traditional batch mode and a Lean mode, he might at least have to ask himself why he wouldn't want to go for the better results of Lean. If he can look at both results and still say he is not interested in getting the better results, then I don't know what to say. He is probably in the wrong job.

So that is why I created UGH. Now let's do a simple recap of what we learned from UGH's Lean journey. To begin with, the primary objective is to achieve better results and become a better company. How? In its simplest form, Lean is about removing the waste from your own value-adding activities in order to allow you to deliver more value to your customers. For example, a company like UGH with a six-week lead time can be converted to one with a two- to three-day lead time. This allows it to deliver a great deal more value to customers and provides tremendous leverage in the marketplace.

To be successful like UGH, you need to understand three simple management principles before you start: (1) Lean is the strategy, (2) lead from the top, and (3) you are trying to transform the people. You have to change their thinking and the way they look at work. You need to teach them how to see the waste and give them the tools to remove it. This will take time, as UGH discovered, and is a major challenge in any Lean turnaround.

Next, just like Jerry and his team did, you need to drive the four Lean fundamentals into every part of the company. They are the basis of everything you do:

- Work to takt time
- One-piece flow
- Standard work
- Pull

If the CEO simply asks everyone the following questions every day, she will be driving the right behavior into the company: "Is everything running to takt time?" "Is everything in a one-piece flow?" "Do we have standard work in place everywhere?" and "Is a pull system in place for the whole value stream?"

UGH gave itself a running start by doing a few simple things up front to grease the skids for its aggressive Lean efforts. The company engaged a strong Lean consultant and hired several experienced Lean hands to form strong KPOs in each factory. This provided the Lean knowledge that was lacking and got people off to a fast start. Trying to implement Lean on your own from within is an almost impossible task. Get help. The other key thing UGH leaders did was organize for Lean up front by switching to a value stream organization. They knew that their move to Lean meant competing on operational excellence, and so they defined the objectives that they felt would create the desired state:

- 100% on-time customer service
- 20% productivity gain each year
- 50% reduction in defects each year
- 20x inventory turns
- Establishing visual controls and 5S everywhere

Once these targets were established, they ran the company on this basis. Every value stream leader was given these goals and had to report his or her progress on them to Jerry and his staff every Friday morning. This aligned all of UGH on the same goals. It also helped to flatten the organizational structure and get everyone working together. You can do the same. Put your focus on future results, achieving the operational excellence goals, and not on looking backward at last month's results. Those results already happened, and you can't do anything about them now.

Once the targets, structure, and Lean knowledge were in place, UGH began aggressive kaizen activity. The UGH team understood the value of kaizen as a method to teach all the associates how to see and remove waste while at the same time getting great short-term results. Lean is a "learn by doing" activity, and the kaizens facilitated both the doing and the learning. Over time they helped transform UGH into a learning organization where people were excited about coming to work to learn and make a contribution. UGH focused its Lean efforts by creating a model line first and a model factory next. It brought associates from other factories to the model factory kaizens and then asked them to go home and implement what they learned.

To leverage the gains, UGH established a profit-sharing program so that all associates could share in the value that they helped create. It paid out every quarter and not only was a big morale booster but gave everyone a sense of teamwork—which is essential in a Lean turnaround. UGH also set an aggressive kaizen schedule. Companies that think they can do one kaizen every six weeks and still achieve something are kidding themselves. Don't be one of those.

If you follow UGH's lead, you can create unfair competitive advantage for your company as well. Remember Mr. Nakao's advice: "If you don't try something, no knowledge will visit you." I hope you have enjoyed the book. As a former book writer I would love to hear about your Lean turnaround. You can contact me at abyrne@jwchilds.com.

And remember, kaizen is good for you.

About the Cast

Most of the members of the UGH management team are based on real people I have known or worked with:

Scott Smith was renamed from Scott Bartosch, my VP of sales at Wiremold, the biggest distributer in the electrical industry; our biggest customer called him "the best VP of sales in the industry"

Steve Mallard was renamed from Steve Maynard, who was Engineering VP at Wiremold. Steve introduced QFD for new product development at both Wiremold and Sturm, Ruger & Company.

Frank Gee was renamed from my VP of Operations at Wiremold, Frank Giannattasio, who did much of the heavy lifting in Wiremold's Lean turnaround.

Judy Rankin is of course a member of the ladies professional golf hall of fame, but for this book she was renamed for Wiremold's great head of HR, Judy Seyler.

Dick Conway was one of my closest friends growing up. He taught me to play golf, something I will always be grateful for. For this book he took the place of Orry Fiume, Wiremold's great and now very famous CFO for coauthoring the book *Real Numbers: Management Accounting in a Lean Organization.*

Barbara Mooney was introduced before in *The Lean Turnaround* under her real name, Barbara Looney. She worked at Wiremold's Walker subsidiary and was responsible for starting a poem competition between herself and Art Byrne about eliminating, rack by rack, Walker's huge work-in-progress inventory area. Her efforts resulted in freeing up 23,000 square feet of space and eliminating $2.6 million of inventory that was freed back into cash.

Ellen Minor in real life is Ed Miller, my VP of Marketing and best strategic thinker at Wiremold.

Mr. Kurosaki in real life is Mr. Kurosaka, the President of the Shingijutsu consulting company and someone I have worked with for the past 30 years. His knowledge and insights in real life are extraordinary.

Jim Boots, UGH's Kaizen Promotion Office (KPO) head, in real life is Jim Booth, the KPO head for one of my portfolio companies where he has been responsible for getting 12 factories to move from 3 inventory turns to over 20 turns and in the process freeing up over $100 million dollars of inventory.

And last but not least, Jerry York has been my best friend since 1963, when we first became teammates on the Boston College hockey team. Today he is also my best golf partner. In real life Jerry has achieved even more than our fictitious UGH CEO. Jerry is the hockey coach of Boston College and this year reached the milestone of 1,000 wins, a feat I believe will never be duplicated. He has also won five national championships and is far and away the best college hockey coach in the history of the game. More than that, Jerry was the perfect fit for our UGH CEO because he embodies the people skills and team building needed not only to build great hockey teams but also to turn around a company like UGH. Leadership skills are leadership skills no matter what business you are in. I think Coach York did an excellent job turning UGH around, and I am confident he will win many more national championships.

Index

L

M

About the Author

Art Byrne has been implementing Lean in various companies since his first General Manager job at the General Electric Company in 1982. As Group Executive of the Danaher Corporation, he, along with one of his Group Presidents, brought Lean to Danaher with the help of four former Toyota executives who had worked with Taiichi Ohno implementing the Toyota Production System in Toyota's suppliers. As CEO of The Wiremold Company, he more than quadrupled sales and increased enterprise value by 2,467 percent in a little over nine years. He is a member of the IndustryWeek Manufacturing Hall of Fame, won a Shingo Prize at Wiremold, and is the author of the bestselling book *The Lean Turnaround*.